Zero Quality Control:
Source Inspection
and the
Poka-yoke System

Zero Quality Control: Source Inspection and the Poka-yoke System

Translated by
Andrew P. Dillon

Productivity Press

New York

Originally published as *Furyō = Ø e no chōsen: Genryū kensa to poka-yoke shisutemu; Zero QC hōshiki e no tenkai,* copyright © 1985 by the Japan Management Association, Tokyo

English translation copyright © 1986 by Productivity Press, a division of The Kraus Organization Limited.

Additional copies of this book are available from the publisher. Discounts are available for multiple copies through the sales department (888-319-5852) Address all other inquiries to:

Productivity Press
444 Park Avenue South, 7th Floor
New York, NY 10016
Telephone: 212-686-5900
Telefax: 212-686-5411
email: info@productivitypress.com

Cover design by Russell Funkhouser

Printed in the United States of America

Library of Congress Cataloging-in-Publication data

Shingo, Shigeo, 1909-1990
   Zero quality control
   Translation of : Furyō zero e no chōsen
   Includes index
   1. Quality control. I. Title
   TS156.S4722513   1985
   658.5'   85-63497
                                 CIP

09 08 07   21 20 19

Publisher's Message

According to Shigeo Shingo, there are three types of engineers in America: *table engineers*, who spend all of their time in meetings arguing about problems on the shop floor; *catalog engineers*, who scour the latest catalogs for new equipment to solve these problems; and *"nyet" engineers*, who vote against almost every improvement suggestion.

Mr. Shingo, inventor of the SMED (Single-Minute Exchange of Die) system and the *poka-yoke* (mistake-proofing) system, and a key developer of the Toyota Production System, was in America at the invitation of three companies to help them search for ways to improve the efficiency of their production systems. He urged his audiences at these companies to become *improvement engineers* and, calling himself "Dr. Improvement," demonstrated the essence of his ideas by spending the majority of his time on the shop floor observing problems, making suggestions, and working with both the workers and management to find solutions. "My medicine works," Shingo remarked, "but only if the patient takes it."

The title of this book refers to three critical and interrelated aspects of quality control as taught by Shigeo Shingo. *Zero Quality Control* (Zero QC) is the ideal production system — one that does not manufacture any defects. To achieve this ideal, two things are necessary. *Poka-yoke* (in English, "mistake-proofing") looks at a defect, stops the production system, and gives immediate feedback so that we can get to the root cause of the problem and prevent it from happening again. *Source inspection* looks at errors before they become defects and either stops the system for correction or automatically adjusts the error condition to prevent it from becoming a defect. Using poka-yoke devices and source inspection systems has enabled companies like Toyota Motors to virtually eliminate the need for statistical quality control (SQC), which has been the very heart of quality control in this country for years.

As you read the text of this brilliant book you will see the amazing simplicity of Mr. Shingo's thinking. It is so simple that you wonder at times what it is that is so new. But do not be misled. I caution you to read slowly and allow the totality of his ideas to penetrate deeply within you. Don't allow the simplicity to fool you. Here in these pages is the logical thinking of a true genius of manufacturing. When you get to the numerous examples of poka-yoke devices offered in Chapter 7, you will begin to see the wonder of how inexpensive and simple ideas can truly prevent defects from occurring.

Just as Mr. Shingo taught us (in his book *A Revolution in Manufacturing: The SMED System*) to separate inside exchange of die (IED) from outside exchange of die (OED) to reduce setups from hours to minutes, here he teaches us another major concept: to detect errors *before* they become defects.

So many of us think that the advantage of Japanese companies over European and American ones is their lower labor costs. But when you begin to realize that quality costs amount to 20 to 30 percent of sales for many American manufacturing firms, you then can see the enormous value of Mr. Shingo's teaching. It is greater quality that gives you the real international competitive edge.

I believe that this book is a great gift from Mr. Shingo to American manufacturing and should save us literally billions of dollars in the years ahead. Quality is the easiest way to improve productivity. In fact, I'll go further and say that quality is essential for survival. I recently heard from a large American automotive manufacturer who stated that his company has over 2,000 suppliers. Their goal is to reduce that number to 200. I believe that the surviving 200 will be only those that can produce increasingly higher quality at successively lower costs. The quickest way for you to improve quality and lower costs is to study very carefully the teachings of Shigeo Shingo.

For many readers, I know that it is difficult to comprehend the idea of "zero defects." Many of us have been taught that nothing is perfect and that producing defects is an inherently unavoidable and therefore acceptable part of the manufacturing process. It reminds me of the story about parachute production during World War II.

How could the pilots be told that there was an error rate of 3 percent in the parachutes they carried? The problem was ultimately solved — and zero defects realized — by asking those who folded the parachutes to test them by jumping from planes occasionally themselves.

Mr. Shingo asks all of you to become improvement engineers. He doesn't ask you to jump from an airplane, but he does ask you to drop the idea that defects are a normal part of manufacturing. He encourages you to read and learn that, as he puts it, "defects = 0 is absolutely possible." Apply these ideas, and you'll find your company healthy and stronger than you ever thought possible.

This book would not have been possible without the assistance of many people. I am grateful to the original publisher, the Japan Management Association, and especially to Kazuya Uchiyama, for making the original materials available to us. Andrew P. Dillon of Yale University provided a careful and accurate translation of the book. Patricia Slote was responsible for managing all editorial and production processes. Nancy Macmillan edited the translation, and Cheryl Berling proofread the text. Russ Funkhouser designed the cover. Nanette Redmond, Ruth Knight, Laura Santi, and Leslie Goldstein of Rudra Press were responsible for typesetting the text, preparing the artwork, and designing the interior of the book. Marie Kascus prepared the index. I would like to thank all of them for their help.

Norman Bodek
Publisher

Foreword

The concept of statistical quality control (SQC) methods seemed revolutionary when I first heard about it in 1951.

Until then, I had paid attention only to extremely low-order "judgment inspections," whose sole conceivable function was to check finished products and eliminate defective ones.

The notion that the only function of an inspection is to eliminate defective goods was demolished when I heard about "informative inspections." This new method reduced defects by providing feedback when they were discovered and acting on the basis of that feedback. This, indeed, was an innovative way of thinking about inspection. I embraced this approach with total confidence that it was a progressive and advanced method with, as was explained, the scientific and theoretical underpinning of inductive statistics.

However much my confidence in SQC methods may have seen its ups and downs over the following 20 years, my faith in it has remained fundamentally unshaken.

By 1961, the implementation of *poka-yoke** methods had made it possible to eliminate defects entirely, and my confidence in SQC methods weakened somewhat as I realized this meant there was a way to reduce defects without relying on statistical methods. Basically, however, I still thought that the SQC approach was the best available.

As poka-yoke methods came into widespread use and defects clearly diminished, I asked myself why this was so. Was it not, I concluded, a result of the use of 100 percent inspections and of the execution of rapid feedback and action? It dawned on me that statistical quality control methods, which combined inductive statistics

---

* See page 45 for a definition of *poka-yoke* (pronounced POH-kah YOH-kay). For the sake of simplicity the word is romanized throughout the remainder of this book.

and techniques of quality control, owed their essential function to the quality control methods and that the role of inductive statistics was secondary.

If informative inspections are the essence of quality control methods, it would be desirable to use 100 percent inspections and to speed up feedback and action to detect abnormalities, thereby enhancing the value of informative inspections themselves. I concluded then, that:

- Fully 100 percent inspections, although ideal for the detection of defects, entail considerable time and trouble.
- SQC methods try to get around this problem by enlisting the aid of inductive statistics and cutting down the task through the use of sampling.
- The new inspection method requires only the aggressive use of poka-yoke measures, procedures that take no time or trouble even when 100 percent inspections are performed.

Freeing myself to a certain degree from the 20-year spell that had led me to think true quality control demands the use of inductive statistics, I proceeded to devise the new concepts of successive checks and self-checks.

Although the incidence of defects can be strikingly reduced through the use of successive checks, self-checks, and other techniques, I looked for ways to cut defects even further. It occurred to me that we were giving feedback and taking action only after defects had been detected, and I wondered whether there were not some inspection system that would prevent defects from occurring in the first place. After all, I thought, defects result from errors, and perhaps there was some way to prevent errors at an earlier stage through the use of control mechanisms. This line of thought brought me first to the idea of source inspections.

It turned out that significant benefits could be obtained by combining source inspections and the poka-yoke system, and in 1977 a result of zero monthly defects was achieved in a 30,000-units-per-month washing machine assembly process at the Shizuoka plant of Matsushita Electric's Washing Machine Division. This gave me confidence in a "Zero Quality Control" system and for the first time freed me completely from the spell of statistical quality control.

I will discuss these developments in detail in the main body of the book. At this point, however, I venture to offer this book to the public because I am under the impression that there are still many people who believe that true quality control requires the use of inductive statistics. I would like these people to understand and take cognizance of the real significance of the functions of quality control.

Since these early developments, quality control campaigns in Japan have brought about dramatic improvements in quality as they have progressed from the use of QC circles to Total Quality Control (TQC), and today our results in this area are the subject of worldwide interest and praise.

By way of explaining the ultimate significance of these issues, I would like to relate a little fable.

> *In olden times, there was a vague belief that making inspections meant joining your hands in prayer in the presence of the God of Judgment Inspections.*

The Origin of the Statistical Quality Control Method

> *There came along a wonderfully efficacious new god, however, the "Statistical Quality Control (SQC) Method." The Informative Inspection became the new object of worship and its sacred temple was surrounded by a latticework wall made of a special alloy known as Inductive Statistics. Bathed in sunlight and sparkling with indescribable hues, this wall was suffused with an awe-inspiring aura.*
>
> *Even when only partial facts were visible, touching the wall had the effect of clearly revealing the overall picture, and this deepened the faith of many people in this new object of devotion.*

SQC Was Enshrined on a Lofty Mountain

> *Because SQC was at first enshrined on the lofty Mountain of Science, it was inaccessible to ordinary people, and only certain scholars and theoretically inclined technicians were able to make the pilgrimage to it.*
>
> *Even so, the word spread that product quality was improving and defects were declining in a plant run by people from Production Village A who had made the pilgrimage. Study groups were therefore formed among people in other Production Villages and everywhere the ranks of believers in SQC swelled.*

Popularization Through QC Circles

> *Still, worship was limited to only certain people.*
> *Thinking to spread the word among the masses, a group of*

*leaders hit on the idea of QC Circle Fairs, in which young
people called Workers would hoist images of the god and the
shrine onto their shoulders and make their way through the
villages. These festivals proved to be a great success and in no
time at all the creed had spread throughout Japan.*

The Development of TQC Fairs

*These fairs were renamed TQC Fairs as they reached beyond
Production Villages to Technical and Financial Villages, and
even to Marketing and Personnel Villages; and Village Chiefs,
Governors, and people higher up joined together to shoulder the
holy shrines. And since the sacred image proved effective against
a multitude of problems, including Quality of Work and Product Quality, TQC Fairs continued to expand and develop.
Visitors came from throughout the world to observe the fairs,
and eventually TQC Fairs came to be held in all countries.*

The Sacred Image Was Hidden Behind the Wall of Inductive Statistics

*Alas, the Temple of SQC-ism, constructed of Inductive Statis-
tics, was so overpoweringly resplendent that it dazzled many
who forgot about worshipping the God of Informative Inspections and believed no benefit could be gained without actually
touching the Temple of Inductive Statistics. Inductive Statistics
had been thrust to the fore, with the result that people not
only forgot about the existence of the God of Informative Inspec-*

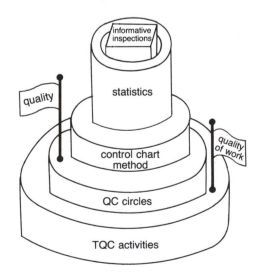

tions — *they gradually fell prey to the delusion that mere participation in TQC Fairs had miraculous effects.*

Before long, however, oversights gradually began to crop up even among those who had touched the wall of the Temple of Inductive Statistics and people began to understand, too, that the God of Informative Inspections had the power to reduce defects but not to eliminate them altogether.

The Development of a QC Method Aimed at Zero Defects

Those who hoped to reduce defects further, even to eliminate them, concluded that perhaps there was a defect inherent in the teachings of the God of Informative Inspections. For the first time, they contemplated the possibility of switching to a new deity, the God of Source Inspections. Simultaneously, they decided to do away with the wall of Inductive Statistics that so solidly encircled the God of Informative Inspections.

Poka-yoke Becomes the Raw Material for Building a New Temple

This time, it was an image of Source Inspections that was enshrined as an object of worship in the temple built of poka-yoke materials. But unlike the case of the relationship between Informative Inspections and Inductive Statistics, in which the object of worship was placed in the temple and then forgotten,

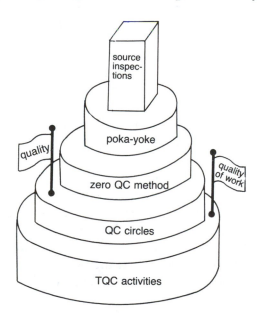

this time the image of Source Inspections was fully exposed on a poka-yoke dais so that anyone could come and do reverence to it.

Movements in which holy shrines were borne by QC circles and by TQC associations grew ever more successful as they sought to spread this new faith.

I seem to have spent a long time with my fable, but I did this because I want readers to understand the relationships among three things:

• Quality control *per se*
• Techniques that support quality control
• Circle activities to promote quality control

The important points, then, are as follows:

1. The SQC method was a conceptual innovation that shook the conventional notion that the only kind of inspection was a judgment inspection.

2. The SQC method is composed of two elements: inductive statistics and informative inspections as a method of quality control. Inductive statistics, however, encircled informative inspections, and what should have been nothing more than a technique obscured the more essential informative inspections, thus impeding the progress of its quality control functions.

This misunderstanding is implicitly illustrated by the fact that, even today, some people maintain that "if you don't use statistics, it's not quality control."

3. To instill the realization that it is actually on the shop floor that quality is built in, people in the workplace organized QC circle activities and then TQC circle activities.

4. Yet while activities to promote quality control expanded, no essential progress was made in quality control functions as such.

5. To advance to the functions of quality control, 100 percent inspections, immediate feedback, and immediate action were adopted and self-check methods were introduced.

This is why the efficacious techniques of the poka-yoke system were developed. As a result of these techniques, inductive statistics has been rendered unnecessary in the area of control.

6. The active pursuit of zero defects led to the development of source inspection methods. These methods were particularly effective when combined with the poka-yoke system.

7. Poka-yoke methods are techniques rather than objectives. It follows that the techniques of the poka-yoke system must not be allowed to obscure the goal of source inspections.

8. QC circle activities and TQC circle activities are extremely valuable in promoting of a Zero QC system formed by linking source inspections and poka-yoke methods. Such movements must be further expanded.

In any event, we can distinguish three separate function types:

- Basic quality control functions
- Techniques for putting quality control functions into practice
- Functions promoting QC movements

Not only should these functions be clearly differentiated, but I believe it is extremely important that they be actively used in effective combination with one another.

I wrote this book in little more than a month. My motivation was a book entitled *Reforming the Workplace at M* which claimed that "putting a poka-yoke system in place was extremely effective in reducing defects," implying that the reduction of defects was an effect only of poka-yoke methods.

There is no doubt that the poka-yoke system can, by itself, be tremendously effective. It can be even more effective when combined with successive checks and self-checks. The achievement of a Zero QC system, however, *requires* that poka-yoke techniques be combined with source inspections. The poka-yoke system must not obscure the functions of source inspections in the way that the SQC method, via inductive statistics, obscured the essential functions of informative inspections.

I have frequently observed misunderstanding of this point and so I have hurried to make this volume public because I believe it would be calamitous for such false impressions to hinder the proper development of Zero QC methods.

I stress this point repeatedly and hope that it will be properly understood by large numbers of readers. (I hope, too, that you will reread this foreward after you have finished the book.)

It took 26 years for me to free myself completely from the spell of inductive statistics. In retrospect, I find that, along the way to eventual attainment of a Zero QC system, I have learned a great deal from my encounters with many people and many tasks.

In this sense, I offer my heartfelt thanks to all those who provided me with valuable opportunities and suggestions.

A glance at bookstore shelves shows QC-related books to be overwhelmingly more numerous than books dealing with industrial engineering (IE), and one cannot help but be struck by how much interest there is in QC.

These books, however, are either explanations of techniques founded on SQC or works relating to the running of QC circles or to the establishment of quality standards. Am I wrong in feeling that there are few books on the functions of quality control itself — and especially on basic studies of the control function?

It is to raise these issues that I present this book, for zero defects can indisputably be attained by faithfully implementing these Zero QC ideas and methods. Surely the fact that zero defects have been a reality for a number of years attests to the validity of the approach.

I sincerely hope that, in the future, we will see more and more studies of the nature of the quality control function. I ask, too, that I may profit from readers' criticisms of this book. Please write to the publisher, Productivity Press, with your comments and observations.

I have recently had frequent occasion to travel abroad, and while I am deeply impressed by the tremendous worldwide interest shown in Japanese QC activities, I fear that some of this interest does not go beyond mere imitation of the superficial aspects of QC circles and TQC activities.

I would far prefer that people gain a proper understanding of the essential functions of quality control and the techniques that underlie those functions.

Like the achievement at Mitsubishi Heavy Industries' Nagasaki Shipyards of the world's fastest shipbuilding operation and like the development of the SMED concept, this book is the product of long years of reflection and actual practice. For me, the work is something of a milestone.

I have reflected long and hard on the many roundabout routes I have taken because I sometimes regarded successful measures as mere operational improvements and failed to transform them into something conceptual. Now, more than ever, I believe one must always pay attention to the conceptual significance of production improvements.

It is because the poka-yoke system has the very real capacity to reduce, and eventually to eliminate, defects that I would like to see it adopted in as many companies as possible.

This is why I have had a number of firms provide actual examples of poka-yoke applications, and I would like to take this opportunity to express my sincere gratitude to those companies for their generosity.

I offer this book to the public in the hope that it may contribute to the further development of appropriate quality control movements around the world.

Shigeo Shingo

Contents

Figures

Zero Quality Control:
Source Inspection
and the
Poka-yoke System

1
Inspections and the Structure of Production

THE FIVE ELEMENTS OF PRODUCTION

Production activities are composed of five elements. These are:

1. *Objects of production*: the products
2. *Agents of production*: the people in charge of making products, as well as the machines, tools, and other equipment that assist them
3. *Methods*: the means by which actions are performed
4. *Space*: where actions are performed and the locations to and from which objects are transported
5. *Time*: the timing of work or how long actions take

When we engage in production we must, first of all, give consideration to these five elements.

Objects of Production

Whenever a change takes place in the products we are making, all our methods change as well. This means that if, having made item A up to now, a model change requires us to start making item B, we will have to alter the way we go about making the items in question. Even when a single item A is involved, a switch, say, from two-piece construction to integrated construction will inevitably have a tremendous impact on production agents, methods, space, and time.

All this means that we need to conduct thorough studies of the objects of production from the standpoint of value engineering (VE).

I recall, in listening to a talk given by a Mr. H around 1948, that I was deeply impressed to hear the speaker say that, in manufac-

3

turing cylinders for motorcycles, he had been told by academicians exactly how much in the way of scrap cuttings would be generated by the operation involved. He, on the other hand, decided to make the cylinders by bending sheet metal, welding it and then grinding it to the required degree of precision, rather than by cutting the metal parts.

The point here is that all he had to do was to satisfy the product's necessary functions, and that there was no reason to look for efficiency in the production of scrap.

In the same sense, we need to examine thoroughly the nature and requirements of the objects of production: how will the products be used, and what qualities must they have to function properly?

Agents of Production

Once the question of the objects of production has been settled, we next have to make the most efficient use of agents of production. We must choose appropriate people to take charge of each process, machines, and tools.

Methods. When both the objects and the agents of production have been decided upon, we have to select the most suitable methods for making the products in question, using the appropriate agents of production.

Space. The next questions concern use of the space where the products will be made. Should we, for example, group similar machines together, or arrange machines in accordance with process flow?

Time. Finally, we need to take into account questions of time. Of prime consideration are issues that have a significant impact on interprocess stocks — for instance, whether we make only what is needed when it is needed and in the quantities needed, or we make predetermined amounts ahead of time. In this situation, it does not matter whether questions of time are given priority over those of space or vice versa.

In any event, production improvement calls for investigation into each of these five elements of production.

The notion of five elements of production is akin to that of the "Five W's and One H," i.e.

Objects of production — *What?*
Agents of production — *Who?*
Methods — *How?*
Space — *Where?*
Time — *When?*

To these may be added an additional element:
Why?

This question of purposes, however, is not necessarily a constituent of things themselves (*Figure 1-1*).

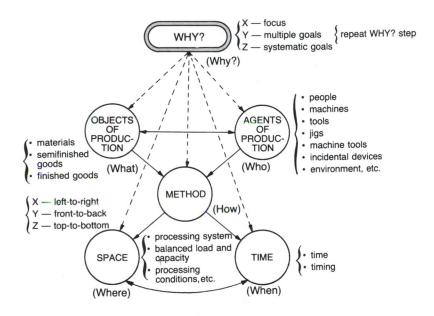

FIGURE 1-1. **The Five Elements of Production and the Five W's and One H**

THE STRUCTURE OF PRODUCTION

Production Is a Network of Processes and Operations

In my lectures, I sometimes ask how many in the audience know how to ride a bicycle. Nearly everyone's hand goes up in response. I then ask how many know how to make any necessary repairs on a bicycle. This time far fewer hands go up. From this demonstration, we may conclude that the ability to ride a bicycle and the ability to repair a bicycle are different. Yet it seems to me that, unconsciously, we mistakenly assume that knowing how to ride a bicycle means knowing how to fix one. It is important to understand, therefore, that to be able to repair a bicycle, one has to understand the structure of the bicycle, the functions of each part, and the functional relationships among all the parts. The question of production is similar. The fact that someone is engaged in production every day does not necessarily mean that that person knows how to fix the system when it breaks down, e.g., when defects occur or efficiency plummets.

For that, one needs a proper understanding of the structure of production, what the functions of each element of production are, and how the various elements relate to one another.

How, then, is production structured? *Figure 1-2* gives us the answer in schematic form. The vertical, or *Y*, axis, shows a flow from raw materials to finished goods and how the objects of production change according to methods, space, and time. This is called a *process*.

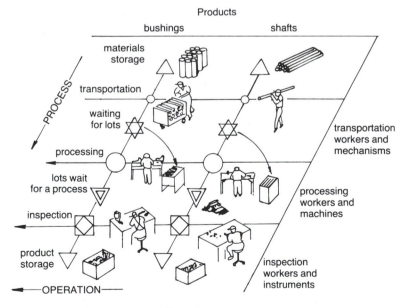

FIGURE 1-2. **The Structure of Production**

In contrast to a process is the flow, shown on the horizontal, or *X*, axis, in which the agents of production change use methods, space, and time to create products. These actions are known as *operations*. Thus, production may be visualized as a network of processes and operations.

Process Elements

We have defined process as a flow by which raw materials are converted into finished goods. All aspects of a process fall into one of the following categories:

1. *Work*: assembly, disassembly, alterations of shape or quality
2. *Inspection*: comparison with a standard
3. *Transportation*: change of location
4. *Delay*: a period of time during which no work, transportation, or inspection takes place

Delays can be further divided into two categories:

Process delays: delays between processes that occur when, in lot operations, items do not move on to the next process until work at the current process has been completed.

Lot delays: delays for the purpose of keeping in step with lots. In lot operations involving, for example, 1,000 items, 999 unprocessed items wait while work is performed on the first item. Similarly, while the second item is being processed, the remaining 998 items are delayed along with the first item on which work has already been completed.

Thus, a process may appear in various guises:

1. Raw materials wait (i.e., are delayed) in a warehouse.
2. They are transported to a machine.
3. They wait by the machine (process delay).
4. The machine performs work on them.
5. If items are processed in lots, lot delays are used to keep in step with the lot as a whole.
6. As soon as machine processing is completed, items are inspected.
7. Finished goods are delayed in a holding area (product storage).

In terms of processes composed solely of work, we might find the following:

1. Materials are shaped by forging.
2. They are cut on a lathe.
3. They undergo heat treatment in an oven.
4. They are ground on a grinding machine.
5. They are assembled in an assembly shop.

In any case, even though more complex combinations show up in the real world, and even though there may be numerous unit processes involved, these various actions can ultimately be categorized under work, inspection, transportation, or delay.

In contrast to processes, operations proceed in the following way:

- Worker A transports raw materials for shafts from a warehouse to the machine. Then he does the same for the raw materials for bushings.
- Lathe operator B cuts shafts. Then he cuts bushings.
- Inspector C inspects shafts after processing. Then he inspects processed bushings.

These actions on materials constitute operations. Since people make use of assistants in the form of machines, actions by which machines work on materials may similarly be referred to as operations. Thus, production activities are composed of complementary Y-axis processes, which provide products with required functions, and X-axis operations, which comprise actions to achieve the desired result.

Operations can be classified as illustrated in *Figure 1-3*. Terms used in the figure may be defined as follows:

> *Preparation, after-adjustment operations*: setup or tooling changes
>
> *Principal operations*: operations repeated in each cycle.

These fall into several categories:

1. *Essential operations*: operations involving actual cutting, inspecting or moving
2. *Auxiliary operations*: mounting and removing items, pushing buttons, etc.
3. *Human margin allowances*: miscellaneous allowances relating to people

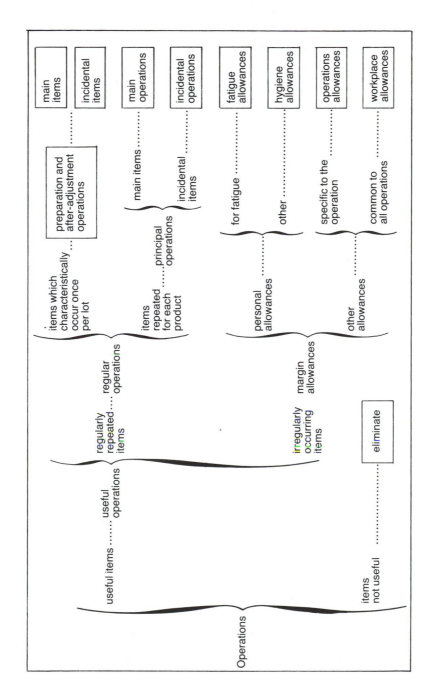

FIGURE 1-3. **The Structure of Operations**

4. *Nonhuman margin allowances*: occasional operations relating to tasks such as clearing away cuttings, wiping off grease, and the like

Operations such as these correspond to the four process phenomena illustrated in *Figure 1-4*.

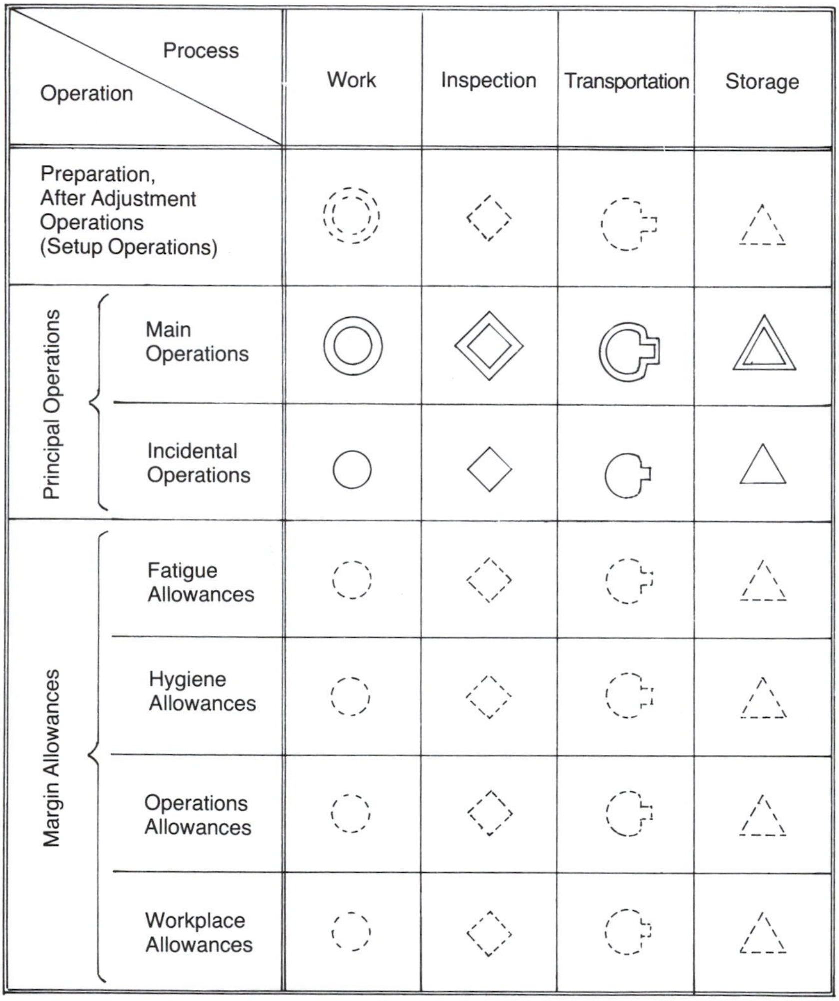

Operation \ Process	Work	Inspection	Transportation	Storage
Preparation, After Adjustment Operations (Setup Operations)	⊙	◇	⌀	△
Principal Operations — Main Operations	◎	◈	⌬	△
Principal Operations — Incidental Operations	○	◇	⌀	△
Margin Allowances — Fatigue Allowances	○	◇	⌀	△
Margin Allowances — Hygiene Allowances	○	◇	⌀	△
Margin Allowances — Operations Allowances	○	◇	⌀	△
Margin Allowances — Workplace Allowances	○	◇	⌀	△

FIGURE 1-4. The Relationship Between Processes and Operations

Some people have claimed that processes refer to large units in production analyses, and operations refer to small units. These theories are simply wrong. No matter how finely you analyze the process by which goods are transformed, it will always remain a process. Thus, in the case of a unit process, the following can be analyzed as process elements:

- Cutting the ends of workpieces
- Cutting inside diameters
- Cutting outside diameters

By contrast, operations elements might include:

- Moving a tool vertically into the end of the workpiece to cut it off
- Moving a boring bit laterally into the workpiece
- Turning a handle on a machine to move a tool used for machining the outside diameter

Thus a process is an integrated flow of objects beyond which appear various people and machines, for example, transport workers, lathe operators, and inspection workers. From an operations point of view, on the other hand, various goods (e.g., shafts and bushings) appear on the other side of workers and machines.

Seen from the front, then, production consists of processes, while the view from the rear shows it to be made up of operations.

It follows that production activities should be classified in terms of qualitative differences, and not in terms of larger and smaller units. This latter error arises from the conventional application of the notion of processes to a wide range of phenomena and from resulting analyses that use relatively large process units.

Processes and Operations in Harmony

The Conflict Between Processes and Operations

We have explained that production is composed of processes and operations. These two elements are occasionally in conflict with one another.

When, for example, rush orders call for shutting down machines to wait for goods to come down the line, machine work rates are sacrificed for the sake of process demands and processes are given priority over operations.

If the situation is reversed and, because of relatively similar setups, a worker has moved up an order that could just as well have been taken care of later, then items that ought to be processed will be delayed and delivery deadlines will be missed. Since in this case operational convenience has led to process delays, operations have taken precedence over the process.

We can, therefore, think of processes as actions that serve customers and operations as actions performed for the sake of plant efficiency. It follows that putting too much emphasis on either one is undesirable, and this is why confusion would arise on the shop floor without the intervention of managers. Front-line supervisors placed at the intersections of processes and operations must constantly seek to keep these opposing demands in harmony with one another.

Operations Supplement Processes

When we describe production activities as networks of processes and operations, we are referring to matters of structural organization. It is process functions, in fact, that attain the principal goals of production, while operations play a supplementary role.

It follows that, no matter how effectively operational functions are performed, production as a whole cannot achieve much success if process functions are inadequate. As long as there are errors in the organization of processes, product flaws will result no matter how perfectly operations are performed. Overly generous precision tolerances for parts will mean excessive play in assembled goods and numerous defects in finished products. Similarly, inappropriate processing procedures will necessitate the expenditure of unnecessary worker time and effort.

These extremely clear examples of process errors make it easy for people to see that process functions take precedence over operations functions. In real-world production activities, however, what we actually see are operations functions, and process functions leave only a faintly visible impression with us. This is because they are hidden by operations and we must make special efforts to be aware of them. Once we accustom ourselves to looking at production activities solely from the point of view of operations, the operations perspective takes over and we end up overlooking process-side deficiencies.

Undue stress laid on operations will cause numerous process-side inefficiencies to crop up. Consider the following cases:

- Concentrating solely on operations, we group similar machines together. In process terms, this sort of homogeneous grouping entails increased transportation, which in turn does nothing but raise costs.
- Single-minded efforts to push machine capacities to the limit will generate process-yield imbalances, and interprocess delays will increase.
- Conducting large-lot production to counter machine time lost to setup changes will increase inventory.

Overemphasis on Operations Characteristics

In 1972, I went as a consultant to the F-M Corporation in the United States. While there, I noticed that machine layout followed a homogeneous arrangement, large-lot operations were being carried out, and huge quantities of stock were visible everywhere. When I asked an IE engineer why his company did not adopt flow operations, he replied simply that if it did, it would not be able to balance its machine capacities.

The following year, when a delegation from the French firm Citroen came to visit the Washing Machine Division of Matsushita Electric, one member of the group asked how long it took between the first processing stroke on the body of a washing machine and completion of the finished product. "About a week?" the visitor guessed.

"Not at all," was the Matsushita plant manager's reply. "In general, it takes about 2½ hours."

His dumbfounded guest was profoundly impressed when he actually visited the plant and witnessed the process that turned out finished washing machines in 2½ hours.

Following the tour, the delegation leader, a Mr. Mermet, described his impressions in a particularly striking way. He said that there were many cases in which Citroen's individual machines were far more efficient than the ones he had just seen. In terms of process flow, however, his own firm lagged far behind Matsushita.

In 1975, I was invited as a consultant to the O Company, an affiliate of Siemens in Stuttgart, West Germany. There, I observed the following procedures:

- Mouthpieces are attached to electric light bulbs at machine 1, and worker A fits parts into the machine for this purpose.
- When this is done, assembly is performed automatically. Worker B takes the assembled units and lines them up on a pallet.
- Pallets are then transported to a storage area for semifinished goods and stored.
- Next, worker C transports pallets containing the semifinished units assembled on machine 1 to machine 2 and inserts them into the machine.
- Final processing is performed automatically, after which worker D transfers the finished products to pallets, lines them up neatly, and transports them to storage.

When I asked the plant manager why he did not link machines 1 and 2, he replied that he had considered the possibility, but that it was impossible because the capacities of the two machines could not be balanced. The capacities of the machines in question were as follows:

Machine 1:   5,500 units/day
Machine 2:   5,000 units/day

"And what," I asked, "is your daily market demand?"

When he told me that he needed 5,000 units per day, I remarked that if machine 1 were to function at full capacity, it would simply produce surpluses that would end up as increased inventory. He must, I suggested, be halting the operation of machine 1 for about 10 percent of the time.

I then proposed that he install a magazine between machines 1 and 2, so that machine 1 would automatically shut down when 100 units accumulated in the magazine, and automatically start up again when only 10 units remained. Providing this type of full work control system, I said, would mean that machine 1 would rest 0.2 seconds for every 2 minutes it worked, and this would balance out the capacities of the two machines. Adopting a system like this would create several advantages:

- Linking machines 1 and 2 would make it possible to save on manpower by eliminating the work done by workers B and C.
- Stock between machines 1 and 2 could be drastically cut — to the semifinished items in the magazine — and no intermediate storage area would be needed.
- Transportation from machine 1 to the semifinished goods storage area and from this intermediate storage area to machine 2 could be eliminated.
- Quality-related feedback would be available immediately, reducing defects.
- Production time could be shortened considerably.

Three months later, the president of O came to Japan to visit K Manufacturing, a company with which his firm has a cooperative agreement, and he told me that he had set to work implementing my suggestions right away. He reported having had significant success in raising productivity, reducing defects, and reducing inventory.

From these examples, we see that there are two aspects of production activities, processes and operations, and even though operations are essentially supplementary to processes, it is operations behavior that is most visible to us. This means that, while we may think that improving operational efficiency will of itself raise productivity, we are neglecting another important aspect to the problem. Indeed, this is perhaps because we forget to acknowledge the priority of efficient processes over efficient operations.

Errors in European and American Production Philosophies

In recent years I have had numerous occasions to visit the United States and Europe and to observe a number of production plants. I have come across many plants where, as described above, operational efficiency is stressed to the neglect of process efficiency. In other words, I have seen a number of cases in which homogeneous machine layouts mean extra transportation or stock accumulates all over plants because batch systems or process systems have been adopted in the hope of pushing machine capacities to the limit.

The general attitude toward such stock is that it is a "necessary evil," but it seems to me that there is almost no sense of guilt involved: that 90 percent of the emphasis is on the "necessary" part and only 10 percent on the "evil." Some people even claim that stock is necessary!

Why should this be so? What is happening is that people are making claims like these:

- Stock can cut losses associated with long setup times.
- Stock can minimize production confusion when defects show up or machines break down.

In response to the argument about long setup times, I would say that if the use of my SMED approach* makes it possible to cut setup times from four hours to three minutes, then the reasons for adopting large-lot production in the first place all but disappear. If, furthermore, it is possible to attain zero defects through the use of the zero defect quality control system described in the present book, and if machine breakdowns can be totally prevented through "no breakdown maintenance," then the *raison d'être* for stock generation simply vanishes.

There is another reason that companies adopt large-lot production, however. This stems from the confusion between high-volume production and large-lot production.

High-volume production refers to the production of the same type of item in large quantities. This mode of production brings expectations of improved efficiency and decreased defects, for it has the advantages that machines, dies, and the like can be depreciated quickly and that skills improve rapidly as a result of labor division and specialization. But it is the prerogative of the market to choose and control high-volume production — not that of the production plant. The only real choice the production plant has is whether to produce in large or small lots. Companies usually use large-lot production to cut their losses when setup times are long. As pointed out above, however, SMED methods have made this approach almost worthless, since it does nothing but increase inventory.

Numerous plants in Japan have learned from and followed in the wake of the industrialized nations of Europe and America, and many plants have uncritically and unconsciously adopted the one-sided Euro-American production philosophy that emphasizes operations. As a result, it seems to me, many one-sided, operations-oriented production approaches have been used by Japanese plants.

---

* See *A Revolution in Manufacturing: The SMED System* (Productivity Press, 1985).

In any event, we need to be be aware that:

- There are two functional sides to production: processes and operations.
- It is in the nature of operations functions to supplement process functions.
- Because operations functions loom large in our sight, we tend to have eyes only for issues of operational efficiency.
- Improving productivity requires that we consider both process efficiency and operations proficiency as we work to achieve harmony between the two.

My argument in this book is that a proper understanding of the structure and functions of production can be decisive in all matters of production improvement. These ideas form the basis, too, of Zero Quality Control methods, including no-defect inspections and source inspections.

Human Work Rates and Machine Work Rates

In managing production activities, it is necessary to take into account the efficiency of both operations and processes.

Obviously it is desirable to have 100 percent efficiency on both sides, but in reality many problems stand in the way. It often happens, too, that giving priority to process efficiency will mean sacrificing operational efficiency. In such cases, it is important to treat operational efficiency as having two separate aspects: human work rates and machine work rates.

In general, costs drop once machinery is depreciated, but human costs, by their very nature, will continue to rise. Figuring that human costs are generally three to four times higher than machine costs, we developed multiple machine operations for the Toyota Production System. The idea was that by putting each worker in charge of several machines, human work rates would be kept at a maximum even if machine work rates fell slightly. Awareness of lower machine work rates led us to do everything we could to build low-cost machines. The goal of many companies in the Toyota group is to build machines at one-tenth of market prices, and in many cases these firms have succeeded.

THE SIGNIFICANCE OF INSPECTIONS

We have explained that production activities form a network of processes and operations. What, then, is the significance of inspections?

Inspections Supplement Processes

As we have seen, production is constructed of a network of processes and operations. Processes, we said, can be further broken down into four categories: work, inspection, transportation, and delay. We also said that inspections consist of comparisons with standards, but this is merely a description of the act of inspection. Within a process, inspections are characterized by the following functions:

- Inspections reveal and prevent defects in the course of work.
- Inspections reveal and prevent defects in the course of transportation.
- Inspections reveal and prevent defects in the course of delays.

In this way, inspections may be said to supplement work, transportation, and delays. Strictly speaking, the inspection function can be thought of as secondary to production, with inspections themselves playing only a passive, wasteful role.

Although from an operations point of view it is necessary to conduct maximally efficient inspection operations, the fact that inspections are of little value on the process side means that even the most efficient inspection operations are nothing more than efficiently wasteful. It follows that we need, first of all, to examine why we are conducting inspections at all. Even more, we need to carry out higher-order investigations aimed at finding methods of work, transportation, and delays that obviate the need for inspections.

Although inspections are supplementary to work, transport, and delays, from this point I am going to focus on the functions of inspections with respect to work, or processing.

On Defects and Inspections

Isolated Defects and Serial Defects

Isolated defects are essentially those that occur only once. An example would be a single part that is defective because one particular unit of raw material was flawed.

Serial defects, in contrast, occur repeatedly. For example, many pieces might lack holes because a broken punch was not detected right away.

Sensory Inspections and Physical Inspections

Sensory inspections are inspections performed by means of the human senses, e.g., judgments of plating adequacy or inspections of paint saturation. It tends to be difficult to set criteria for inspections of this kind, because different people will make different judgments and even the same person might make different judgments on different days.

Physical inspections involve the use of measuring devices, such as calipers or micrometers.

Subjective Inspections and Objective Inspections

Subjective inspections are made by the same person who performed the work. This method always suffers from the dangers of compromise and inattention.

Objective inspections, on the other hand, are made by someone other than the operator who performed the work. This method provides for more rigorous inspections — with fewer lapses of attention — than does the subjective method.

Process-Internal Inspections and Process-External Inspections

Inspections carried out at the same process where the work was performed are process-internal inspections, and inspections carried out at a different process are process-external inspections. Because process-internal inspections permit rapid transmission of information, or feedback, in the event a defect occurs, they are more efficient in reducing defects.

Statistical Inspections and Nonstatistical Inspections

In carrying out inspections — especially sampling inspections — the number of samples may be chosen either in accordance with statistical theory or not. Obviously, it is more rational to determine the number of samples on the basis of statistical theory.

100 Percent Inspections and Sampling Inspections

An inspection of every processed item is a 100 percent inspection, and the method of extrapolating from an appropriate number of samples constitutes sampling. Inspection labor costs can be considerably reduced where it is permissible to conduct sampling inspections. It is sometimes claimed that 100 percent inspections generally take a great deal of trouble and increase the risk of oversights.

Feedback and Action

When a defect occurs, information to that effect sent back to the work process is known as inspection feedback. Such feedback is most effective when it is given promptly, for it permits countermeasures to be devised and methods altered at the work process where the defect occurred. This devising of countermeasures is known as action.

Measurement and Judgment

Measurement refers to the determination of numerical values through the use of measuring devices such as calipers or micrometers after work has been completed. A decision to accept or reject the item is then made on the basis of these numerical results.

Since inspections essentially involve distinguishing acceptable from unacceptable goods, however, it is not always necessary to make numerical measurements. Sometimes a simple gauge-like judgment tool is adequate for determining whether an item is acceptable. When inspections focus on judgments rather than measurements, automated inspections can make use of extremely simple and inexpensive devices.

Quantity Inspections and Quality Inspections

Checks to ascertain that needed quantities suffer from neither excesses nor shortages are quantity inspections, while quality inspections include checks such as the following:

- Is the part machined to within permissible limits?
- Has the surface been ground to within permissible limits?
- Is the degree of hardness obtained in heat treatment suitable?

- Are any parts missing from the assembly? Are all parts present the right ones?
- Are there any scratches? Is the part clean?

Quality inspections may even involve judgments made with the aid of numerical measuring devices as long as what is being checked is product quality.

2

Management Functions and Quality Control

MANAGEMENT FUNCTIONS

Management functions can be visualized in terms of the following: stages of action, the movement from individual to group activities, and five categories of executive management.

The Seven Stages of Action

The stages of individual action within a business organization can be characterized in the following way:

Volition. As used here, this term refers to the choice to begin some new task or the decision to increase profits.

Policy. When volition has been invoked and one is determined to act, a policy is set by a desire to do a specific task and a desire to do it a specific way.

Programming (or planning). Planning and programming are carried out for the purpose of giving concrete shape to and developing the policy. Ideal methods are devised and standard operations are put in place.

Execution. Actual processes and operations are performed in accordance with plans set up in the programming stage.

Control. Execution alone is inadequate. Control must accompany execution to ensure that processes and operations faithfully adhere to standards set up in the programming stage.

Monitoring. The results of controlled execution are checked and the answers to questions such as the following are reflected in the programming (or planning) stage of the next cycle:

• Were there any flaws in execution?
• Were the control methods appropriate and effective?
• Were there any problems relating to programming?

Satisfaction. A comparison of the results of monitoring with initial policy targets and then evaluation will establish "100 percent satisfaction" or "70 percent satisfaction," etc. At the same time, this will invoke new volition and start off the next cycle.

Cycles like the one described above are constantly repeated as human beings continue their activities (*Figure 2-1*).

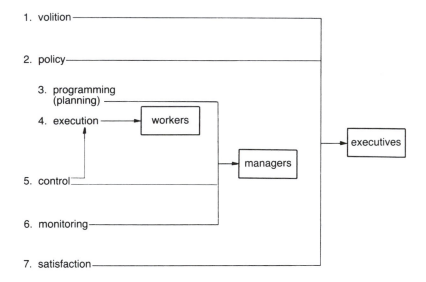

1. volition
2. policy
3. programming (planning)
4. execution → workers
5. control
6. monitoring
7. satisfaction

managers

executives

FIGURE 2-1. The Seven Stages of Action

From Individual Activities to Group Activities

Production activities soon increase to the point where they cannot be sustained by individuals, and it is here that people cooperate to carry out production.

In the early days, it may have been that everyone performed the same sort of task, but as the number of people involved grew, group activities were organized and hierarchical divisions of labor emerged.

Thus, different functions are shouldered by different groups (*Figure 2-2*):

Executives: volition, policy, satisfaction

Managers: programming (or planning), control, monitoring

Workers: actual execution of productive processes and operations

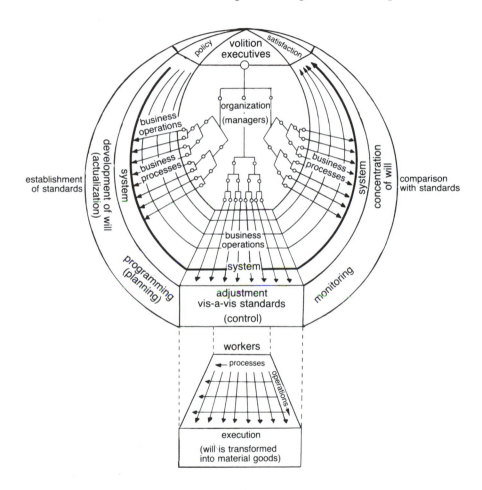

FIGURE 2-2. **The Structure of Management**

Like "extended individuals," groups spiral through the seven stages of action with the aim of improving the performance of the organization as a whole. The control functions of such an organizational unit may be illustrated by the tetrahedral structure shown in *Figures 2-3* and *2-4*.

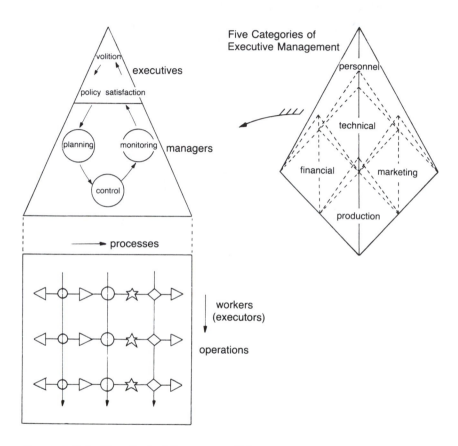

FIGURE 2-3. Tetrahedral Structure of Management

As tasks are divided up within the cycle of action of this organizational unit, individuals, as members of the organization, bear part of the responsibility for the organization as a whole. As in the case of molecular activity, then, it is the sum of each individual's "seven stages of action" (i.e., volition, policy, programming [or planning], execution, control, monitoring, and satisfaction) that determines the direction of the organization as a whole.

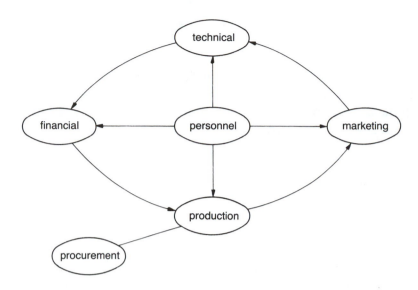

FIGURE 2-4. The Five Categories of Executive Management

The results of individual management functions (programming [or planning], control, monitoring) and execution corresponding to control likewise affect the ultimate achievements of the whole organization.

The Categories of Executive Management

Although our examples up to this point have mainly been of production issues, we can also distinguish among five categories of executive management:

Technical. The manager needs first to ensure the availability of technical capacity to carry out functional product design and to actually manufacture the product.

Financial. The next requirement is capital. A finance department will be needed to handle this issue.

Production. After technical capacity and capital have been secured, the next problem to come up is production. Between finances and production is situated a capital procurement function that, because it plays an intermediate role, belongs neither to finances nor to production.

Marketing. Next, a marketing department is set up to provide the goods produced to the market. Since marketing, or sales, is the ultimate aim of production, close communication links must always operate between marketing and production.

Personnel. Since each of the functions above is run by people, a personnel department is needed to manage the entire business from the viewpoint of people. This group is interwoven with the four other groups because its function is comprehensive management from the point of view of everyone in the company.

Each of the five categories of management outlined above forms its own "tetrahedral organization," while together, they make up an overall tetrahedral structure.

INDIVIDUAL MANAGEMENT FUNCTIONS AND THE SCIENCE OF STATISTICS

As mentioned above, management functions can be categorized as programming (or planning) functions, control functions and closely related execution functions, and monitoring functions.

The Programming (or Planning) Function

Programming involves drawing up production plans and establishing standard process and operations systems.

The establishment of such standards goes beyond abstract process systems (e.g., cutting off ends, cutting inside diameters, cutting outside diameters) to determine permissible deviations in the form of tolerances. It might be determined, for example, that deviation within the range of 150 ± 0.05mm is permissible for outside diameters.

At this programming stage, however, when the work conditions required for the manufacture of goods are not yet established, it is extremely effective and, I think, highly recommended that one make use of SQC (statistical quality control) techniques based on the science of statistics. Statistics can be effective in a number of situations:

- It is extremely helpful to use experimental planning methods based on statistics to examine what sort of conditions need to be specified.
- Statistical methods are extremely effective, in cases involving several work conditions, in determining significant differences when choosing optimal methods.
- When standard work methods are being determined, consideration of which factors need to be examined in setting up a work methods chart is another extremely effective technique for ensuring consideration of all factors.
- The construction of histograms can, of course, be quite convenient for correctly evaluating the current state of work methods and for looking into improvements.

The next important issue, I think, concerns how to link the programming (or planning) function to control on the one hand and to execution functions on the other. For this, we have to compile standard work process manuals and standard operations manuals. The instructions in these manuals must be thoroughly understood by personnel in charge of control and execution, and actual instruction and training should be carried out so that error-free execution can take place. If these efforts are inadequate, defects due to misunderstandings or incomplete understandings may arise even when the standards themselves are perfectly appropriate.

The Control Function and the Execution Function

It is an inescapable fact that, in the real world, defects in production actually occur at the stage of control and execution. No matter how admirably the planning may have been carried out, the products are actually made at the control and execution stage, and the conceptual approach and techniques chosen have a decisive impact on the quality of the finished product.

Although the actual results of production activities are ultimately determined by the results of the execution stage, execution is inseparably linked to, and influenced by, control. In the performance of the execution function, both managers and workers are constantly subject to the influence of the control function. Managers observe the operational methods used by workers and regulate their execution, and the workers strive to carry out their tasks in accordance with the standards that have been set for them. When errors occur, moreover, they carry out repairs themselves.

The control function is sometimes assisted by internal devices that detect abnormal conditions and errors. This, in fact, is the significance of the poka-yoke approach we will discuss later on.

The following are instances in which defects may occur during the execution stage:

- Standards devised in the planning stage are flawed.
- Control or execution is not carried out in accordance with standards set during the planning stage because those standards were imperfectly or improperly understood.
- Standards established by programs (plans) are observed, but deviations from permissible tolerances occur.
- Standards set by the planning function are correctly understood, but inadvertent mistakes occur.

Situations like these simply invite defects. Consequently, defects will occur unless preventive countermeasures are put in place. This is where the fulfillment of control functions is of considerable significance.

Furthermore, since the control capacities of managers and workers themselves often have no effect on inadvertent mistakes, we can say that the wisest way to deal with such errors is to uncover them through the use of detection measures designed for that purpose. At Arakawa Auto Body, a 3.5 percent defect rate was cut to 0.01 percent in the space of two years — a reduction due principally to the installation of poka-yoke devices. This example, I think, shows the surprising extent to which defects due to inadvertent mistakes actually occur on the shop floor.

Next, it is important to consider effective linkage between control and execution functions on the one hand and the monitoring function on the other. It turns out that sampling checks are often carried out at this stage. Yet in terms of theory, even if errors occur at the control and execution stages, such errors will be overlooked. Of course, the number of samples chosen will be based on statistical theory. Even so, from the point of view of all-out efforts to attain zero defects, this approach cannot, in spite of its roots in probability theory, lead to the total elimination of defects.

Feedback and action involving the results of quality checks, moreover, often take place at distant processes, and this means large control cycles and delayed improvement in the level of management. Effective measures for improving the level of management include the following:

- Wherever possible, check 100 percent of the results of control and execution.
- Shorten the time between control and execution results on the one hand and monitoring on the other.

The Monitoring Function

The role of the monitoring function is to compare the results of control and execution with the plans in order to locate flaws. Thus, if there are any deficiencies in planning or undesirable results of control and execution, it must be determined whether the flaws are in control or in execution and suitable countermeasures must be devised. It is nonsense to say merely that "appropriate monitoring has been carried out," for defects will be prevented in the future only by relaying information on abnormal conditions back to the processes involved (feedback) and then taking prompt and suitable countermeasures (action).

Improvement efforts will come alive only when one begins to work toward obviating future defects. Such efforts will push the management cycle of planning, control, and monitoring to a higher level, producing an upward spiral of improvement.

The Deming Circle and Management Functions

The "Deming Circle," named for its advocate,* is widely spoken of in the field of quality control (*Figure 2-5*).

---

* Dr. W. Edwards Deming is the American statistician who went to Japan in the 1950s to teach the basics of statistical quality control.

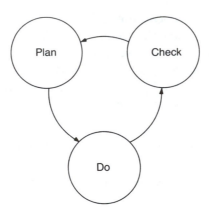

FIGURE 2-5. Deming Circle

The circle consists of three elements: plan, do, and check. It is claimed that moving around this circle will achieve successively higher management.

What I maintain, however, differs from Deming's approach in two respects:

- The execution ("do") function exists independently of "management."
- Among management functions, the execution ("do") function is inseparable from the control function (*Figure 2-6*).

In real life, the control function is allotted primarily to managers, while the execution function is assigned mostly to workers. The execution function, meanwhile, is constantly influenced by the control function. Sometimes the control function is assigned to the workers in charge of execution.

But does the control function unquestionably belong among management functions, and must it be thought of as distinct from the execution function?

It turns out that recognizing the existence of this control function and making it more efficient is the crucial concept of a Zero QC system that will eliminate defects.

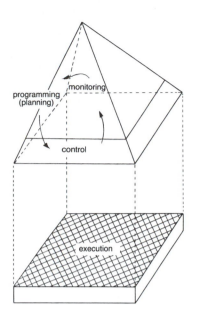

FIGURE 2-6. Management Cycle

The argument either that the Deming Circle does not recognize the control function or that a similar control function is inherent in the Deming Circle's "do" phase is acceptable on its own terms, but I fear many people tend to take Deming's "do" function at face value and overlook the existence of a control function.

Adherence to this approach would permit us, at the stage of control and execution, to expect quality maintenance, but not quality improvement. If we want to improve quality, then we would have to move around the cycle to do it at the planning stage.

These considerations will make it easier to understand the significance of installing poka-yoke devices at the stage of control and execution. There is no doubt that poka-yoke techniques constitute an effective means of regulating wide variations in quality. That, however, is a quality maintenance function. Anyone wishing to improve quality will have to give consideration to poka-yoke at the planning stage.

3

Inspections Don't Reduce Defects

INCREASING THE NUMBER OF INSPECTORS (QUANTITATIVE ENHANCEMENT)

A plant manager at A Industries complained during one of my visits that he simply could not find any way to reduce defects.

"What have you tried?" I asked.

He told me that an inspector at the very end of the process in question separated the good products from the defective ones, but that about 100 units out of every 1,000 were defective. At that point, the plant manager ordered an increase in the number of inspectors. The next day, the number of defective units dropped to 80 and the second day it fell to 60. He felt somewhat relieved to be on the right track, but on the fourth day the number of defective items rose again, this time to 120 (*Figure 3-1*).

"What on earth am I supposed to do to cut defects?" he asked.

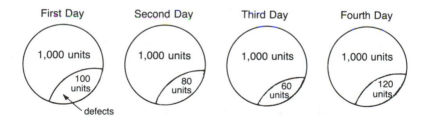

FIGURE 3-1. Inspections and Defects

This is what I told the plant manager:

"Two inspectors may be able to catch defects that might slip by one inspector, and using the two inspectors may, indeed, eliminate

35

such oversights and keep you from mixing defective items in with with the good ones you send to customers.

"That issue, however, is unrelated to the question of reducing defects.

"In any event, there isn't much point in inspecting goods at the end of the process. Since defects are generated during the process, all you are doing is discovering those defects. Adding inspection workers is pointless, because there's no way you're going to reduce defects without using processing methods that prevent defects from occurring in the first place.

"It follows, then, that when a defect shows up, you've got to send information to that effect back to the work stage so that processing can be corrected.

"At any rate, it's an unalterable fact that processing produces defects and all that inspections can do is find those defects. That's why approaching the problem only at the inspection stage is meaningless."

CONDUCTING MORE RIGOROUS INSPECTIONS (QUALITATIVE ENHANCEMENT)

On a visit I made to V Industries, a manufacturer of packing materials, the inspection department head, Mr. Wakabayashi, brought up the following question.

It seemed that after products had been shipped to the parent company, defects were sometimes found during inspections conducted when the items were received. Mr. Wakabayashi was troubled because he had even had to visit the parent company in Kyushu to repeat inspections.

"Why," I asked him, "do you think it is that your parent company finds defects when it takes delivery of your products? I can think of two possible reasons. Either your parent company is finding defects that slipped unnoticed out of your plant, or it views as defective some products that you judged to be satisfactory.

"You seem to be using sensory inspections to judge the appearance and hardness of your packing materials. Have you got samples of the acceptable limits?"

I told him that he ought to have such samples and that someone from the inspection department should be present when quality standards were set up. I also chided him when he admitted that, although the head of the technical department had gone to the meeting in question, no one from the inspection department had been there.

He immediately suggested dispatching a representative from the inspection department to the parent company to reach an agreement on quality and, in particular, on samples of acceptable limits.

His department was then able to pass or fail products on the basis of these samples and this completely eliminated defects found during delivery inspections at the parent company. When I left him, he told me his goal was to cut in-house defects in half. I wished him luck.

When I visited V Industries the following month, Mr. Wakabayashi showed me inspection statistics and proudly announced that he had met his goal for cutting in-house defects. We congratulated one another on his achievement.

Afterwards, during a tour of the plant, I noticed a great deal of #2810 packing material — the product that had caused the trouble before — discarded in waste bins beside a vulcanization press. I remarked to the operator that there seemed to be a lot of defects. "Were the raw materials at fault?" I asked.

"No," he replied. "It's just that management's been getting fussy with their inspections recently, so we throw out any material that doesn't seem right."

In the past, the defect rate had been high because all clearly defective goods were discarded and the rest of the items were submitted for inspection. Now any items that seemed the least bit odd were thrown away, including some that were perfectly good.

Despite statistics showing that defects had been cut in half, the plant's "absolute defect rate" had not only not decreased, it had risen. Alarmed by this, I summoned Mr. Wakabayashi to the shop floor and had him take a look at what was going on.

"It's complete nonsense for you to be pleased by a 50 percent reduction in the statistical defect rate," I told him. "Nothing at all has been accomplished unless you've lowered the plant's absolute defect rate."

In response to my comments, Mr. Wakabayashi immediately made the following improvements (*Figure 3-2*):

1. A shared conveyor was installed along the front of several vulcanization presses.

2. If each press handled, say, four units of packing material, the conveyor would immediately carry those four pieces together to the

next process. In the past, no items were transported to the next lot until the entire lot had been processed.

3. At the next process, deburring, surface irregularities were removed and units were immediately sent on to the inspection process.

4. At the inspection process, products that passed inspection were placed, along with other items of the same type, on a turntable-type holder.

5. When a defect was discovered, a button was pushed and the offending operation was halted.

6. The die was then checked by an inspector, the supervisor of the operation, and the operator. After removal of the cause of the defect — e.g., the removal or grinding down of any residue or scratches on the die — the operation resumed.

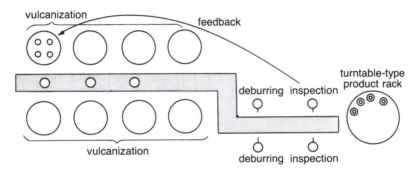

FIGURE 3-2. Processing and Inspection Feedback

Thus, news of the discovery of a defect was immediately fed back to the operation in question and that operation did not resume until action had been taken to prevent the defect from recurring.

Operating methods were altered, moreover, so that if a crack appeared in one of the four dies, that die would not be used.

As a result of these changes, the plant's absolute defect rate dropped to one-tenth of its previous level and the rate of inspection defects fell sharply as well.

The crucial lesson in this episode was that it did not matter how rigorously inspections were carried out: defects are generated at the work stage and all inspections can do is find those defects.

The example above shows that defects will not be reduced merely by making improvements at the inspection stage, although such improvements may, of course, eliminate defects in delivered goods.

To reduce defects within production activities, the most fundamental concept is to recognize that defects are generated by work and all inspections can do is to discover those defects. Zero defects can never be achieved if this concept is forgotten. This is a vital point and can never be stressed enough. The idea it expresses, moreover, is the cornerstone on which the Zero QC system is built.

4
Approaching the Zero QC Method

PRELIMINARY STAGE: THE OLD METHOD (JUDGMENT INSPECTIONS)

I was taught that an inspection within a process is the act of comparison with a standard, principally to eliminate defective goods. When 100 percent inspections took too much trouble, I used appropriate sampling inspections. I imagined that the occurrence of a certain level of defects was inevitable in any work done by humans, and thought that we should pay attention so as to not produce defective items as we work. At the same time, I vaguely assumed that we could reduce defects by making inspections more and more rigorous. In short, I thought that judgment inspections were the only kind of inspections there were.

STAGE 1: ENCOUNTER WITH THE STATISTICAL QUALITY CONTROL (SQC) METHOD

In 1951, when I was in charge of education for the Japan Management Association, a Mr. A from Nippon Electric Company came to my office and asked me if I had heard about quality control. I replied that I understood the term to mean efforts to inspect products, make high-quality goods, and eliminate defects.

"That's not good enough," he told me. "It's not quality control unless you use statistics." He then proceeded to explain the American-style statistical quality control (SQC) method to me. He told me about experimental planning methods, determination of significant differences, factor charts, histograms, and control charts for informative inspections. For the next several hours, I listened to him explain

41

such things as standard limits and control limits, control charts and 3 SD limits, $\overline{X}$.R control charts, P control charts, and sampling inspections based on statistical science.

What particularly impressed me was the revolutionary idea of informative inspections that could reduce defects in the future. With this approach, control charts would be drawn up and, whenever values appeared outside of the control limits, information to that effect would be fed back to the process involved and work methods would be improved. I was further struck by the truly revolutionary technique of determining whether a situation was normal or not through classification according to 3 SD control limits. At the most basic level, I was enormously impressed by the theoretical backing provided by the science of inductive statistics. It seemed to me, too, that the theory-based techniques of experimental planning methods and the determination of significant differences were extremely effective.

Mr. A told me he had total confidence in this theoretical sampling inspection system, in which sampling inspections that used to depend solely on intuition were put on a scientific, statistical footing.

His final words left a powerful and lasting impression. "From now on," he stressed, "if it doesn't use statistics, it's not quality control."

For a long time afterwards, I believed that quality control systems that used the science of statistics were the ultimate in quality control methods. I believed, furthermore, that informative inspections constituted a revolutionary control system for raising quality, and inductive statistics provided the most rational technique available. I invited Dr. Eisaburo Nishibori to the Japan Management Association and devoted myself to studying the statistical quality control (SQC) method.

STAGE 2: ENCOUNTER WITH POKA-YOKE METHODS

In 1961, I visited Yamada Electric in Nagoya. There, the plant manager told me the following story.

"One of the operations we do involves the assembly of an extremely simple push-button device that we deliver to our parent company, Matsushita Electric, in Kyushu. The device is composed of two buttons, an *on* button and an *off* button, under each of which we have to enclose a small spring. Sometimes, though, one of our workers forgets to put in a spring. When Matsushita Electric discovers a switch without a spring, we have to send an inspector all the way to Kyushu to check every switch that was delivered.

"This is a real pain in the neck, so whenever it happens, we tell workers to be particularly careful and for a while things improve a bit. The same thing happens again before long, though, and these chronic defects are getting to be a real nuisance. Matsushita bawls us out every time for making mistakes in such a simple operation, and recently I had to go to Kyushu myself to apologize. Is there anything we can do to keep these defects from occurring?"

I immediately went into the plant to observe the assembly of the switches.

The operation was an extremely simple one. A worker would insert two small springs and then install the buttons. As I watched, however, a worker neglected to put in a spring before installing the button. The head of the manufacturing department saw this, too. In a panic, he scolded the worker for forgetting the spring and then had the switch reassembled.

I thought about what I had seen for a moment and then turned to Mr. Y, the manufacturing department chief.

"What," I asked him, "does it mean for a human being to 'forget' something?"

Mr. Y looked puzzled and replied, "To 'forget' means . . . well . . . it just means to forget, doesn't it?"

When I asked him to explain, he was unable to answer and finally fell silent. After a brief pause, I suggested to him that there were really two kinds of forgetting. The first involves simply forgetting something. Since people are not perfect, they will, on rare occasions, inadvertently forget things. It is not that they forget things intentionally; they just happen, inadvertently, to forget now and then.

"Haven't you ever, in your whole life, forgotten anything?" I asked Mr. Y.

"Sure I have," he replied. "I forget things now and then. My wife always chews me out about it."

I observed that, that being the case, he was probably in a poor position to complain to his wife that his workers were forgetting things.

The other type of forgetting, I told him, involves forgetting that one has forgotten. We are all familiar with this kind of forgetting. It is the reason, for example, that we make checklists for ourselves.

If people had the omnipotence of gods, they would be able to remember everything and they would not need checklists.

"When I go to play golf," I said, "I carry a checklist with me in a notebook. When I am about to leave, I mostly depend on my memory when I'm getting together the equipment I need. Afterwards, though, I look at my checklist and when I notice, for example, that I have forgotten my gloves, I immediately get my gloves and put them in my bag. That way, I have all my equipment with me when I get to the golf course.

"The same thing applies to this operation. Rather than thinking that workers ought to assemble the switches perfectly every time, you should recognize that, being human, they will, on rare occasions, forget things. To guard against that," I suggested, "why not take the idea of a checklist and incorporate it into the operation?"

The next question was how this could be done, so I had them put the following suggestions into effect (*Figure 4-1*):

- A small dish was brought and, at the very beginning of the operation, two springs were taken out of a parts box containing hundreds of springs and placed on the dish.
- Switch assembly took place next; then springs were inserted and buttons installed.
- If any spring remained on the dish after assembly, the worker realized that that spring had been left out, and the assembly was then corrected.

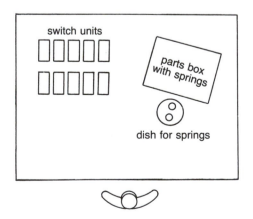

FIGURE 4-1. Ensuring Spring Insertion

This change in the operation completely eliminated the problem of missing springs and the parent company made no more claims on the subject.

Since springs in the earlier operation had been taken out of a parts box containing hundreds of other springs, there had been no way of knowing whether a spring had been removed or not. The new operation made it possible to know that a part had been forgotten and so eliminated the problem of missing springs.

Whenever I hear supervisors warning workers to pay more attention or to be sure not to forget anything, I cannot help thinking that the workers are being asked to carry out operations as if they possessed divine infallibility. Rather than that approach, we should recognize that people are, after all, only human and as such, they will, on rare occasions, inadvertently forget things. It is more effective to incorporate a checklist — i.e., a poka-yoke — into the operation so that if a worker forgets something, the device will signal that fact, thereby preventing defects from occurring. This, I think, is the quickest road leading to attainment of zero defects.

In terms of management functions, this sort of poka-yoke device fulfills a control function that supplements the execution function.

This poka-yoke concept is actually based on the same idea as "foolproofing," an approach devised mainly for preserving the safety of operations. In the early days, I used the term "foolproofing" (in Japanese, *bakayoke*), but around 1963, when Arakawa Auto Body adopted a "foolproofing" device to prevent seat parts from being spot-welded backwards, one of the company's part-time employees burst into tears when her department head explained that a "foolproofing" mechanism had been installed because workers sometimes mixed up left- and right-hand parts. "Have I really been such a fool?'" she sobbed. She ended up staying home the following day and the department head went to see her there.

He tried all sorts of explanations. "It's not that you're a fool," he told her. "We put the device in because anybody can make inadvertent mistakes." Finally, he managed to persuade her.

When the department head told me this story, it was clear to me that "foolproofing" was a poorly chosen term. But what name would be suitable? After some thought, I gave the name *poka-yoke* (mistake-proofing) to these devices because they serve to prevent (or "proof;" in Japanese, *yoke*) the sort of inadvertent mistakes (*poka* in Japanese) that anyone can make.

Since the word *poka-yoke* (pronounced POH-kah YOH-kay) has been used untranslated in the English version of my book, *A Study of the Toyota Production System*, and appears in the French, Swedish, and Italian-language editions, it is now current throughout the world.

In the years following the development of the idea, poka-yoke devices were used widely. Because the adoption of appropriate poka-yoke devices results in the total elimination of defects, I began to have some doubts about the conventional view of exclusive reliance on SQC methods.

I think the source of this doubt lay in the fact that the poka-yoke approach uses 100 percent inspections to guard against inadvertent mistakes. I had come to assume that if we admit the existence of inadvertent mistakes, then 100 percent inspections are superior to sampling inspections based on statistical theory. Nevertheless, my belief that SQC provided the best quality control methods available remained largely unshaken. At the time, I thought that the total elimination of defects had been an effect of 100 percent inspections. If, instead, I had noted the significance of checking actual working conditions, the concept of "source inspections" would surely have been developed sooner.

It is clear to me now that my belief that SQC methods were unsurpassed impeded development in the direction of source inspections.

STAGE 3: ENCOUNTERS WITH SUCCESSIVE AND SELF-CHECKS

Application of the poka-yoke concept in numerous plants brought success that exceeded my expectations. Unfortunately, however, although poka-yoke devices were fine in situations permitting the use of physical detection methods, there are a surprising number of things that can only be checked by means of sensory detection methods. The poka-yoke approach cannot be applied in such cases.

Despite the fact that SQC methods had achieved markedly better results than conventional judgment inspection methods, I still felt there was something missing. In particular, I wondered why it was that, appropriately applied, the poka-yoke method was capable of eliminating defects entirely while SQC methods could only lower defect rates. I concluded that, although the SQC system was characterized by informative inspections, the answer to the question lay in the fact that the detection of abnormalities was performed selectively and corrective action took place slowly. If that was the case, I thought, then more rapid action would be provided by *self-checks*. It seemed to me that the answer lay in having the processing operation worker carry out both checks and action.

Given the long-standing emphasis on the objectivity of inspections, however, this concept was flawed by the idea that, if the worker involved carried out his or her own inspections, he or she might be apt to compromise on quality, or might inadvertently let defects slip by. This is why stress had always been laid on the need to guarantee the independence of inspections — on the idea that inspections had to be performed by disinterested inspectors.

Since this inevitably slowed down corrective action, it occurred to me that the need for objective inspections did not require that inspections be carried out — as is common — at the end of the work process. Why not have the closest person perform inspections? The "closest person," i.e., the operator at the next process, could just as well take on the job of inspector. This would have the benefit that information about any abnormality discovered could be relayed immediately to the worker at the previous process. This is how the *successive check system* was devised. This method garnered considerable success in subsequent experimental applications at a number of plants (*Figure 4-2*).

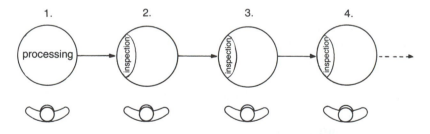

FIGURE 4-2. Successive Checks

In 1963, I went as a consultant to Matsushita Electric's Moriguchi Television Division. Mr. Kishida, the head of the division, told me that his plant had adopted a SQC system because of a 15 percent process defect rate. The SQC methods, along with the enthusiastic use of control charts and QC Circle activities, had brought the defect rate down to 6.5 percent, but afterward it had just stayed there. Mr. Kishida was still not satisfied and he asked me if there were some other methods he might use.

After a good deal of thought, I proposed that he try a successive check system. I explained the method to him and the new system was rapidly put into place. One month later, the interprocess defect rate fell to 1.5 percent. Three months later, that rate had dropped to 0.65 percent, and the defect rate at the last process had gone as low as 0.016 percent.

Emboldened by the success of the successive check system, I realized that a *self-check system* would allow even faster corrective action to take place. Self-checking, though, was said to be flawed by workers' tendencies to make compromises and inadvertently overlook problems.

Those issues related to sensory inspections, however, and it dawned on me that, in cases where poka-yoke devices could be used, a self-check system was even better than a successive check system. With this in mind, I actively developed poka-yoke devices and worked to expand the use of successive check systems. In instances where it was technically or economically unfeasible to apply poka-yoke methods to self-check systems, we tried hard to incorporate poka-yoke functions into successive check systems.

This way of using self-check systems and successive check systems proved to be markedly more successful than SQC systems using control charts.

Yet these self-check systems and successive check systems remained approaches based on the idea of informative inspections, and in that sense were founded on the same concepts as were SQC-based control chart systems. The reason that they were far more successful in reducing defects resided in large part, I think, in the fact that the detection of abnormalities was carried out by means of 100 percent inspections rather than sampling inspections, and when abnormalities occurred, corrective action was taken extremely rapidly.

Considerations such as these were already outside the scope of inductive statistics, and I felt my confidence in statistically based SQC systems collapsing rapidly. Yet I was still spellbound by my preconceived notion that quality control methods backed by scientific statistical theory were superior. I still could not completely escape this idea.

STAGE 4: SAMPLING INSPECTIONS DO NOTHING BUT MAKE INSPECTION PROCEDURES MORE RATIONAL

In 1964, Mr. Tokizane, managing director at the headquarters of Matsushita Electric's Television Division, told me that he didn't want a single television made by his company to be defective.

"I feel that way," he said, "because an individual customer generally buys only one television set. If that one set is defective, then that customer may assume that all Matsushita television sets are lemons. I won't allow defects in even one set, and so I'm in the plant nearly every day keeping an eye on workers."

I replied that I thought his attitude seemed reasonable, but then something about the use of statistically based sampling inspections had suddenly occurred to me: no matter how scientific a basis sampling inspections may have, the entire method rests on the notion that a certain level of defects is inevitable, whether it be one television set in 10,000 or one in 100,000.

Yet here was Mr. Tokizane, saying that he could not allow even one defective television set — even if it were one in 10,000 or one in 100,000. The idea that sampling inspections were extremely rational measures backed by the science of inductive statistics contradicted Mr. Tokizane's perfectly justifiable assertion that he would not allow a single defective television set in his company.

Unable to resolve this conflict, I fell to thinking as I headed home from Osaka by train. My confusion continued until we reached the outskirts of Tokyo, when suddenly it hit me: the statistical basis of sampling inspections meant only that such inspections made inspection techniques more rational; it did *not* make quality assurance more rational. Sampling inspections, in other words, may represent a rationalization of methods, but in no way do they represent a rationalization of goals.

The superiority of 100 percent inspections clearly dawned on me as I realized that they, and not sampling inspections, had to be used if one wished to put quality assurance on a more rational basis.

The justification for using sampling inspections was that 100 percent inspections would take too much trouble and cost too much. Why not, then, use 100 percent inspection techniques like poka-yoke ones — techniques that require little in the way of trouble or expense? This realization for the first time released me from the spell of sampling inspections and the inductive statistics behind them.

STAGE 5: ENCOUNTER WITH SOURCE INSPECTIONS

As explained above, I had been concentrating on the use of 100 percent inspections and on speeding up feedback and action. My thinking had never gone beyond the concept of informative inspections, and although I had given considerable thought to reducing defects, I had not adopted the more radical position of wanting to eliminate defects entirely.

As I went about applying poka-yoke methods, however, I noticed that the installation of suitable poka-yoke devices had the effect of reducing defects to zero. Was there some approach, I wondered, in which carrying out suitable inspections would make it possible to eliminate defects altogether?

Then it hit me. Why not just perform inspections at the sources of defects? Thus, around 1967, I arrived at the concept of *source inspections*. It had dawned on me that the occurrence of a defect was the *result* of some condition or action, and that it would be possible to eliminate defects entirely by pursuing the cause. The causes of defects lie in worker errors, and defects are the results of neglecting those errors. It follows that mistakes will not turn into defects if worker errors are discovered and eliminated beforehand.

I began advocating source inspections based on this fundamental notion and, in terms of actual techniques, installed a variety of poka-yoke systems that proved to be enormously successful.

In 1971, I joined the Japan Management Association's first overseas study group in visits to various plants in Europe. During that trip, we toured the facilities of Wotan, a molding machine manufacturer in Düsseldorf, West Germany.

During a question-and-answer period following the tour, a Mr. K of the M Spring Company — one of our group who always asked lively questions — stood up and asked the people at Wotan if they carried out quality control.

"Of course we do," the manufacturing division chief representing the company replied.

"But," continued Mr. K, "in touring your plant I didn't see a single control chart."

"Control chart? What on earth is that?"

Mr. K then triumphantly proceeded to explain control charts while the Wotan representative listened in silence. When Mr. K had finished, the Wotan executive responded:

"That's a very interesting idea, but don't you think it's fundamentally wrong-headed?"

Mr. K bristled. "Fundamentally wrong-headed?! What are you talking about?"

"The idea you just described deals with defects after they occur," the Wotan representative explained. "The basic idea behind our approach to quality control is to prevent defects from occurring in the first place."

"How in the world do you do that?" Mr. K asked.

Our host said that, rather than checking quality after a task had been completed, they checked whether operating methods were suitable before the job started.

As I listened to the Wotan representative, I recalled a scene I had just witnessed in the machine shop. When the operator in charge of a radial boring machine had put drills in place and was ready to begin, he motioned to a roving quality control officer, who came over to the machine and, using a chart as a guide, checked both drill positions and the positions of stoppers used to determine hole depths. Only when he gave the OK sign did the operator start the machine. As I listened to the division chief's words, I realized that it was this type of operation he was talking about.

The Wotan representative then asked Mr. K what the process defect rate at his company was.

"Only about 2.5 percent," said Mr. K proudly.

"I see," our host replied. "but the process defect rate at my company isn't any higher than 0.3 percent."

That took the wind out of Mr. K's sails and he was silent for the rest of the question-and-answer period.

I realized that the idea of checking operating conditions before the operations rather than after them was precisely the same as my concept of source inspections. I remember taking courage from this realization and thinking that this attested to the superiority of the source inspection concept. It was at that point, in fact, that my philosophy with regard to source inspections took definite shape.

At the same time, I repeatedly heard people say that the SQC system "builds quality into the process." But where was the evidence?

My claim was that a process is a flow in which raw materials are converted into finished products, and that any errors in process standards would naturally generate defects. That issue, of course, has to be addressed when standards are determined, that is, at the planning stage.

In the course of actual production activities, however, quality is shaped by means of "operations" that fulfill execution functions supplementary to processes. As execution functions, moreover, operations are heavily influenced by the regulatory effects of control functions. It follows from this, surely, that it is correct to say that quality is built into processes.

Furthermore, as the phrase "time is a shadow cast by motion" implies, saying that something takes a long time refers to carrying out motions that require a long time to perform. In the same way, we can say that "quality is a shadow cast by motion."

What is more, since motions are affected by operating conditions, we can conclude that the fundamental concept of source inspections resides in the absolute need for control functions that — once errors in operating conditions (i.e., in the objects of production, agents of production, methods, space, or time) are discovered — resolve those errors and prevent them from turning into defects.

In terms of techniques for bringing this about, the use of poka-yoke methods is tremendously effective.

It is in this way that we finally arrive at a Zero QC system aimed at zero defects (*Figure 4-3*).

STAGE 6: THE ACHIEVEMENT OF A MONTH WITH ZERO DEFECTS

In 1977, I hurried to the Shizuoka plant of Matsushita Electric's Washing Machine Division when I heard that the facility had achieved a continuous record of one month with zero defects in a drainpipe assembly line operation involving 23 workers.

When I got there, I found that this significant goal had been attained by the use of source inspections, self-checks, and successive checks, and by the installation of effective poka-yoke devices — ingenious and relatively inexpensive mechanisms that everyone had cooperated in coming up with. These devices were installed according to the characteristics of the processes involved. This success resulted from the extraordinary efforts of supervisors working under Mr. Izumi, the department head, as well, of course, as those of the

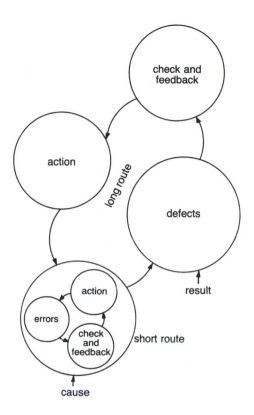

FIGURE 4-3. Cycle for Managing Errors and Defects

foreman, Mr. Muneo Iwabori, who directed actual work on the shop floor.

Before Matsushita's accomplishment, I had secretly been afraid that it might be impossible for a drainpipe assembly line employing so many workers and handling 30,000 units each month to actually go through an entire month with zero defects. Seeing this achievement gave me an unprecedented jolt, therefore, and I drew boundless confidence and courage from the realization that, given the proper conceptual approach and appropriate techniques, and given suitable leadership and general enthusiasm and cooperation, people can in fact achieve things that have been thought to be impossible.

The Matsushita Washing Division's Shizuoka plant continued zero defect production for over six months, and I confidently appealed to a number of other plants with the assertion that they, too, could achieve zero defects for the space of one month. Lo and behold, these plants began to achieve zero defect production for one month, and even for several months running. To myself, I thought how difficult such success would be to achieve with SQC methods based on inductive statistics.

STAGE 7: BASIC CONCEPTS FOR A ZERO QC SYSTEM

A Zero Quality Control system is built on the following basic ideas:

1. Use source inspections, i.e., inspections for preventing defects, to eliminate defects entirely. This does not mean dealing with the results of defect generation, it means applying control functions at the stage where defects originate.

2. Always use 100 percent inspections rather than sampling inspections.

3. Minimize the time it takes to carry out corrective action when abnormalities appear.

4. Human workers are not infallible. Recognize that people are human and set up effective poka-yoke devices accordingly. Poka-yoke devices fulfill control functions that must be effective in influencing execution functions (*Figure 4-4*).

A RESPONSE TO INDUCTIVE STATISTICS

When I first heard about inductive statistics in 1951, I firmly believed it to be the best technique around, and it took me 26 years to break completely free of its spell.

Considered from an independent vantage point, several observations can be made with respect to inductive statistics:

- Inductive statistics remains an excellent technique.
- Active use should be made of statistics in the sense that the technique is extremely effective in the planning phase of management.
- Nevertheless, statistics is not always effective in control and execution phases. In fact, it can surely be said that an infatuation with statistics has impeded the progress of the management function itself.

Characteristics of Quality Control Methods

inspection method					judgment inspections	control charts	successive checks	self-checks	source inspections (zero QC)
object of checks	**number of samples**	**inspection agent**	**inspection technique**	**speed of action**		informative inspections			
results	(statistical or other) sampling	others	sensory	long-term	✡	✡	—	—	—
results	(statistical or other) sampling	others	sensory	momentary	—	✡	—	—	—
results	(statistical or other) sampling	others	sensory	immediate	—	—	—	—	—
results	(statistical or other) sampling	others	material	long-term	✡	—	—	—	—
results	(statistical or other) sampling	others	material	momentary	—	✡	—	—	—
results	(statistical or other) sampling	others	material	immediate	—	—	—	—	—
results	(statistical or other) sampling	self	sensory	long-term	—	—	—	—	—
results	(statistical or other) sampling	self	sensory	momentary	—	—	—	—	—
results	(statistical or other) sampling	self	sensory	immediate	—	—	—	—	—
results	(statistical or other) sampling	self	material	long-term	—	—	—	—	—
results	(statistical or other) sampling	self	material	momentary	—	—	—	—	—
results	(statistical or other) sampling	self	material	immediate	—	—	—	—	—
results	all items	others	sensory	long-term	✡	—	—	—	—
results	all items	others	sensory	momentary	—	—	—	—	—
results	all items	others	sensory	immediate	—	—	◉	—	—
results	all items	others	material	long-term	✡	—	—	—	—
results	all items	others	material	momentary	—	—	—	—	—
results	all items	others	material	immediate	—	—	◉	—	—
results	all items	self	sensory	long-term	—	—	—	—	—
results	all items	self	sensory	momentary	—	—	—	—	—
results	all items	self	sensory	immediate	—	—	—	◉	—
results	all items	self	material	long-term	—	—	—	—	—
results	all items	self	material	momentary	—	—	—	—	—
results	all items	self	material	immediate	—	—	—	◉	—
causes	(statistical) sampling	others	sensory	long-term	—	—	—	—	—
causes	(statistical) sampling	others	sensory	momentary	—	—	—	—	—
causes	(statistical) sampling	others	sensory	immediate	—	—	—	—	—
causes	(statistical) sampling	others	material	long-term	—	—	—	—	—
causes	(statistical) sampling	others	material	momentary	—	—	—	—	—
causes	(statistical) sampling	others	material	immediate	—	—	—	—	—
causes	(statistical) sampling	self	sensory	long-term	—	—	—	—	—
causes	(statistical) sampling	self	sensory	momentary	—	—	—	—	—
causes	(statistical) sampling	self	sensory	immediate	—	—	—	—	—
causes	(statistical) sampling	self	material	long-term	—	—	—	—	—
causes	(statistical) sampling	self	material	momentary	—	—	—	—	—
causes	(statistical) sampling	self	material	immediate	—	—	—	—	—
causes	all items	others	sensory	long-term	—	—	—	—	—
causes	all items	others	sensory	momentary	—	—	—	—	—
causes	all items	others	sensory	immediate	—	—	—	—	—
causes	all items	others	material	long-term	—	—	—	—	—
causes	all items	others	material	momentary	—	—	—	—	—
causes	all items	others	material	immediate	—	—	—	—	—
causes	all items	self	sensory	long-term	—	—	—	—	—
causes	all items	self	sensory	momentary	—	—	—	—	—
causes	all items	self	sensory	immediate	—	—	—	—	—
causes	all items	self	material	long-term	—	—	—	—	—
causes	all items	self	material	momentary	—	—	—	—	—
causes	all items	self	material	immediate	—	—	—	—	◉ ◉

FIGURE 4-4. Characteristics of Quality Control Methods

- A major feature of SQC systems is the capacity for information inspections, and it is extremely important to pursue this function to the limit.
- In any case, inductive statistics is an excellent technique for making methods more rational; it does not necessarily have anything to do with rationalizing the attainment of goals.

5

More on Inspection Systems

We will now discuss three inspection methods:

- Inspections that discover defects: *judgment inspections*
- Inspections that reduce defects: *informative inspections*
- Inspections that eliminate defects: *source inspections*

INSPECTIONS THAT DISCOVER DEFECTS: JUDGMENT INSPECTIONS

Even today, many plants conduct judgment inspections, i.e., inspections whose sole purpose is to categorize finished products as defective or acceptable after processing has been completed. The point of this method is to keep defective goods from moving on to customers or subsequent processes, and in this sense it is an effective tool. It remains inherently a kind of postmortem inspection, however, for no matter how accurately and thoroughly it is performed, it can in no way contribute to lowering the defect rate in the plant itself. This inspection method is consequently of no value whatsoever if one wants to bring down defect rates within plants.

Furthermore, the question of whether one chooses to perform judgment inspections by sampling or by the 100 percent technique is totally unrelated to the essential nature of the inspection method. The question involves only a choice of methods that bear on the issue of whether inspection labor costs can be reduced.

Even though the true purpose of judgment inspections is simply to find defective goods, many plants set up independent inspection processes that also inspect items that are not defective. Surely this is tremendously wasteful.

What is wrong, I often wonder, with the idea of getting rid of all inspections performed at special processes that have to check all items either between work processes or at the end of the final work process? We have long assumed that "inspection" is synonymous with judgment inspection. Yet, in fact, the judgment inspection is the lowest order of inspection and we have to escape from its clutches as soon as we can. All we need to do to accomplish this is to realize that the effective use of informative and source inspections will itself keep defective goods from moving on either to customers or to subsequent processes.

There are some cases in which it is thought that judgment inspections have been made considerably more rational by having been automated. In the manufacture of the H automobile, M Industries in Japan maintains a technical cooperation arrangement with the L Company in the United States, to which it furnishes door lock technology. The head of manufacturing of the L Company came to Japan at one point and boasted that his firm had streamlined operations by automatically inspecting all assemblies in a final inspection process, thereby preventing even a single defective item from being delivered to the parent company's plant. He was somewhat taken aback when Mr. Kurozu, plant manager at K Industries, explained that at his company, poka-yoke devices had been provided at every process so that defects did not occur in the first place. Since absolutely no defect could move to the next process, he explained, the shipping of defective items to the parent company was prevented by a simple function inspection at the final process. When the two men then compared defect rates at their companies, it turned out that the L Company's defect rate was far higher.

In the final analysis, the fact that the L Company's inspections had been automated meant only the automation of judgment inspections. This may have reduced inspection labor costs, but it was of no use whatsoever in reducing the defect rate in the plant.

INSPECTIONS THAT REDUCE DEFECTS: INFORMATIVE INSPECTIONS

An informative inspection is an inspection in which, when a defect occurs, information to that effect is fed back to the work process involved, which then takes action to correct the method of operation. One can expect, consequently, that the adoption of this system of inspections will have the effect of gradually reducing production defect rates.

Informative inspections can be divided into three categories:

- Statistical Quality Control Systems (SQCS)
- Successive Check Systems (SuCS)
- Self-Check Systems (SeCS)

What follows is a detailed description of each, complete with examples.

Statistical Quality Control Systems (SQCS)

The characteristics of so-called SQC systems include, first of all, the notion of informative inspections, which use statistically based control charts to reduce future defects by feeding back information about defects to the offending processes; work methods are then corrected accordingly. Also characteristic of SQC systems is the use of statistics to set control limits that distinguish between normal and abnormal situations. The number of samples taken to detect abnormal values is similarly determined according to statistical principles. Thus, the use of statistical principles may be considered to be the essential condition identifying a method of inspection as an SQC method.

Specification Limits and Control Limits

In using a control chart system, two limits have to be established:

- *Specification limits*: tolerance limits demanded by product functions
- *Control limits*: limits within which normal operations will fall; for example, the outside diameters of all processed rods might fall within the range of 30mm ± 0.06mm

In this case, if specification limits are greater than control limits, all items processed under usual work conditions may be satisfactory. If, on the other hand, specification limits are narrower than control limits, it is possible that, under usual processing conditions, portions of production outside the specification limits will show defects. In any event, operating conditions should be examined and improvements made at the planning stage, so that control limits fall within specification limits.

Establishing Control Limits

Generally used 3 SD control limits are established in the following manner (*Figure 5-1*):

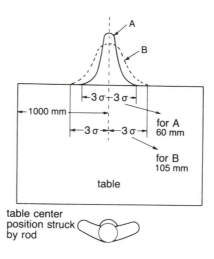

FIGURE 5-1. **Strike Distribution Curve**

1. One thousand attempts are made to strike the table's center point with a shaft.
2. The center is set at 1,000mm from the edge and values for each strike point are recorded.
3. These observed values are summed and the mean value is found to be 1,000mm.
4. The differences between the observed values and the mean value are found. Their sum is 0.
5. These deviations, or differences between the mean value and observed values, are squared.
6. These 1,000 squared deviations are added and then divided by 1,000. From the square root of this can be found the standard deviation (SD), which shows the degree to which the observed values are scattered. In this case, the SD for worker A is 20mm. (*Figure 5-2*).

A			B		
observed value x (mm)	deviation x − m (mm)	deviation squared (x − m)²	observed value x (mm)	deviation x − m (mm)	deviation squared (x − m)²
990	− 10	100	985	− 15	225
995	− 5	25	1020	20	400
1012	12	144	1100	100	10000
1000	0	0	905	− 95	9025
1001	1	1	910	− 90	8100
1007	7	49	1050	50	2500
......	......	......	......	......	......
......	......	......	......	......	......

For A: $1000\,\overline{)1000000}$ gives 1000 → mean value (m); deviation sum 0; $1000\,\overline{)400000}$ gives 400 → deviation squared per strike; $\sqrt{400} = 20$ → standard deviation (σA).

For B: $1000\,\overline{)1000000}$ gives 100 → mean value (m); deviation sum 0; $1000\,\overline{)1225000}$ gives 1225 → deviation squared per strike; $\sqrt{1225} = 35$ → standard deviation (σA).

FIGURE 5-2. **Calculation of Standard Deviation (SD)**

7. If a similar experiment carried out by worker B yields a standard deviation of 35mm, then we can say that A's strikes are less scattered than B's.
8. If we draw lines three standard deviations apart on either side of the center line, both A's SD (60mm) and B's SD (105mm) are found to fall within the range 3 SD = 99.73 percent.
9. Thus, a mere 0.27 percent of strikes — or about three strikes in 1,000 — fell outside the 3 SD limit.
10. Since we are dealing with a phenomenon that under ordinary conditions shows up only 3 times out of 1,000, it seems highly probable that it is an abnormal situation. Therefore we may think of this 3 SD limit as marking the boundary between normal and abnormal.

In reality, the use of statistics allows us to find control limits more simply than this, but in any case the basic approach is the same: control limits are established, and the results of actual operations are measured and their values recorded. If an abnormality is observed in those values, the information is fed back to the process where the abnormality occurred. A check of actual results is then carried out by means of sampling techniques based on statistical theory.

Thus, the compilation of control charts is a necessary condition in SQC methods.

$\overline{X}.R$ Control Charts, and P Control Charts

As seen above, under ordinary operating conditions, the mean of measured values $\overline{X}$ falls within the specification limits. If the spread of measurements also falls within three SD's, then defective items will not be produced under ordinary operating conditions.

The appearance of a value outside the control limits is taken as an abnormality, and feedback is accordingly sent to the process where the value appeared. This allows defects to be reduced by means of improvements made when abnormal conditions are discovered in the course of checking operating methods.

In such cases, defective items will show up as a matter of course either when the control limit $\overline{X}$ is considerably more distorted than the specification limit $\overline{X}$, or when the $\overline{X}$ is fine, but the scatter, that is, the 3 SD range, is so large that it extends beyond specification limits. The reason for using a control chart system, therefore, is that it permits quality improvements and the vigorous promotion of defect reduction by a reconsideration both of conditions making up $\overline{X}$ values and of conditions accounting for large SDs.

In Japan, the adoption of this sort of control chart method has improved the level of quality control considerably.

Like these $\overline{X}.R$ charts is a defect rate control chart used in the workplace called a *P control chart*. In this approach, abnormal values are eliminated from defect rates and control limits are established by taking statistically based samples of these defect rate values for ordinary conditions. Then defect rates in actual shop operations are observed and no action is taken if values are within control limits. When abnormal values show up outside control limits, that information is fed back to the process where defects occurred. The process is examined and improved so that no more abnormal values occur.

This strategy has several advantages. It makes it possible to keep defect rates from rising, and, because action is taken when abnormal values show up, the causes of defects can be corrected. This makes possible a decrease in the overall defect level.

The other side of the coin is that, while it is understandable to want to prevent defect rates from rising, a somewhat more cynical view of the matter makes it look as though the point of this approach is to preserve past defect rates. Why not take a more aggressive stance and ask why defects cannot be cut further and further — even eliminated? The sin involved in getting caught up by this passive approach, surely, lies in a false sense of security stemming from reliance on the high-powered scientific techniques of statistics. This false sense of security causes one to misunderstand the true nature of what is going on.

In Toronto in 1982, I gave a two-day series of talks to a group of senior executives from large American firms. A number of questions concerning Japanese total quality control (TQC) methods came up in those two days, and at one point I asked an executive of the D Aircraft Company who was sitting in the front row whether his firm engaged in quality control.

"Of course we do," he replied.

"In that case," I continued, "do you use control charts?"

"Yes."

"How about P control charts?"

"Yes, we draw up P control charts, too, depending on the process."

"I see," I said. "Tell me, why do you draw up P control charts? After all, P control charts are designed to maintain previous defect rates. They certainly won't actively lower defect rates, will they?"

For a moment, he looked as though he did not understand what I was saying. I remember being struck by the forced smile that came over his face when he said, "OK. Well, maybe you've got a point there. . . ."

Control Charts Serve Only as Mirrors

In 1955, I had some business to attend to at Nippon Steel's Kamaishi refinery and happened to run into Dr. Eisaburo Nishibori at the inn I was staying at in Sendai. At the time, Dr. Nishibori was in charge of quality control at the Japan Management Association.

In talking with Dr. Nishibori, I learned that he was going to the Kamaishi refinery that day, and the next day he was traveling to

Hirosaki, in Aomori Prefecture, to consult at F Chemical Industries, where enthusiastic QC activities were under way. That night he was scheduled to be in Sapporo, in Hokkaido.

I told him that I, too, would be at the Kamaishi plant and then stay in Sapporo the following night, because I was going to visit the Toyobane mines in the Jozan Valley.

The next evening, I chanced to run into Dr. Nishibori again, just as I arrived at my hotel. I asked him how the quality control situation was progressing at F Chemical Industries.

"Well," he replied, "they've got a young quality control department head who's pursuing QC really enthusiastically. I asked if I could take a look at the plant and he showed me around right away. The thing was, that in a plant of about 150 people, there were control charts posted everywhere. When I asked him how many control charts they drew up, he told me they used about 200.

"When we got back to the conference room, the department head asked for my impressions. I told him I thought he was putting a lot of effort into the job, but there was one important control chart he wasn't making.

"'Missing an important control chart?' he said. 'What chart is that?'

"'What I mean is that you don't have a control chart for your control charts.'

"He stared back at me with a blank look on his face, so I explained that he wasn't distinguishing between necessary control charts and unnecessary control charts.

"'Oh, that!. . . ,' he said. Then he sank into thought.

"The point was that this fellow figured all he had to do to perform quality control was to draw up control charts, so he taught his shop foremen how to construct the charts and they posted the charts everywhere.

"If you think about the role a control chart plays, though, it is clear that it essentially serves as nothing but a mirror. All it does is reflect prevailing conditions. That's it. Pasting hundreds of 'mirrors' on the walls or the ceiling or the floor isn't going to guarantee improvements in quality.

"When you look in a mirror and see that your face is dirty, you take a washcloth and wipe your face. That's when the dirt comes off. Looking at your face reflected in a succession of mirrors is utterly pointless unless you do something about it in the form of corrective action."

Dr. Nishibori's admonition made a deep impression on me.

Even today, I sometimes run into young technicians who believe that drawing up control charts is the same thing as quality control. Surely, such people are letting themselves be infatuated by techniques and are not pursuing the true significance of control charts.

Informative Inspections Come to Life Through Action

As I stated earlier, defects will not be reduced unless we first understand the current state of quality and then take appropriate action. Yet control chart methods use sampling to check for abnormalities. Even though this approach may be supported by statistical science, the fact remains that abnormalities appear irregularly and randomly. Since you cannot predict when they will show up, the probability that statistical sampling will find abnormalities at just the right time is far lower than with 100 percent sampling. Moreover, control chart methods as generally practiced involve a considerable time lag between the discovery of an abnormality and the corrective action. That means that it takes a long time before improvements are made. During this period, a substantial number of defects will probably appear.

Thus, the effectiveness of a control chart approach in reducing defects is considerably diluted by a synergism between the time it takes for sampling to turn up abnormalities and the lag between the discovery of such events and corrective action. Indeed, this is surely the main reason that, despite a basic conceptual shift from the old notion of judgment inspections to the innovative idea of informative inspections, it has not been possible to achieve quantum improvements in quality with statistically based methods.

In the final analysis, although statistical science served simply to make methods of inspection more rational, our mastery of its excellent and innovative techniques transformed methods into objectives. We ended up concentrating solely on the applications of technique. As this happened, it seems to me, the basic objectives and functions of informative inspections were simply forgotten.

Pluses and Minuses of SQC Systems

On the plus side, in contrast to the old idea of inspections that distinguished between defective and acceptable items, an appeal to the new, pioneering notion of informative inspections has shown the possibility of defect rate reductions, and this fact has yielded phenomenal developments. Moreover, the pioneering techniques given to us by statistical science are of considerable value. In the planning phase of management, application of analytical techniques such as the experimental planning method and the determination of significant differences has led to real improvements in the establishment of standard work processes and operating procedures. We should also recognize that statistics gives us a highly reliable means for determining appropriate sample sizes for establishing control limits and for finding abnormalities.

At the same time, the method involves several minuses. The first is that the effectiveness of SQC systems as statistical techniques at first led many people to proclaim that "if it doesn't use statistics, it's not quality control." Even today, certain people show the aftereffects of this malady.

The beliefs that you cannot carry out quality control without drawing up control charts, or that sampling inspections are rational because they are backed up by statistical science, led people to forget that these are no more than streamlined inspection methods and that they do not make quality assurance any more rational. I think there can be no doubt that the confidence such people had in the powers of statistical science was a bit excessive.

Moreover, the major conceptual advance represented by informative inspections was obscured by the shadow of inductive statistics. As a result, people neglected qualitative improvements in informative inspections, that is, the performance of 100 percent checks or increases in the speed of corrective action.

The use of mathematical techniques such as those of inductive statistics dominated discussions among both scholars and certain theory-oriented technicians who excelled in "desktop" mathematical processing. This frequently ended up alienating shop technicians and front-line supervisors, especially shop foremen, group leaders, and team leaders, who have to bear the responsibility for quality control. I often used to hear shop foremen and group leaders complain that merely hearing the words "quality control" gave them headaches. The fact that quality control efforts in Japan were led by certain highbrow theorists with no real connection to the workplace has been, I suspect, one reason for the tardy pursuit of real quality control systems aimed at zero defects.

Around 1965, I visited C Industries in Nagoya. There, I heard the following story from President Eguchi, on leave from the T Bank:

"About 30 years ago," he said, "one of the directors of my bank started his own company.

"This man's son had a promising future, for he was unusually bright and graduated at the top of his class at N University. At first, he worked for a firm in the Y Automobile group for about 10 years and then his father brought him into his own company, where, after a few years, he was promoted to managing director, with nearly all aspects of production under his jurisdiction.

"About four years ago, this man's son began advocating the massive adoption of QC methods, and he started bringing in consultants from universities and the like. Morning, noon, and night, all he would ever talk about was *kyuu shii* (QC) this and *kyuu shii* (QC) that. Well, recently the whole plant ended up coming to a standstill (*kyuushi*). I mean, QC is fine, but that was a bit extreme. I think the problem was that he was performing QC only in terms of superficial techniques without understanding what true quality control was all about. I'm always warning our technical people to steer clear of that shallow kind of quality control."

This poor fellow's failure served as yet another lesson to me, for he had let himself be carried away by statistical appearances without really understanding the nature of quality control.

Successive Check Systems (SuCS)

The Birth of the Successive Check Method

By 1960, I knew that SQC methods made it possible to lower defect rates dramatically, but I could not rid myself of the nagging thought that there must be some other, more streamlined way to achieve such reductions. In thinking about what that way might be, I observed that the essence of SQC methods had to lie in informative inspections. Drawing courage from the case in which a poka-yoke device had eliminated defects in the spring insertion operation at

Yamada Electric, I succeeded in distancing myself to a certain extent from the spell of statistics by realizing that there were ways of reducing defects that lay outside SQC methods. My feeling that SQC systems were overlooking something led me to conclude that such methods suffered from two shortcomings:

1. Abnormalities are found by means of sampling inspections. Yet wouldn't it be better to use 100 percent inspection techniques? The problem is that 100 percent inspections are expensive and they generally take a lot of time and trouble. If low-cost 100 percent inspections could be devised, wouldn't they be preferable? "That's it!" I thought. "That is why effective poka-yoke devices ought to be used!" I determined then and there to design poka-yoke mechanisms.

2. The other point is that a look at SQC methods as they are actually applied shows that feedback and corrective action — the crucial aspects of informative inspections — are too slow to be fully effective.

Theoretically, I thought, the best way to speed up feedback and action would be to have the worker who processes items carry out 100 percent inspections and then immediately take action if he or she found any abnormality. Then I recalled the old rule that holds that objectivity is essential to the performance of inspections. Indeed, this is why, in the past, inspections have had to be performed by independent inspectors, rather than by the workers involved in the actual processing.

A worker who inspects something that he or she has worked on might make compromises on quality or might, through inadvertence, miss defects.

If that is the reasoning, I thought, then it is still not necessary to have independent inspectors. An inspection can be carried out by any worker other than the one who did the processing. If this task is given to the nearest person, then one could have a *successive check system* of the following sort:

1. When A is finished processing an item, he or she passes it on to B at the next process.
2. B first inspects the item processed by A and then carries out the processing assigned to him or her. Then B passes the item on to C.

3. C first inspects the item processed by B and then carries out the processing assigned to him or her. When that work is finished, C passes the item on to D.
4. In this way, each successive worker inspects items from the previous process.
5. If a defect is discovered in an item coming from the previous process, the defective item is immediately passed back to the earlier process. There, the item is verified and the defect corrected. Action is taken to prevent the occurrence of subsequent defects. The line is shut down while this is going on.

This type of system largely makes up for the deficiencies of SQC methods because it makes it possible to conduct 100 percent inspections, perform immediate feedback and action, and have inspections performed by people other than the workers involved in the processing. This system is all the more effective when poka-yoke devices are applied to it. Indeed, these methods have led to truly significant reductions in defect rates.

Like control chart systems, this successive check system involves a variety of informative inspections. Yet surely this new method represents a conceptual advance over control chart systems. Another advantage of successive check systems is that they can be applied even in cases where sensory inspections are unavoidable.

Examples of Successive Check Systems: Matsushita Electric Industrial Company, Ltd.

From the birth of the concept of successive check systems in about 1960, such systems were applied in a number of plants and yielded one success after another. During this period, I visited Matsushita Electric's Morikawa television division, where the division head, Mr. Kishida, told me of some difficulties his firm was having "We used to have a process defect rate of around 15 percent in our television assembly operation," he told me. "Control chart methods and vigorous QC Circle activities cut that rate to about 6.5 percent, but defects have leveled off there and we can't figure out how to get the rate any lower."

I explained the successive check method and he promptly agreed when I suggested that he try the approach in his plant. Since the assembly operation had been accompanied by inspection operations, implementation of the new method increased assembly tact time by roughly 10 percent, from 30 seconds to 33 seconds. After one month's implementation of successive check methods, process defects fell from 6.5 to 1.5 percent, and assembly tact time returned to the original 30 seconds on the twenty-third day. Tact time returned to its previous value because checks became simpler as defects gradually decreased, and familiarity made it possible to check items extremely quickly. Although I had at first thought that checks would add time to the procedure, this was because I worried about psychological backlash involving a need to increase tact time because checks would be performed after the original assembly operation had been completed.

Three months later, the innovations had resulted in stunning success (*Figure 5-3*). Interprocess defects had fallen to 0.06 percent, and defects at the final process to 0.016 percent.

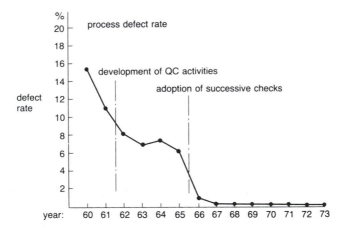

FIGURE 5-3. Effect of Successive Checks

Ordinarily, the implementation of a successive check system leads without exception to a lowering of the defect rate to one-fifth to one-tenth of the previous value in the space of a single month. I often hear factory officials say that such results could never be achieved with SQC methods.

Check Target Selection and Action

Sometimes, however, people have little success with the application of successive check systems. Several points should be kept in mind when dealing with such problems.

Selection of check targets. It is inappropriate to use successive checks to check for too many things. In the final analysis, checking for too many things will undermine the effectiveness of the method, for either nothing will get checked or the number of things workers forget to check will grow.

The fact that checking takes time means that eventually some checks will be neglected.

It is appropriate, therefore, to extract major points from statistics on defects discovered at the final process and to limit the number of points checked in each process to two or three. The examination of defect statistics for the purpose of selecting important points to check should take place every two to four weeks.

Important safety points, however, should always be checked, and should be checked last. These include parts such as automobile brakes, in which defects might cause accidents.

Feedback and action. Two extremely important factors in successive checks are the performance of 100 percent checks, and prompt execution of feedback and action.

Successive checks means far more than merely checking items in succession. When defects are discovered, it is critical that workers operating previous processes be alerted promptly so they recognize the defects in question and correct operating conditions accordingly. Defects will never be reduced if the workers involved do not modify operating methods when defects occur. To this end, processing lines are halted while the workers themselves make the necessary corrections. Lines do not move again until those corrections have been made.

In general, managers and workers on the shop floor are loath to shut down lines, but there are three reasons why such measures must be adopted:

1. Shutting down a line makes it possible for managers to identify the offending process rapidly and clearly. They can then exercise effective leadership so that quick and powerful improvements can be implemented.

2. A worker will be that much more attentive to the task in the future because of the responsibility he or she feels for shutting down the line.
3. The fact that defects will cease to be generated after a temporary line shutdown will more than compensate for the loss incurred as a result of the shutdown.

Failing to shut down the line and take corrective action is just the same as subduing the symptoms of appendicitis with ice. The ice will work, but the pain will recur and eventually considerable time will be lost. It is better in the long run to have the appendix removed, because then the symptoms will not return. For reasons such as these, it is extremely important to take basic, thorough corrective action when abnormalities appear.

Checks Based on Sensory Inspections

In cases involving scratches, paint quality, or other issues where judgments must be made by means of sensory inspections, samples of acceptable limits should be made up and judgments made on the basis of comparison with such limit samples. Even then, however, judgments on the margin will be difficult to make.

This is how the problem was handled at V Industries:

1. C checks the operation performed by B at the previous process.
2. At the final process, specialized inspection worker A passes judgment on checks made by C.
3. At the end of each day of operations, A, B, and C meet to examine and discuss the outcomes of that day's checks.

Defects Increase in the Initial Stage of Successive Checks

I often hear the complaint that defects actually increase in the initial period following the adoption of successive checks. We have to distinguish here between two categories of defects: *interprocess defects*, which are discovered between processes, and *final process defects*, which are discovered at the final inspection of a process. In the initial period, it is nearly always interprocess defects that increase. This is perfectly natural, since defects that had escaped unnoticed in the past are now being discovered. Without exception, however, final process defects will drop by 80 to 90 percent after the first month. As implementation proceeds, interprocess defects will gradually decrease as well.

In general, the implementation of successive checks proceeds as follows:

1. In the first 10 days or so after implementation, interprocess defects increase, but final process defects fall to roughly one-third of their previous level.
2. In the next 10 days, interprocess defects fall to about one-half of their previous level and final process defects drop to roughly one-fifth.
3. In the next 10 days (i.e., after one month), inter-process defects fall to about one-fifth and final process defects to roughly one-tenth of previous levels.

Thus, an initial increase in interprocess defects should actually be a cause for satisfaction because it means that defects that used to slip by unnoticed are now being found.

Consideration for Workers

It is imperative to gain the thorough understanding and compliance of workers in the implementation of successive checks. Failure to do this will undermine interpersonal relations in the shop by creating an atmosphere in which each worker feels as though he or she is always being criticized by the worker at the next process. It is therefore necessary for everyone to understand that inadvertent human errors are more easily detected by others and that workers help one another by checking each other's work.

In the initial phases of successive check implementation at the M Company, a part-time worker, N, was distressed because she had forgotten to attach labels on three occasions in one day. She felt she had caused trouble for everyone else because the line had been shut down each time. "Maybe this job is too much for me," she said. The next day, she stayed home from work.

When this happened, her supervisor promptly went to visit her and assured her that it had not been her fault. He persuaded her to return to the job, and for a month afterwards she did not make a single mistake.

Many workers feel better about checks performed by the next worker down the line because they have the impression that it is more like having friends tell you to be careful than having complaints made about you by specialized inspectors. Workers often say it is better to be warned immediately than to hear complaints long after defective work is done. They support successive checks because their compliance in the identification of defects allows improvements to be made immediately and lowers defects.

Signals to Managers

A group leader at Q Electric once gathered workers at the end of the day because numerous soldering defects were showing up in a chassis assembly process. He warned them several times to be more careful in the soldering operations. Nevertheless, defects did not decrease and, convinced that part-time workers simply did not have the skill required, the group leader more or less gave up.

When successive checks were introduced, the group leader noticed that the conveyor frequently shut down near worker C in process number 3. He therefore stood behind C to observe. He saw that C would press solder against the soldering iron, melt it, and then drop it on the wound portion of lead wires. He explained to C that soldering involved using the soldering iron first to heat the part to be soldered. The solder would melt and flow when the part was sufficiently hot. He then performed the operation himself so that C would understand. From then on, defects were almost completely eliminated.

The group leader who told me this story said that although he had initially thought that part-timers were hopeless because they did not have the necessary skill, it was, in fact, technical leadership that had been lacking. When he realized this, he changed his attitude and, as a result of observations he made in the shop, he discovered a number of similar phenomena. Appropriate leadership eventually reduced defects by 90 percent.

Thus, the fact that a conveyor was stopping in the midst of successive inspections rapidly and accurately signaled the presence of a problem to the manager. Subsequent prompt implementation of effective action led to a reduction in defects.

A Decrease in the Number of Items Held Back for Correction

On a television assembly line at T Industries, inspections used to be carried out at the final process and items to be fixed would be repaired by specialized repair workers.

Since the line was engaged in high-diversity, low-volume production, considerable numbers of items to be repaired accumulated at the final process. This led to frequent model mixing, model errors, and insufficient quantities of finished goods.

The use of successive checks, on the other hand, means that defects are dealt with between processes. No more items are held back and no trouble with model mixing or mismatched quantities ever occurs. The system achieved the further result that a drop in the defect rate means an increase in the number of units produced.

Cases in Which Checks Cannot Be Made at the Next Process

Although in principle successive check systems call for checks to be made at the next process, in actual operations this may not be possible. In such cases, one has no choice but to carry out the checks at the nearest possible subsequent process.

When defects are discovered, however, it is imperative to shut down the line right away. The defective item must then be shown to the worker where the defect originated. Once this worker has recognized the problem, he or she can immediately improve processing methods.

The checking of important items, moreover, should be carried out not only by the worker at the next process, but also by the worker at the process after that. This method of "double checking" is extremely effective.

Where the correction of defects requires a long time, an off-line repair worker can do the needed work after the worker where the problem originated has taken a look at the circumstances under which the defect occurred.

It may be necessary, too, to perform successive checks by selecting one item in five (or one in ten) when the operating cycle is unusually rapid.

Basic Principles Underlying Successive Check Methods

Successive check methods rest on the following principles:

1. Always conduct 100 percent inspections.
2. Judgments about defects are made objectively by a disinterested person.
3. When a defect occurs, information to that effect is immediately fed back to the processing worker where the defect originated. That worker then takes stock of the situation and takes corrective action.
4. Processing from then on thereby ceases to generate defects.

An Example of Successive Checking

One operation at Orient Technologies involved gluing support braces into the inside corners of television-set cabinets (*Figure 5-4*).

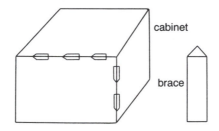

FIGURE 5-4. Brace Attachment

Although 16 such braces had to be glued in, occasionally an inspection worker at the final process would warn that in the course of a day, say, eight cases had been detected in which braces had not been glued in. When this happened, Ms. Takizawa, the very able and spirited worker in charge of the operation, would strongly protest that that was impossible. Even when it was pointed out to her that there were no traces of glue on the defective cabinets, she would not listen, insisting instead that someone must have wiped off the glue at some intermediate process. The adoption of successive checks meant that the worker at the next process was able to indicate missing braces to Ms. Takizawa immediately and return the defective pieces to her. When she examined them then, she saw that, indeed, she had left out some braces.

Now even the strong-willed Ms. Takizawa could not utter a word of rebuttal when she saw braces missing on cabinets she had just sent on to the next process. She realized she had perhaps been a bit overconfident and began paying more attention to the job. From that point onward, no more cabinets showed up with missing braces.

When considerable time used to elapse before cabinets were inspected, Ms. Takizawa had simply been unable to believe that she had left out braces. Now, when cabinets she had just worked on were returned to her and she could verify oversights with her own eyes, she realized that she was capable of errors. Defects were reduced because she then worked more carefully.

Thus, it is 100 times more effective to have defects recognized by the workers themselves than to have them pointed out by a supervisor.

Surely, this example provides a fine explanation of the basic principles involved in successive checks.

Self-Check Systems (SeCS)

Movement Toward Self-Inspection Systems

Although sweeping reductions in defect rates are possible with successive check systems, the nature of informative inspections remains such that rapid feedback and swift action are desirable. For this, it would be ideal to have the actual worker involved conduct 100 percent inspections to check for defects. As I said earlier, however, it has long been held that there are two flaws to be reckoned with: workers are liable to make compromises when inspecting items that they themselves have worked on, and they are apt occasionally to forget to perform checks on their own.

If it were possible to guard against these flaws, then a self-check system would be superior to a successive check system. In cases where physical, rather than sensory, inspections are possible, so-called poka-yoke devices can be installed within the process boundaries, so that when abnormalities occur, the information is immediately fed back to the worker involved. This makes instant corrective action possible, since it permits abnormalities to be discovered within the processes where they occur rather than at subsequent processes. This sort of self-check system represents a higher-order approach than a successive check system, and its use can cut defect rates even further.

This has been proved by results in many companies, perhaps in part because people have less psychological resistance to discovering abnormal situations themselves than to having them pointed out by others. In addition, being able to see the reality of an abnormal situation with one's own eyes allows one to understand its true causes, and more appropriate and effective countermeasures can be worked out and implemented.

With successive checks, there may be cases in which the actual circumstances of defect generation have already vanished by the time information is relayed back by a worker at the next process. Countermeasures may therefore be inadequate because a worker's confirmation of the facts has to rely on guesswork.

In any event, the use of self-check methods makes possible the extremely rapid achievement of far lower defect rates than with control chart methods.

Self-check systems, however, suffer from the defect that they are difficult to use where the detection of abnormalities depends on sensory methods. Even so, self-check methods can be used in a surprising number of instances if we make efforts either (1) to adopt high-level detection techniques for items that absolutely require sensory inspections, or (2) to select basic operating conditions that can be measured physically. This means that, rather than becoming ensnared in present circumstances, it is far preferable for us to consider problems from many angles and actively study ways in which self-check systems can be adopted.

Examples of Self-Check Systems

V Industries. V Industries produced a product called a stem tightener. The 6.5 percent defect rate for this product was high and the company was looking for some way to reduce it.

Operating procedures were as follows:

1. Pour teflon powder into the center of the lower die.
2. Smooth off the die surface to standardize the amount of powder poured in.
3. Press down the upper die to form the product.
4. Expel the product with an expulsion device and remove it from the lower die.
5. Have the expulsion device push the product to a chute.

The problem was that, although inside and outside diameters were reliable, defects would show up in the form of fluctuations in product thickness. The principal cause was that the amount of teflon powder poured into the dies was not uniform. A single worker was in charge of three machines, and since the machines carried out forming operations automatically, this worker occasionally measured and adjusted product thickness. Even so, large numbers of defects continued to be generated.

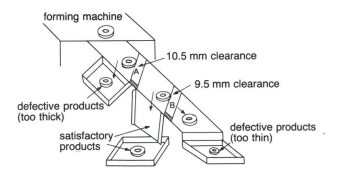

FIGURE 5-5. **Stem Tightener Inspection**

The improved operation proceeded as described below (*Figure 5-5*). Since the specified thickness for the product was t = 10mm ± 0.5mm, the chute for carrying away formed products was equipped as follows:

1. Combination gauge/guide A was attached to the upper end of the chute.
2. The space between gauge A and the chute was 10.5mm.
3. Combination gauge/guide B was attached to the lower end of the chute.
4. The space between gauge B and the chute was 9.5mm.
5. When a formed item is expelled and moves down the chute, products thicker than 10.5mm are unable to pass beneath gauge A and are led by A into a defects bin at the left of the chute.
6. Products thinner than 10.5mm pass underneath A.
7. Products thicker than 9.5mm are led by gauge B into a bin for acceptable parts to the left of the chute.

8. Parts that are thinner than 9.5mm pass underneath gauge B and are led to the defects bin in the middle.
9. When defective products show up in either defective parts bin, they come in contact with limit switches that notify the worker that a defect has occurred by stopping the line and sounding a buzzer.
10. When this happens, the worker hurries to the machine, finds the cause of the defect, and then fixes it. Machine operations start up again after repairs have been completed.

The cause of thickness defects lay in fluctuations in the amounts of teflon powder poured in. The principal reasons for this were that:

• So-called bridging in the materials hopper meant variations in amounts of teflon poured in.
• Blockages in the mesh of the box-type vibrating sieve used for pouring powder into the die caused variations in the amounts of powder falling into the die.

The following improvements were made:

• A device to prevent bridging was mounted on the materials hopper.
• A W-shaped flat spring was installed in the middle of the box-type vibrating sieve. Vibrations cause it to clean the die constantly and mesh blockage no longer occurs.

As a result, V Industries was able to reduce the previous 6.5 percent defect rate to 0.4 percent, i.e., to one-fifteenth of its former figure. A number of actions were important in attaining this strikingly low defect rate:

• 100 percent inspections are performed.
• Feedback and action take place as soon as defects occur.
• The new system prevents the occurrence of serial defects by promptly shutting down machines and taking corrective action whenever a single defect occurs.
• Suitable countermeasures can be devised because the circumstances surrounding defect generation are clearly visible.

T Industries. At T Industries there was an operation in which four 3ø holes were drilled around the outside of products called capsules. The operation was automated and involved a single worker in charge of ten machines.

Small drill diameters occasionally led to broken drills or to incompletely drilled holes due to drill detachment. *Figure 5-6* shows "normal" operations in which a machining verification device has been mounted on the hydraulic drilling unit.

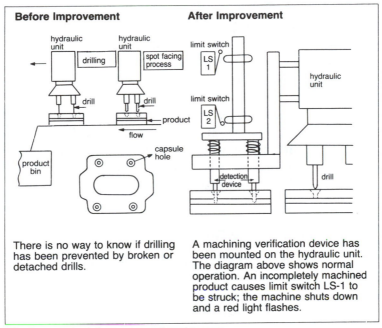

Before Improvement

After Improvement

There is no way to know if drilling has been prevented by broken or detached drills.

A machining verification device has been mounted on the hydraulic unit. The diagram above shows normal operation. An incompletely machined product causes limit switch LS-1 to be struck; the machine shuts down and a red light flashes.

Effects: Hole defects were reduced to zero.

Cost: Cost was zero because discarded parts were used.

FIGURE 5-6. **Preventing Missed Capsule Holes**

When incomplete drilling occurs, a verification rod strikes limit switch LS-1, which shuts down the machine and signals the worker by means of a flashing red light. Corrective action is taken at once and the machine begins operating again after repairs have been made. After the repairs, undrilled items are once again processed on the machine. This method eliminated undrilled products.

Thus, the effective application of poka-yoke devices to self-check systems means that 100 percent checks are carried out and that machines are halted when defects occur. This, together with prompt corrective action, makes it possible to prevent serial defects from occurring. As a result, striking reductions in defect rates can be obtained. In addition, in situations where corrections can be made, zero defects can be achieved with a minimum of effort.

SOURCE INSPECTIONS: INSPECTIONS THAT ELIMINATE DEFECTS

Source inspections can be described as inspection methods that, rather than stimulating feedback and action in response to defects, are based on the idea of discovering errors in conditions that give rise to defects and performing feedback and action at the error stage so as to keep those errors from turning into defects.

Zero QC systems can be set up by combining these source inspections with 100 percent inspections and immediate feedback and action. In terms of practical measures to achieve this end, the use of poka-yoke devices is extremely effective. Indeed, it is poka-yoke methods that first make it possible to bring about zero defects.

The Significance of Source Inspections

Many people maintain that it is impossible to eliminate defects from any task performed by humans. This view stems from the failure to make a clear separation between errors and defects. Defects arise because errors are made; the two have a cause-and-effect relationship.

I claim that it is impossible to eliminate all errors from any task performed by humans. Indeed, inadvertent errors are both possible and inevitable. Yet errors will not turn into defects if feedback and action take place at the error stage. In this way, I am advocating the elimination of defects by clearly distinguishing between errors and defects, i.e., between causes and effects. This is the principal feature of source inspections.

The problem can be visualized in the following way. Management systems in the past have carried out control or management in large cycles (*Figure 5-7*):

- An error takes place (cause).
- A defect occurs as a result.
- This information is fed back.
- Corrective action is taken accordingly.

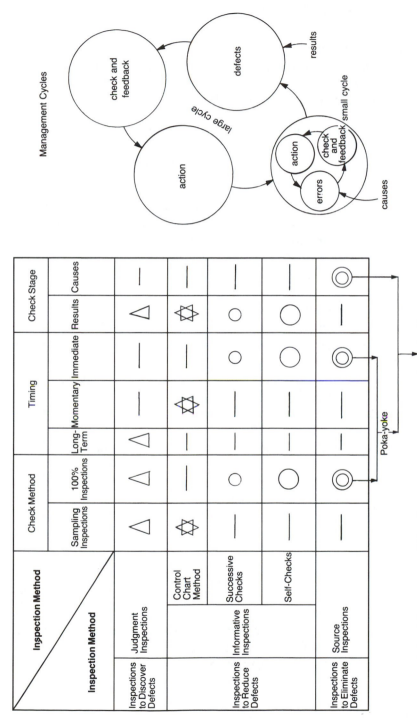

Management Cycles

FIGURE 5-7. **Errors and Management Cycles**

In source inspections, however, control or management is carried out in small cycles:

- An error takes place (cause).
- Feedback is carried out at the error stage, before the error turns into a defect.
- Corrective action is taken accordingly.

Zero defects are achieved because errors do not turn into defects, and management cycles are extremely rapid.

In general, we can imagine five situations in which defects occur:

1. Cases in which either inappropriate standard work processes or inappropriate standard operating procedures are established at the planning stage. An example of this might be the setting of unsuitable heat-treatment temperatures. Since all products become defective in this sort of situation, real operations can not begin, of course, until these conditions are corrected.

2. Cases in which actual operations show excessive variation even though standard methods are appropriate. An example might be the occurrence of occasional defects owing to excessive play in machine bearings. Here, too, operations can begin after proper maintenance has been performed.

3. In cases where sections of raw materials are damaged or material thicknesses fluctuate excessively, thorough inspections must be carried out when such materials are received.

4. In cases where friction in machine bearings results in excessive play or worn tools throw off measurements, overall tool management and maintenance need to be carried out.

5. Some defects clearly occur in cases of inadvertent errors by workers or machines, e.g., when chips clog parts. Such events are unpredictable and occur randomly, which makes them difficult for sampling inspections to capture. Here, 100 percent inspections are indispensable.

The various situations described above recall something I have already said. The reduction in the defect rate at Arakawa Auto Body from 3.5 percent to 0.01 percent in the space of two years resulted from the adoption of source inspections, self-checks, successive checks, and poka-yoke devices. This fact proves, does it not, that the majority of defects are of the inadvertent error type (5)?

Most of the remaining 0.01 percent of defects are those involving dirt, scratches, or other things that are difficult to eliminate. The above methods completely do away with mismatched assemblies, missing parts, and similar defects.

Thus, the most effective strategies for reaching zero defects are using source inspections to move through management cycles at the level of causes, and using source inspections in combination with 100 percent inspections and poka-yoke devices to speed up feedback and action.

Vertical Source Inspections and Horizontal Source Inspections

Source inspections fall into two categories: vertical and horizontal.

Vertical Source Inspections

The idea behind vertical source inspections is to try to control upstream processes in cases where they contain the causes of defects. At Iwao Ceramics, a manufacturer of ceramic tiles, a fairly large number of defects turned up in the form of warped products. Examination of firing oven temperatures and product stacking methods reduced the defect rate somewhat, but something was lacking. At that point, Mr. Tatebayashi, head of the Manufacturing Division, looked into whether there might be problems in processes upstream. His survey revealed that so-called nurturing times (needed for added water to penetrate the clay uniformly) were insufficient. Revised operations significantly lowered the defect rate by controlling and inspecting the uniform distribution of water in the clay before it proceeded to the forming stage.

At V Industries, a considerable number of defects showed up in the manufacture of cylindrical teflon packing materials because distortions occurring in the firing process twisted products and left them without cutting margins. Here, too, investigations into firing temperatures and the speed of temperature changes did not have much effect.

At this point it was observed that the molded raw materials to be fired were of uneven density, and a number of improvements were made:

- The raw teflon powder was precisely weighed so as to conform to specified weights.
- Vacuum packing methods were used to minimize the intrusion of air into the powder during packing.
- The teflon powder used for packing was made to flow evenly and vibrated so that it would pack down tightly enough.
- The speed of press compression was reduced and simultaneous compression from the top and the bottom was provided.

When these preformed products were subsequently fired, there was much less warping and twisting than in the past, and no products were missing a cutting margin.

Thus, it is always necessary to examine source processes in accordance with the quality flows in cases where source processes have a much greater impact on quality rather than do the processes nearest at hand.

Horizontal Source Inspections

Horizontal source inspections refer to an inspection method based on the idea of detecting defect sources within processes and then conducting inspections to keep errors from turning into defects.

A vacuum cleaner packaging operation. Mr. Shimizu, the head of the Production Technology Department at Matsushita Electric's Vacuum Cleaner Division, once told me that parts occasionally turned out to be missing at the final packaging process for finished vacuum cleaners. He was annoyed by this because products with parts missing were sometimes even shipped to customers. I immediately went to the plant and observed the packaging operation. The operation proceeded as follows:

- About 10 small accessories and an instruction manual were placed in a cardboard carton, along with larger items such as the body of the vacuum cleaner and the hose.
- When packing was completed, the top was closed and sealed with plastic tape.
- The fully packed carton was then weighed on a scale set up on a nearby roller conveyor.
- When the weight was too low, the carton would be reopened and checked for missing parts. Any missing parts were then added.

The problem was that the accuracy level of the scale did not make it possible to detect the omission of small parts. Vacuum cleaners missing such parts were occasionally sent to customers and this resulted in complaints.

"I thought of using a more accurate scale," said Mr. Shimizu, "but I hesitated because of the high cost."

After observing the operation for a while, I turned to Mr. Shimizu and said I thought that the basic idea behind the method he used was wrong.

"What! The basic idea is wrong? What are you talking about?" he answered.

"The method you're using tries to carry out inspections after defects have already occurred," I explained. "Why don't you make your inspections in such a way that you prevent defects from happening in the first place?"

Mr. Shimizu is extremely bright and he caught on immediately.

"Yes," he said, "I get it. I'll change the operation right away."

The improved operation proceeded as follows:

- Bowed springs were installed in front of boxes containing small parts so that every time a part is removed from a box, a spring is pressed and a limit switch is activated (*Figure 5-8, A*).
- A spring is provided on the holder in the box containing instruction booklets. The movement of a hand taking an instruction booklet pushes the spring and trips a limit switch (*Figure 5-8, B*).
- Thus, the movement involved in taking each small part trips a limit switch and for each motion a green signal lamp lights up (*Figure 5-8, C*).
- If a part is missing, a stopper does not descend, the packing carton halts, and a buzzer sounds (*Figure 5-8, D*). When the part not indicated by a green lamp is added, the stopper descends.
- Gummed tape is then applied and the carton is shipped out.

After these improvements were made, defects were eliminated and the operation has continued with zero defects for several years since.

Bending cover edges. This operation involved bending one edge of a cover used in an automobile. Right and left covers were the same shape, the only differences being that on right-hand covers a hole was on the right and on left-hand covers it was on the left. This led workers occasionally to bend the wrong edges of covers.

A. Bowed Spring Poka-yoke

B. Instruction Booklet Poka-yoke

C. Instruction Booklet Insertion Lamp

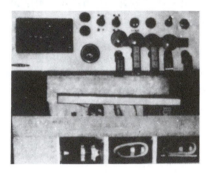

D. Conveyor Stopper

FIGURE 5-8. **Improvements in Vacuum Cleaner Packaging Operation**

Sometimes one cover in every several dozen was defective in this way.
The operation was improved as follows (*Figure 5-9*):

- For right-hand covers, a sensor that activates a limit switch was installed at the position of the right-hand hole.
- For left-hand covers, a sensor that activates a limit switch was installed at the position of the left-hand hole.
- When the edge of a right-hand cover is to be bent, a switch causes current to flow to the right-hand limit switch sensor. When the edge of a left-hand cover is to be bent, current flows to the left-hand limit switch.
- If a part is positioned backwards, the part presses against the sensor, causes a buzzer to sound, and switches off power to the bender. When this happens, the machine will not operate even when the start button is pushed.

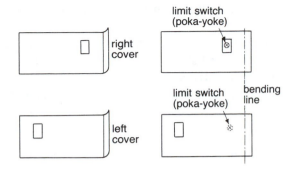

FIGURE 5-9. A Poka-yoke Device for Bending Cover Edges

These improvements resulted in the elimination of defects, and for the first time, the operation became one that even novices could perform flawlessly.

Carburetor assembly. In this operation, a small ball valve was inserted in an automobile carburetor and then a cap was installed. Defects sometimes occurred, however, when workers forgot to insert ball valves before installing caps. Function tests at a subsequent process would uncover gasoline leaks and the unit would have to be reassembled after it was taken apart and a ball valve inserted.

The operation was improved as follows (*Figure 5-10*):

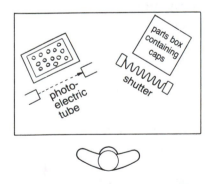

FIGURE 5-10. A Poka-yoke Device for Guaranteeing Ball Valve Insertion

- A photoelectric switch was installed in front of a box containing ball valves.
- A shutter was attached to the front of a box containing caps.
- When a worker's left hand reaches into the box to take out a ball valve, the movement trips the photoelectric switch and the shutter for the cap box opens. Unless the worker reaches into the valve box, the shutter on the cap box will not open and caps cannot be removed.

This made it impossible for a worker to perform the operation if he or she had forgotten to take out a ball valve. Not a single instance of missing ball valve insertion has shown up in the several years since these improvements were made.

Seat assembly. Seat assembly operations at Arakawa Auto Body took the form of so-called mixed production, with seats for Coronas, Corollas, Celicas, Carinas, and other models all moving along the same line. This meant that workers had to pay extraordinarily careful attention to attaching the appropriate fittings to each seat. Even so, incorrect parts were occasionally attached.

The following improvements were made:

- Small foil disks were pasted to the lower portions of *kanban* according to the model involved.
- *Kanban* insertion racks were set up, with a reflector-type photoelectric switch for each model mounted on the front.
- When the *kanban* arrives along with a seat body, a worker takes the *kanban* and inserts it in the *kanban* insertion rack. This causes a lamp to light on the front of the parts box containing fittings for the model indicated. At the same time, the shutter for only that box opens (*Figure 5-11*).
- The worker then takes parts out of the box indicated by the lamp and attaches them to the seat.
- Tact time is 30 seconds. If 20 seconds elapse and no parts are removed from the box, a buzzer sounds and seats are prevented from moving to the next process because a conveyor stopper is not withdrawn. (When a seat comes in contact with the stopper, furthermore, the assembly conveyor shuts down.)
- Since no shutters open except the one for the correct parts box, it has become impossible to attach incorrect fittings to seats.

FIGURE 5-11. **Poka-yoke for Attachment of Seat Fittings**

Even on a mixed production line handling a variety of models, the above improvements eliminated model mismatches and made it possible for workers to perform the operation without anxiety. Incorrect parts were not attached to seats even when regular workers were absent and other workers substituted for them. This method is known at Arakawa as the *passport system*, and it has proven to be a considerable success in a number of applications.

The examples cited above share several common features:

- Each makes use of a source inspections approach in which the idea is to discover errors at their source and then carry out feedback and action before the errors turn into defects.
- The use of poka-yoke devices allows information concerning the appearance of defects to be fed back immediately, and prompt corrective action is then taken. In addition, 100 percent inspections are used.
- In general, the cost of constructing poka-yoke devices came to ¥ 30,000 ($150) or less. In expensive cases it was no more than ¥ 100,000 ($500) or so.

The use of source inspections and poka-yoke devices has made it possible to go for several years without the occurrence of a single defect.

When these ideas are applied to machine maintenance, breakdowns can be eliminated as well. For example, a thermistor attached to the bearing section of a machine might set off a buzzer and shut down the machine whenever the temperature exceeded 20° C. This would protect against breakdowns involving "baking."

In such situations, the approach is to distinguish between abnormalities (or problems) and breakdowns, and then to run through control cycles at the causal stage by discovering abnormalities where they occur and carrying out feedback and action. By preventing breakdowns from occurring even when abnormalities show up, this conceptual approach makes it possible to make zero breakdowns a reality. In this area as well, poka-yoke methods can be very effective.

THE ESTABLISHMENT OF A POKA-YOKE SYSTEM

As I have explained so far, poka-yoke systems involve carrying out 100 percent inspections and requiring immediate feedback and action when errors or defects occur. This approach therefore neatly solves the problems posed by the old-fashioned belief that 100 percent inspections take too much trouble and cost too much.

Because of the considerable effect obtained by actually installing poka-yoke devices, however, many people are under the false impression that simply putting in such devices will eliminate defects.

Yet in the final analysis, a poka-yoke system is a means and not an end. Poka-yoke systems can be combined with successive checks or with self-checks, and can fulfill the needs of those techniques by providing 100 percent inspections and prompt feedback and action. Successive checks and self-checks, however, can function only as informative inspections, in which feedback and action take place after a defect has occurred. In fact, they make the occurrence of at least one defect inevitable. Of course, in cases where repairs can be made it looks as though no defects occurred, but in an absolute sense, these methods are inherently unable to attain zero defects.

It follows that source inspections and poka-yoke measures must be combined if one wishes to eliminate defects. It is the combination of source inspections and poka-yoke devices that makes it possible to establish a Zero QC system.

Thus, in spite of the fact that poka-yoke methods themselves are extremely effective, final results will depend considerably on the inspection system with which poka-yoke methods are combined. Insofar as is possible, it is imperative to try to combine source inspections and the poka-yoke system, and the use of poka-yoke methods with self-checks or successive checks should be limited to instances constrained by technical or financial impediments.

One must never forget, finally, that the poka-yoke system refers to a means and not to an end.

SAMPLING INSPECTIONS AND 100 PERCENT INSPECTIONS

The persistence of defects in production activities creates the need to find and eliminate those defects. Since it is impossible to zero in on defects automatically, defects will not be found unless 100 percent of the items involved are inspected. Generally speaking, acceptable items are overwhelmingly more numerous than defective ones, so this sort of 100 percent inspection entails considerable "wasted" work. In addition, 100 percent inspections require a great deal of trouble and high labor costs.

These problems have given rise to a technique called sampling inspection, backed by the scientific discipline of inductive statistics. In this approach, highly reliable inspections that take little trouble and are of the same level as 100 percent inspections can be carried out by means of sample sizes indicated on acceptable quality level (AQL) charts; the size of the sample depends on how often defects occur.

According to the extremely logical AQL approach, the relative sample size can be low when the defect rate is high, and relative sample size is increased when the defect rate is low. This method lowers both the cost and the bother of inspections considerably.

Yet even when sample size is determined by the proportion of defects, the defects occur at random intervals. If sampling methods call for one item in 25, for example, or if sampling is random, it is extremely difficult to match sampling with the occurrence of abnormalities or defects.

There would be no problem were AQL charts to incorporate statistically based ways to handle such situations, but in the final analysis, even statistically based sampling methods are nothing but rational means of inspection; in no sense do they make quality assurance more rational. This is because the fundamental approach of sampling inspections is based on probability theory and does not account for one occurrence in 100,000 or one in one million.

Thus such methods may reduce defects, but they can never eliminate them. It used to be thought that 100 percent inspections would raise inspection costs because they require considerable work. Now, however, the use of poka-yoke devices makes for trouble-free and low-cost inspections. This means that so-called sampling inspections have lost their *raison d'être* and the fact that they are backed by scientific statistics becomes meaningless.

Naturally, the possible use of sampling inspections as a second-best strategy should be considered in situations where the application of poka-yoke measures would be extremely difficult, but it should be understood that these are not the method of choice.

I would like readers to free themselves from blind faith in the sampling inspection as a superior and extremely rational method, and I want to stress the importance of understanding clearly that no matter how rational a means of inspection it may be, a sampling inspection is not necessarily appropriate from the point of view of zero-defects-oriented quality assurance. This is especially true in modern automated assembly processes, for even one rare defect can cause an automatic machine to break down or can cause constant temporary shutdowns. Furthermore, since inspection itself is a wasteful act, it is wasteful to set up independent inspection processes. It is important to keep in mind that inspection processes should be attached to work processes so as to eliminate the need for a separate inspection process.

MODEL CHANGES AND THE "IT SYSTEM"

A new-model television set was to be assembled at the Ibaraki Division of A Electronics. On this occasion, Mr. Yamagata, head of the Manufacturing Department, gathered his front-line supervisors and told them what he expected of them.

"We are going to assemble 30,000 of the new-model television sets," he told them, "but initially we are going to make just 50 of them.

"I want things done so that absolutely no defects are passed on to subsequent processes. Not only that, if a defective item is discovered by a successive check or a self-check, I want it sent back to the previous process immediately and allowed to move forward only after the defect has been corrected.

"While you are working on this," he concluded, "I don't want you to be concerned with output levels or with labor costs."

All conceivable poka-yoke devices were installed and self-check and successive check routines were adopted.

Progress toward the daily production target of 1,000 sets was steady:

> First day : 285 sets
> Second day : 473 sets
> Third day : 815 sets
> Fourth day : 978 sets
> Fifth day : 1,012 sets

Daily production after the fifth day exceeded the target of 1,000, and by the end of the month the previously unimaginable production figure of 1,270 sets had been achieved.

In the past, the idea had been to maintain production volumes, and so items had been sent along regularly to subsequent processes. This meant that products needing repair piled up at the final process and there, pressed by the volume of repairs needed, skilled workers worked overtime to correct errors. They were so overworked that occasionally defective products were shipped out and then claims would come back to the company. The new method, however, was tremendously successful and no claims were made involving television sets manufactured through the use of this "IT system."

Later, at an IE institute held in Utsunomiya, I happened to hear a talk given by Mr. Ohta, the foreman actually in charge of this "IT system" experiment.

"I really resisted it," Mr. Ohta told me, "when we were told we couldn't have any defects in the assembly of those 30,000 new-model television sets. I would have said it simply wasn't possible.

"Since they told us that we only had to try the new methods with 50 sets and that output didn't matter, I decided to give it a try.

"In starting the assembly work, we fixed all of the defects that showed up initially and then corrected any problems we had with parts. For errors in operating methods, we put an experienced leader in charge of five workers and he both provided guidance on operating methods and rapidly set up poka-yoke devices. All this led to unexpectedly good results, and we're much more confident now about future model changes."

Listening to Mr. Ohta talk about this "IT system" made me think that it was like taking contaminated blood from a newborn infant and replacing it with healthy blood. The baby would develop a little more slowly at first, but before long things would go smoothly and it would grow into a strong, healthy child.

Any company that deals with model changes has to display new lines of products in its outlets, so there is a tendency to concentrate on raising production figures, to work nights and overtime to "get the numbers right." Yet it is methods like this "IT system" that lead to greater success, methods that are not bound to output numbers and are aimed at preventing defects from occurring.

Indeed, K Electric in Kyushu used this "IT system" with tremendous success when it had to accommodate a model change in home stereo equipment and output was not rising.

INSPECTIONS AND AUTOMATION

As I mentioned earlier, the head of manufacturing of the American L Company — a firm making inroads in Japan by producing door locks for the Japanese firm H Technologies — came and visited the Osaka plant of M Metals and Mining, a company that manufactures the same door locks in Japan. After he had toured the plant and various preliminaries had been gotten out of the way, the L Company representative was told proudly by a Mr. Kurozu, the plant manager, that at M Metals and Mining, all finished products were inspected automatically by machine so that not a single defective item was sent on to customers. The American silenced Mr. Kurozu by responding that his company used poka-yoke methods to carry out source inspections, self-checks, and successive checks at each process and that absolutely no defective items moved from one process to the next, so they did not need special inspections at the final process to keep defective goods from being sent to customers.

Ultimately, the fact that the L Company used automated inspection equipment for judgment inspections may have had the advantage of cutting labor costs by eliminating inspection personnel, but there was no way it could be expected to reduce or eliminate defects.

We see, then, that reducing inspection personnel and reducing or eliminating defects are entirely different issues. Whether defects will be reduced or eliminated depends on the kind of inspection methods used, not on whether the inspections are or are not automated.

Automation can be applied to source inspections, to informative inspections (including control chart methods, successive checks, and self-checks) or to judgment inspections. But the automation of inspections is ultimately a matter of economizing on labor; it has no connection with the lowering of defect rates.

If automation has any effect at all on defect reduction, it may make it possible to conduct 100 percent inspections and thus prevent the shipment of defective goods to customers. It may also allow all abnormalities to be detected and therefore increase the frequency of feedback and action. But that is all.

Recently, I met the director of the N Association's publishing division and he told me that the managing director of the D Company had said that defects would not be reduced unless inspections were automated. I remember feeling that there are many people in the world who, failing to understand that inspection automation and defect rate reduction are different issues, still cling to the delusion that automation will reduce defects.

6

Using Poka-yoke Systems

POKA-YOKE SYSTEM FUNCTIONS

A poka-yoke system possesses two functions: it can carry out 100 percent inspections and, if abnormalities occur, it can carry out immediate feedback and action. The effects of poka-yoke methods in reducing defects will differ depending on the inspection systems with which they are combined: source inspections, self-checks, or successive checks.

Since poka-yoke systems are extremely powerful techniques by themselves, this chapter will concentrate on describing them.

TYPES OF POKA-YOKE SYSTEMS

Poka-yoke systems fall into regulatory function categories, depending on their purposes, and setting function categories, according to techniques they use.

Poka-yoke Regulatory Functions

Two regulatory functions are performed by poka-yoke systems.

Control Methods

These are methods that, when abnormalities occur, shut down machines or lock clamps to halt operations, thereby preventing the occurrence of serial defects. Such methods have a more powerful regulatory function than do those of the "warning" type discussed below, and maximum efficacy in achieving zero defects is obtained by the use of these control-type systems.

Although I have defined control methods as ones that shut down machines to halt operations, the shutting down of machines is by no means the only possible strategy, as the following example illustrates.

The Stereo Equipment Division of A Electronics had an insertion machine that automatically inserted parts such as transistors and diodes into printed circuit boards. The machine would stop when pitch errors occurred in the insertion of bent parts legs into the circuit boards, or when insertion mistakes cropped up because legs were crooked. This had the effect of drastically lowering the machine's work rate. This was the stage things were at when I spoke to the head of the Manufacturing Department.

"In a fully automated system," I told him, "when an abnormality shows up, the mechanism itself has the capacity to detect the trouble and take steps to deal with it.

"In contrast, the 'preautomation' approach I am advocating has the mechanism itself detect the trouble, but then human beings take steps to deal with it. Both methods recognize that abnormalities will occur. After all, there is no machine in the world that will operate 100 years without any abnormal situations arising.

"The abnormal situations in your case are so-called isolated defects. They can also be fixed, so we're not talking about a machine where abnormalities continue to occur just because one error shows up.

"If that's the case, why not make a mark on the board when an abnormality occurs and let the machine continue to operate? The problem boards can be automatically spotted and separated from the good ones. The trouble can be resolved by hand and the machine is not shut down. Wouldn't this sort of approach improve the work rate and be more profitable in the end?"

Methods for the operation were promptly revised and a 30 percent increase in the work rate was achieved.

Thus, control methods do not always imply shutting down machines. A variety of strategies is available.

This example describes an approach taken when isolated defects occurred. It was also a case in which the abnormalities could be corrected. If we were dealing with a case in which abnormalities kept on occurring, i.e., a case of serial defects, then, of course, it would be necessary to use a method that shut down the machine. In a case such as that of unfinished holes resulting from a broken punch, a control method should be used and the machine would have to be shut down.

Warning Methods

These methods call abnormalities to workers' attention by activating a buzzer or a light. Since defects will continue to occur if workers do not notice these signals, this approach provides a less powerful regulatory function than control methods.

In cases where workers' attention is captured by means of light, blinking lights can attract attention more powerfully than steady ones. Ultimately, this method is effective only when workers take notice, and the passive aspect of light signals makes it necessary to regulate placement, intensity and color, etc. On the other hand, sound can actively call out to people, but since it cannot be effective if it is drowned out by other noises in the workplace, it is necessary to regulate volume, tone, and intermittency.

There are a surprising number of cases, too, in which it is more effective to change musical scales or timbres than to turn up the volume. In this sense, there are frequently situations where good results can be obtained through the use of music box-type tones. Light and sound can also be used in combination with one another.

In any event, control methods display far more powerful regulatory effects than do warning methods, so control-type measures should be used as much as possible. The use of warning methods may be considered either where the impact of abnormalities is slight or where technical or economic factors make the adoption of control methods extremely difficult.

Poka-yoke Setting Functions

The setting functions of poka-yoke systems can be divided into three categories.

Setting Function Types and Examples

1. **Contact methods.** Methods in which sensing devices detect abnormalities in product shape or dimension by whether or not contact is made between the products and the sensing devices are called contact methods.

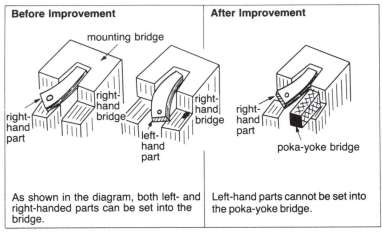

Before Improvement	After Improvement
As shown in the diagram, both left- and right-handed parts can be set into the bridge.	Left-hand parts cannot be set into the poka-yoke bridge.

Effects: Confusion of left and right parts was reduced to zero.

Cost: ¥ 300 ($1.50)

FIGURE 6-1. **Preventing Erroneous Brake Wire Clamp Mounting**

Example: Preventing Errors in Brake Wire Clamp Mounting
   The fact that both left- and right-handed brake wire clamp mounting jigs could be set into a bridge occasioned errors in which left and right parts would be mixed up (*Figure 6-1*).

Example: Ensuring the Presence of Hardware Mounting Screws in Television Cabinets
   The construction of cabinets for television sets at Daito Woodworking, Ltd. included the task of attaching four hardware fittings for the television tube in the front frame, securing each of the fittings with four screws, and then applying tape over the top of the fittings.
   Sixteen screws were attached in all, and on rare occasions one or more screws would be left out. Since tape was then applied over the top of the fittings, such errors were not found when the units were shipped to the parent company and only came to light in the assembly process (*Figure 6-2*).
   Mr. Morikawa of Daito made the following improvements:

- Sixteen limit switches were mounted on the jig underneath the sites where screws were to be attached to the frame.
- After glue has been applied to the four side sections and they are joined to form the frame, pneumatic cylinders press them together and each of the fittings is secured with four screws.

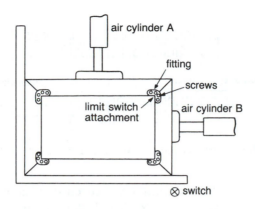

air cylinder A

fitting

screws

limit switch
attachment

air cylinder B

⊗ switch

FIGURE 6-2. **Screws and Poka-yoke Device**

• In the event that even a single screw is missing, the otherwise completed frame cannot move to the next operation because a switch will not have been turned.

Adopting this strategy made it impossible to make defective cabinets, and no more instances of missing screws occurred.

2. *Fixed-value methods.* With these methods, abnormalities are detected by checking for the specified number of motions in cases where operations must be repeated a predetermined number of times.

Example: Ensuring Application of Insulation Tape
At the O Plant, insulation tape was applied to television cabinets in 10 places. In the past, 8cm strips of insulation tape had been lined up on a rod and these would be taken off as needed and applied to the cabinet. Sometimes strips were not applied, however, so the following poka-yoke approach was adopted (*Figure 6-3*).

Strips of tape were first applied to the rod in groups of 10, so that if a worker failed to apply one strip to the cabinet, he or she would quickly notice that one of that group of 10 remained on the rod. From that point onward, workers never neglected to apply all 10 strips.

Next, sets of legs for television sets were manufactured and then packed in cardboard cartons of 50 sets each. An assembly instruction sheet had to be inserted in each small box containing a

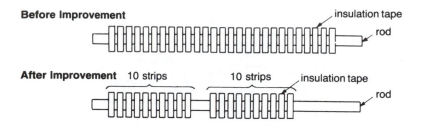

Before Improvement   insulation tape

                                                              rod

After Improvement   10 strips   10 strips   insulation tape

                                                              rod

FIGURE 6-3. Insulation Tape and Poka-yoke Device

set of legs, but the parent company warned that occasionally these instruction sheets were missing. To deal with this problem, the following poka-yoke procedure was devised:

• Instruction sheets are counted and separated into groups of 50 beforehand.

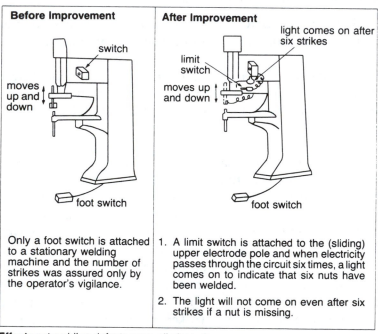

Before Improvement

switch

moves up and down

foot switch

Only a foot switch is attached to a stationary welding machine and the number of strikes was assured only by the operator's vigilance.

After Improvement

light comes on after six strikes

limit switch

moves up and down

foot switch

1. A limit switch is attached to the (sliding) upper electrode pole and when electricity passes through the circuit six times, a light comes on to indicate that six nuts have been welded.

2. The light will not come on even after six strikes if a nut is missing.

Effect: nut welding defects were eliminated
Cost: ¥ 7,000 ($35)

FIGURE 6-4. Device to Ensure the Welding of Nuts

- A packet of 50 instruction sheets is taken out each time a new carton is packed.
- If any instruction sheets remain after a carton is packed, then one or more of the small boxes is missing a sheet. When this happens, the packed items are checked. This put an end to complaints from the parent company.

Example: Ensuring the Welding of Nuts

Although six nuts had to be attached in a welding process, nuts were occasionally left out (*Figure 6-4*).

3. *Motion-step methods.* These are methods in which abnormalities are detected by checking for errors in standard motions in cases where operations must be carried out with predetermined motions. These extremely effective methods have a wide range of application, and the possibility of their use should by all means be examined when poka-yoke setting functions are considered.

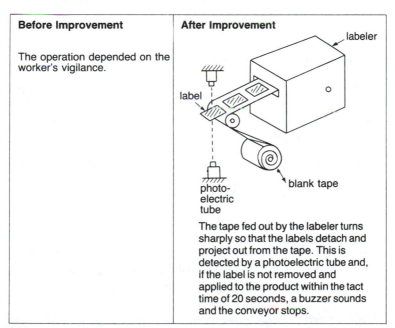

Before Improvement	After Improvement
The operation depended on the worker's vigilance.	labeler, label, photo-electric tube, blank tape The tape fed out by the labeler turns sharply so that the labels detach and project out from the tape. This is detected by a photoelectric tube and, if the label is not removed and applied to the product within the tact time of 20 seconds, a buzzer sounds and the conveyor stops.

Effect: label application failures were eliminated.
Cost: ¥ 15,000 ($75)

FIGURE 6-5. **Device to Ensure Attachment of Labels**

Example: Ensuring the Attachment of Labels
Workers sometimes failed to apply labels and this error would be discovered at an inspection process (*Figure 6-5*).

The examples above show that a wide variety of poka-yoke methods can be devised. Many more examples from a number of companies will be presented in the next section.

DETECTION MEASURES FOR POKA-YOKE SYSTEMS

The following describes detection measures for setting up poka-yoke systems.

Various Detection Measures

A variety of desired functions and corresponding methods is shown in the following Classification of Detection Measures (*Figures 6-6* and *6-7*).

Detection Method Functions

Below are simple explanations of the functions of the various detection methods.

Contact Detection Methods

Limit switches, microswitches. These confirm the presence and position of objects and detect broken tools, etc. Some limit switches are equipped with lights for easy maintenance checks (*Figures 6-8* and *6-9*).

Touch switches. Activated by a light touch on their antenna sections, touch switches can detect object presence, position, breakage, dimensions, etc., with high sensitivity (*Figure 6-10*).

Differential transformers. When put in contact with a product, a differential transformer picks up changes in the degree of contact as fluctuations in lines of magnetic force, thus enabling it to detect objects with a high degree of precision (*Figure 6-11*).

Detection Measures			Presence — Passage (line)	Presence — Passage (plane)	break	Confirmation of Position	Measurement	Overlap	Shape	Foreign Matter	Damage	Color Mismatch
Contact Methods	limit switches		●		●	●	●					
	microswitches		●		●	●	●					
	touch switches		●		●	●	●	●				
	differential transformers		●		●	●	●	●				
	trimetrons						●					
	liquid level relays					●						
Non-contact Methods	proximity switches		●		●	●	●	●				
	photoelectric switches	transmission types	●		●	●	●					
		reflection types	●		●	●	●	●			●	●
	beam sensors	transmission types	●		●	●	●					
		reflection types	●		●	●	●	●			●	●
	fiber sensors		●		●	●	●	●	●			●
	area sensors		●	●								
	positioning sensors					●						
	dimension sensors					●	●		●			
	displacement sensors		●			●	●	●			●	●
	metal passage sensors		●	●						●		
	color marking sensors		●			●						●
	vibration sensors		●		●	●						
	double feed sensors		●					●				
	welding position sensors					●	●		●			
	tap sensors						●					
	fluid elements		●									

FIGURE 6-6. **Classification of Detection Measures (A)**

Detection Measures \ Detection Functions		Pressure	Temperature	Electric Current	Vibration	Cycles	Time	Timing	Information
Pressure Gauges	pressure gauges	●							
	pressure-sensitive switches	●							
Temperature Gauges	thermometers		●						
	thermostats		●						
	thermistors		●						
	thermocouples		●						
Current Meters	meter relays			●					
	current eyes			●					
Vibration Gauges	vibration sensors				●				
Counting Gauges	counters					●			
	preset counters					●			
	stepping relays					●			
	fiber sensors					●			
Time Gauges	timers						●		
	delay relays						●	●	
	timing units							●	
	time switches						●		
Information Devices	buzzers								●
	lamps								●
	flashing lamps								●

FIGURE 6-7. Classification of Detection Measures (B)

The SL micro limit switch is a highly versatile limit switch combining the compact size and economy of a microswitch with the ease of use, safety, and sturdiness of a limit switch. Ideal for automatic assembly processing machines, food processing machines, metered wrapping machines and other machines for industry, as well as for other applications in the field of energy-saving equipment calling for compact size, light weight and ease of use, the easy-to-use short lever type is especially well suited to situations in which mounting space is limited. Under simultaneous development, moreover, is a contactless-type switch of uniform dimensions to respond to the shift toward electronic equipment and mechanical devices. These can be put to a wider range of uses than ever.

FIGURE 6-8. Limit Switches

optional blinking lamp capability

| vertical-type limit switch | VL mini limit switch with lamp | lights when motion is detected | lights when no motion is detected |

Small Lamps Can Be of Great Value

Considerable time and trouble are involved where limit switch operating life is linked to serious accidents and, especially, cases in which many limit switches are attached in high, out-of-the-way places.

In such cases, the compact size, precision, light weight, effectiveness, economy and other characteristics of VL mini limit switches come into play, and the scope of their use is further enlarged by their ability to verify motion and by the addition of a lamp for easy maintenance checks.

Characteristics

1. 100V/200V Dual Use High-Intensity Neon Lamp
   The reflective efficiency of the lamp holder has been increased, so that even at 100V the diamond-cut structure of the lens portion allows light to diffuse to yield sufficient intensity. In addition, the neon lamps are long-lived, with lives of 20,000 hours or more.
2. Displays Can Indicate Either the Presence or Absence of Motion
   In spite of its compact construction, the lamp holder housing snaps in place with a single movement. By merely changing the direction in which the lamp holder is attached, the lamp can indicate either motion or no motion (only the no motion indicator can be used, however, when connecting both NO and NC loads).
3. Watertight Lamp Section
   Superior watertightness is provided by molding the lens and cover simultaneously and by pasting a nameplate to the top.
4. No Special Connections Needed for Lamp Circuits
   The use of a coil spring connection method means that lamp circuit connections take no time or trouble.

FIGURE 6-9. Limit Switches (With Lamp)

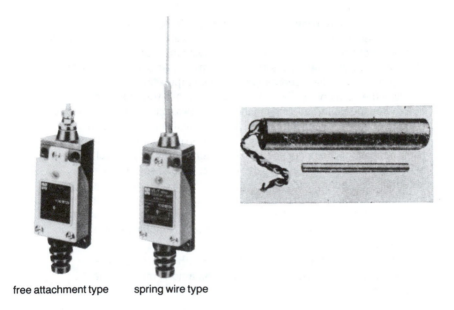

free attachment type   spring wire type

FIGURE 6-10. **Touch Switch**   FIGURE 6-11. **Differential Transformer**

Trimetrons. A dial gauge forms the body of a trimetron, and limit values can easily be set on the plus and minus sides as well as at the true position. This is a convenient detection device because these limits can be selected electronically, allowing the device to both detect the acceptability of measurements and exclude them (*Figure 6-12*).

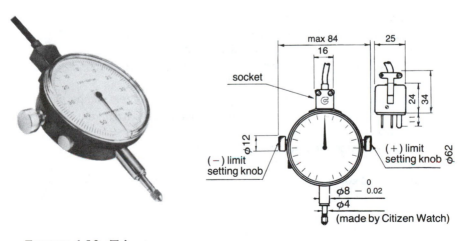

FIGURE 6-12. **Trimetron**

In measurement devices using calipers, micrometers, and dial gauges, measurement cannot be automated or streamlined. To automate measurement devices, one has to use a device that can provide electronic output of the results of measurements. As such a device, the trimetron is a sensitive needle-type gauge incorporating electrical contacts (i.e., switches). The device is capable of a wide range of automated measurement and machine-control functions. In response to the size of objects being measured, the electrical contacts turn on or off and send signals to external devices. These signals can cause lamps to blink, indicating whether or not the dimensions of the objects fall within allowable tolerances. They can also open and close sorting gates to automatically separate acceptable products from defective ones. Other functions include shutting down machines automatically when objects being processed have reached specified dimensions and controlling the actions of machines by reading the movement of machine tool tables or tool posts.

Thus, the trimetron is a signal indicator with built-in contacts for sending signals for three-way discrimination among measurement conditions.

Features
- Durable dustproof, waterproof construction
- Connection with a light box allows pass/fail judgments to be read by means of red/white/green lamps without the need to read a scale
- Shockproof spindle
- Contacts capable of high resolution one micron measurement

Possible Applications of the Trimetron
- Can increase speed and decrease energy for inspection of large numbers of parts
- Automatic selection of three steps
- High-precision auto-shutdown mechanism combining automatic measuring mechanism and reversible motor
- High speed/low speed/stop three-step speed adjustment responds to cutting dimensions on automatic lathe
- Continuous monitoring and warning mechanisms (buzzers, lamps, etc.)
- Multipoint monitoring device monitors simultaneously at different locations
- Can be incorporated into specialized machines

FIGURE 6-12 cont.

Light with Trimetron

output connector

Model TLB-7 Control Type

This control-type light box is capable of three-way control of external devices. It displays pass/fail judgments by means of red, white, and green lamps and at the same time activates a built-in relay to send out off/on signals.

Thus, if used on a sorting machine, it can activate solenoids for opening and closing sorting gates, thereby automatically sorting objects three ways. In addition, it can control dimensions by making continuous measurements of rolling materials and, if material thickness exceeds limits, by sending signals to buzzers to alert workers to shut down machines or alter the distances between rollers. Apart from this, it can measure objects being processed and send a signal to halt processing when specified dimensions have been attained. It is also capable of controlling the movement of tables and tool posts on machine tools.

FIGURE 6-12 cont.

Liquid level relays. These can detect liquid levels without using floats (*Figure 6-13*).

Contactless Detection Measures

Proximity switches. These systems respond to changes in distances from objects and to changes in lines of magnetic force. For this reason, they must be used with materials susceptible to magnetism (*Figure 6-14*).

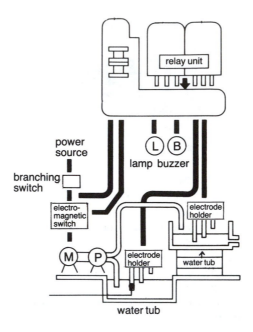

FIGURE 6-13. Liquid Level Relays

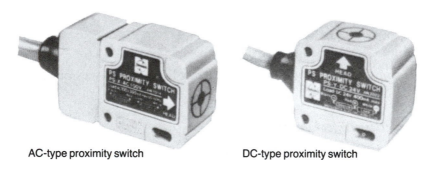

AC-type proximity switch   DC-type proximity switch

FIGURE 6-14. Proximity Switches

Photoelectric switches (transmission types and reflection types). Photoelectric switches include transmission types, in which a beam transmitted between two photoelectric switches is interrupted, and reflection types, which make use of reflected light beams. Photoelectric switches are widely used for nonferrous items, and reflection types are especially convenient for distinguishing color differences. They can even judge welds and the like by means of color differences (*Figure 6-15*).

Sample Applications

to verify passage of objects	to inspect transparent objects	to verify supply of parts	to check feeding of wafers

FIGURE 6-15. **Photoelectric Switches**

Beam sensors (transmission types and reflection types). These detection systems make use of electron beams. Beam sensors, too, include transmission and reflection types (*Figures 6-16* and *6-17*).

Fiber sensors. These are sensors that use optical fibers (*Figure 6-18*).

Area sensors. The majority of sensors detect only linear interruptions, but area sensors can detect random interruptions over a fixed area (*Figure 6-19*).

Positioning sensors. These are sensors that detect positioning (*Figure 6-20*).

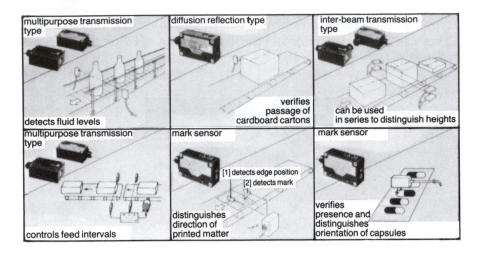

FIGURE 6-16. Beam Sensors

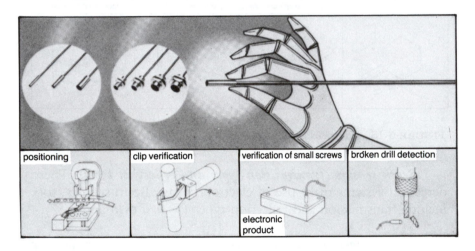

FIGURE 6-17. Proximity Beam Sensors

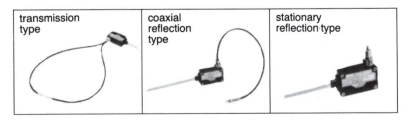

FIGURE 6-18. Fiber Sensor

Sample Applications

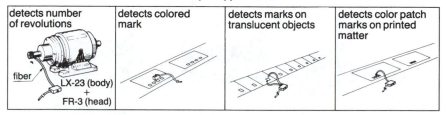

| detects number of revolutions | detects colored mark | detects marks on translucent objects | detects color patch marks on printed matter |

FIGURE 6-18 cont.

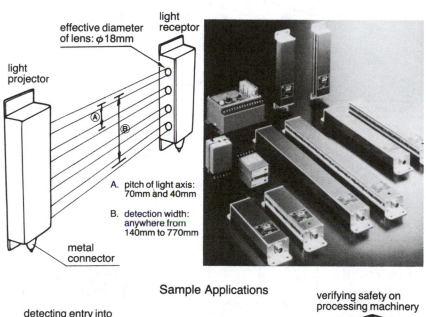

light receptor

effective diameter of lens: ϕ18mm

light projector

A. pitch of light axis: 70mm and 40mm

B. detection width: anywhere from 140mm to 770mm

metal connector

Sample Applications

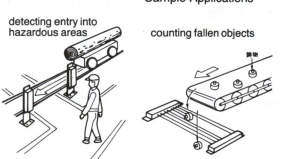

detecting entry into hazardous areas

counting fallen objects

verifying safety on processing machinery

FIGURE 6-19. Area Sensors

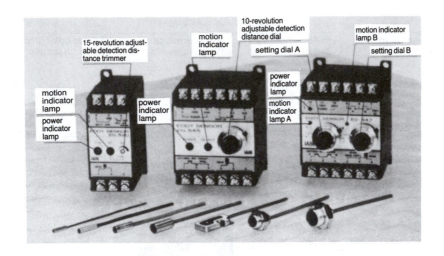

Sample Applications

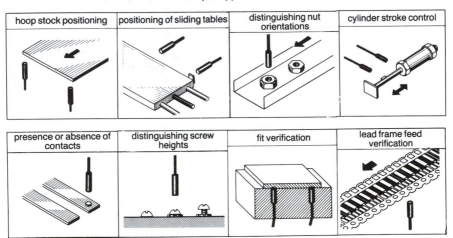

FIGURE 6-20. Positioning Sensors

Dimension sensors. These are sensors that detect whether dimensions are correct (*Figure 6-21*).

 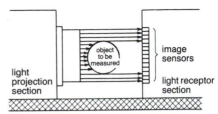

An on-line measuring device that uses sharp parallel light beams to capture an object's equivalent image on an image screen.

The device is composed of a detection unit and a control unit. The detection unit is further made up of a light projection unit and a light receptor unit. Sharp parallel beams are emitted from the light projection unit and captured by the receptor unit. When an object interrupts the parallel light beams, a projected image is formed on the receptor unit. An image sensor scans the image 500 times a second and performs calculations to measure its outside diameter. This system eliminates mechanical moving parts and permits miniaturization as well as measurement with an extremely high degree of reliability.

Features

- Capable of high-precision, contactless measurement: built-in 2048-bit CCD image sensor
- Can accurately measure objects moving at high speeds: averages measurement values made 500 times a second and is therefore unaffected by vibration
- Simple operation: integrated sensor unit and projection unit eliminates need for troublesome light sources
- Upper and lower limit values can be set freely: upper and lower digital comparators are standard equipment, so product inspection is simple
- Data processing capability: standard equipment BCD output can link with printers or computers

Sample Applications

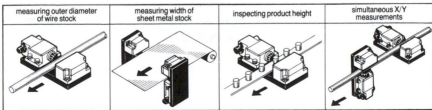

FIGURE 6-21. Dimension sensors

Contactless, high-precision measurement

Contactless method measures without coming in contact with the target object and has resolution of 1 mm

Can measure any material, color

Measures metals, plastics, ceramics, papers, rubbers, etc.

Sample Applications

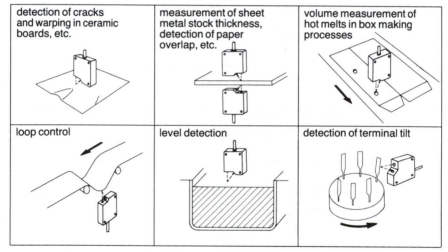

| detection of cracks and warping in ceramic boards, etc. | measurement of sheet metal stock thickness, detection of paper overlap, etc. | volume measurement of hot melts in box making processes |
| loop control | level detection | detection of terminal tilt |

FIGURE 6-22. Displacement Sensors

Displacement sensors. These are sensors that detect warping, thickness, and level heights (*Figure 6-22*).

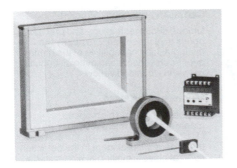

These are contactless sensors that detect only metal in motion. They are perfect for verifying high-speed movement and for counting small metal objects.

Sample Applications

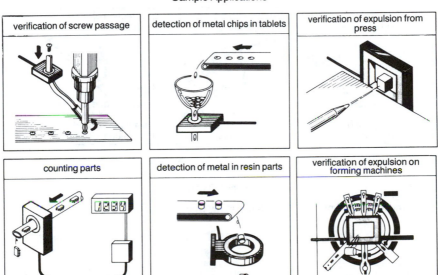

FIGURE 6-23. Metal Passage Sensors

Metal passage sensors. These can detect whether or not products have passed by and can sense the presence of metal mixed in with resin materials (*Figure 6-23*).

Can distinguish nearly all colors

Unique circuit technology and precision optics give these sensors nearly the distinguishing capabilities of the human eye. Such sensors can even distinguish between white and yellow.

High-speed response

Capable of making high-speed judgments at 10 microseconds (1/100,000th of a second), the power of these sensors is evident in the detection even of objects moving at high speeds.

Sample Applications

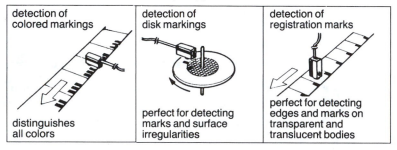

detection of colored markings	detection of disk markings	detection of registration marks
distinguishes all colors	perfect for detecting marks and surface irregularities	perfect for detecting edges and marks on transparent and translucent bodies

Sensor Types

multipurpose type	high-sensitivity type	piano wire type

FIGURE 6-24. Color Marking Sensors

Color marking sensors. These are sensors that detect colored marks or differences in color (*Figure 6-24*).

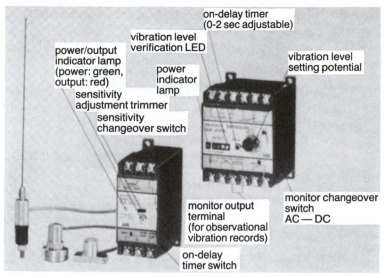

A totally new concept in vibration sensors, where vibrations are transformed into switch signals

Sample Applications

verification of back gauge contact	detection of discharge errors	detection of width distortions	seam position detection
record of changes in elapsed time/years	detection of breaks and missing bits	detection of the start of processing	verifying materials in hoppers

FIGURE 6-25. Vibration Sensors

Vibration sensors. These can detect the passage of goods, the position of welds, and snapped wires (*Figure 6-25*).

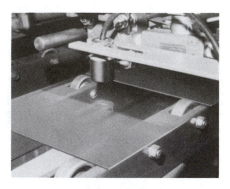

Sample Applications

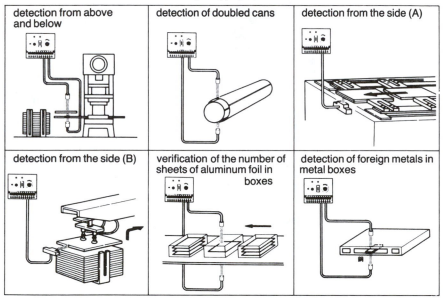

FIGURE 6-26. Double-Feed Sensors

Double-feed sensors. These are sensors that detect two products fed at the same time (*Figure 6-26*).

Welding position sensors. Because these can pick up changes in metallic composition without coming in contact with the object involved, they can detect joints that are invisible on the surface (*Figure 6-27*).

Sample Applications

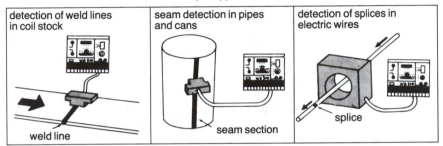

detection of weld lines in coil stock	seam detection in pipes and cans	detection of splices in electric wires
weld line	seam section	splice

FIGURE 6-27. Welding Position Sensors

Tapping errors can be detected simply by inserting the sensor into the screw hole. The detection zone widens circumferentially (laterally) and detects tapping errors with high degrees of precision and certainty.

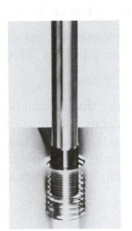

This permits sizable reductions in inspection times and equipment costs. Since this is a contactless device, moreover, the sensor head can be used for a long time without wearing down. It is unaffected by grease or dust.

Features:

• *A high-speed and highly precise contactless device*: revolutionary improvement over the old method of checking tap holes one by one by inserting a master. The principle of detecting changes in lines of magnetic force emitted laterally (circumferentially) from the tip of the cylindrical head permits contactless, high-speed sensing. Can be used semipermanently without wearing down the head.

• *Resists grease and dust*: Magnetic action is unaffected by grease or dust. Detects reliably even on machines with considerable cutting oil. The head construction's waterproof, oilproof seal mechanism is of superior reliability.

FIGURE 6-28. Tap Sensor

Tap sensors. These are sensors that detect incomplete tap screw machining (*Figure 6-28*).

Fluid elements. These devices detect changes in air streams occasioned by the placement or removal of objects and so can detect broken drill bits and the like (*Figure 6-29*).

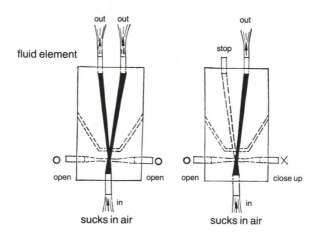

FIGURE 6-29. Fluid Elements

Measures for Detecting Pressure, Temperature, Electric Current, Vibration, Numbers of Cycles, Timing, and Information Transmission

Detection of pressure changes. The use of pressure gauges or pressure-sensitive switches permits detection of oil pipe flow interruptions, etc.

Detection of temperature changes. Temperature changes can be detected through the use of thermometers, thermostats, thermistors, thermocouples, etc. (*Figure 6-30*). These can be used to check surface temperatures of dies, electronic parts, and motors, to perform machine maintenance checks, and for all other kinds of industrial temperature measurement control.

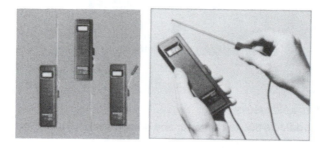

FIGURE 6-30. Surface Temperature Gauges

Detection of electrical current fluctuations. Meter relays are extremely convenient for being able to control the causes of defects by detecting the occurrence of electric currents (*Figures 6-31* through *6-37*).

In spot welding, moreover, conditions that give rise to defects can be pinpointed by using "current eyes" or "nugget testers" to detect secondary currents passing through weld points (*Figure 6-32*).

Features

- Monitors weld results
- Detects defects due to chip wear and branch flows
- Displays abnormalities by causes
- Can be used for galvanized and high-tensile sheet steel
- Mounting of sensor on base of welding machine gun yoke means no loss of operating efficiency

Functions

- A current eye monitors weld quality by detecting voltage changes in welds that correlate closely with weld strength. In addition to providing a reliable means of detection, the device can detect defects due to chip wear and branch flows.
- This apparatus also simplifies weld monitoring by storing a wealth of test data on changes in the thickness and quality of the materials welded and by displaying principal causes involved when defects occur.

Principles

- Changes in voltage between chips and weld strength (nugget diameter) are in the relationship illustrated in *Figure 6-33*. When current is first applied, resistance due to heat is great and resistance decreases as the passage of current grows. This phenomenon shows up as voltage changes.
- The current eye judges the quality of the weld by capturing the area of the welding efficiency component shown in *Figure 6-34* that closely correlates with welding strength even between chips.

FIGURE 6-32. Current Eye

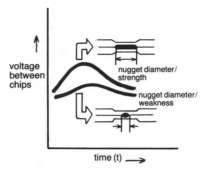

FIGURE 6-33. Voltage Between Chips and Nugget Diameter

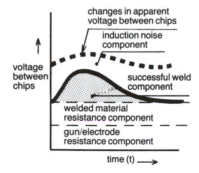

FIGURE 6-34. Constituents Voltage Between Chips

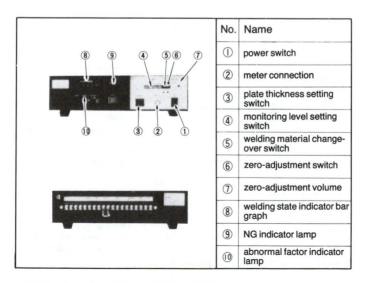

No.	Name
①	power switch
②	meter connection
③	plate thickness setting switch
④	monitoring level setting switch
⑤	welding material change-over switch
⑥	zero-adjustment switch
⑦	zero-adjustment volume
⑧	welding state indicator bar graph
⑨	NG indicator lamp
⑩	abnormal factor indicator lamp

FIGURE 6-35. Exterior View of Meter Relay

Method of Use

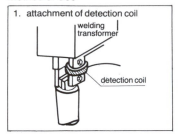

1. attachment of detection coil
   welding transformer
   detection coil

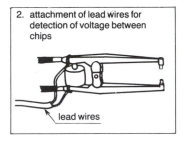

2. attachment of lead wires for detection of voltage between chips

   lead wires

1. attachment of detection coil
2. detection of voltage between chips
   lead wire attachment
3. gun pressurization signal connection
4. decision output terminal connection
5. zero-adjustment
6. set monitoring conditions
   • set for plate thickness
   • set for materials
   • set welding monitor level
7. welding operation
8. monitor welding
   • if abnormality appears, (no good) lamp lights up
   • abnormal factor indicator lamp lights up

FIGURE 6-36. Method of Use of Meter Relay

Item	Summary
range of applicable thicknesses	0.5-2.0mm (thin strip criteria)
applicable materials	soft steel, high-tensile steel, galvanized steel sheeting
current range	0-25KA, 1 range
resistance welding time	6-50 cycles
nugget diameters monitoring accuracy	(bar graph value × 0.053mm) ± 1.3mm (welding conditions:0.8mm RMWA for soft steel plate; proportional to welding conditions)
monitoring levels	2 levels: upper limit, lower limit
repeat time	0.1 sec
indicators	weld condition bar graph, abnormal factors
output	all G, NG relay contacts
power source voltage	AC 100 ± 10V
dimensions/weight	325mm × 100mm × 295mm 3.5kg

(Toyota Auto Body)

FIGURE 6-37. Specifications of Meter Relay

Detection of abnormal vibration. In cases where abnormal machine vibration can cause defects, it is convenient to use the vibration sensors mentioned above.

Detection of counting abnormalities. For this purpose one should use counters, preset counters stepping relays, or fiber sensors (*Figures 6-38, 6-39* and *6-40*).

Manual reset model is equipped with a
stopper to prevent inadvertent zeroing
due to erroneous operation.

plug-in model
type MC6M (hand reset type)

flush-mounted model
type MC6KF (electromagnetic reset
type with hand operation)

The 25.50 count model with maximum fixed-figure calculation speed (100 counts/second) is capable of continuous signaling.

FIGURE 6-38. Counter

main body of PMC preset counter   plugged in to PMC panel socket

FIGURE 6-39. Preset Counter

FIGURE 6-40. **Stepping Relay**

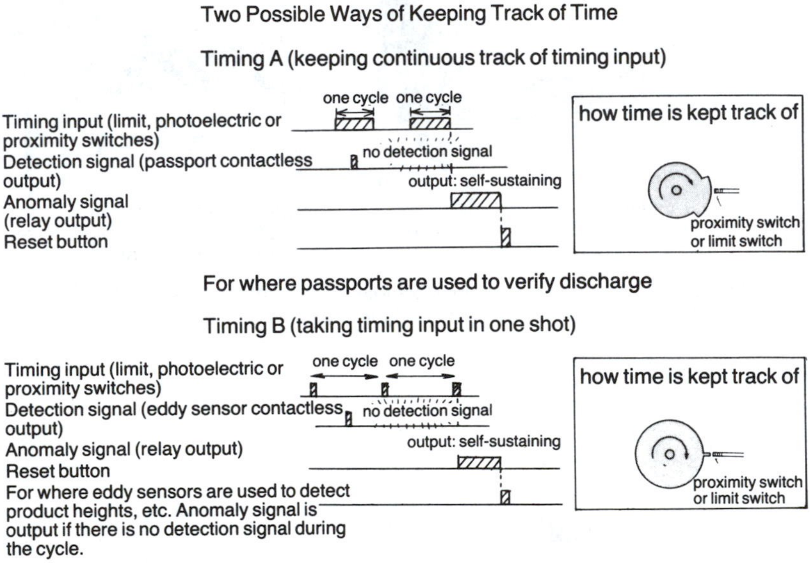

Two Possible Ways of Keeping Track of Time

Timing A (keeping continuous track of timing input)

one cycle one cycle

Timing input (limit, photoelectric or
proximity switches)

Detection signal (passport contactless
output)

no detection signal

Anomaly signal
(relay output)

output: self-sustaining

Reset button

how time is kept track of

proximity switch
or limit switch

For where passports are used to verify discharge

Timing B (taking timing input in one shot)

one cycle one cycle

Timing input (limit, photoelectric or
proximity switches)

Detection signal (eddy sensor contactless
output)

no detection signal

Anomaly signal (relay output)

output: self-sustaining

Reset button

For where eddy sensors are used to detect
product heights, etc. Anomaly signal is
output if there is no detection signal during
the cycle.

how time is kept track of

proximity switch
or limit switch

FIGURE 6-41. **Timing Units**

Time and timing detection. Timers, delay relays, timing units,
and time switches can be used for these purposes (*Figure 6-41*).

Measures for the transmission of information regarding abnormalities. Either sound or light can be used, but whereas sound actively captures workers' attention, defects may continue to be generated if a worker fails to notice a light. The use of color somewhat improves the attention-getting capacity of a steady light, but the summoning power of a blinking light is far greater still.

Above, I have described a variety of detection devices in widespread use. Detection methods and capacities have been rapidly improving of late and I hope that people do their own research and actively gather data so such devices may be used appropriately.

Most of the above examples were taken from the catalogues of the following companies (in alphabetical order):

Citizen Watch Co., Ltd.
Gomi Denki Keiki, Ltd.
Lead Electric, Ltd.
Matsushita Electric Works, Ltd.
Omron Tateishi Electronics Co., Ltd.
SUNX, Ltd.
Toyota Auto Body, Ltd.
Yaskawa Electric Mfg Co., Ltd.

7

Examples of Poka-yoke Systems

COMPANIES CONTRIBUTING EXAMPLES OF POKA-YOKE SYSTEMS

Since I thought that explaining poka-yoke methods by means of examples would be extremely effective when it came to actually adopting a poka-yoke system, I asked some progressive companies that have already achieved considerable success to submit examples. In addition to expressing my sincere thanks to all those firms that have consented to the publication of their examples, I would like to list the names of those companies as a token of my gratitude.

Aizo Industries, Ltd.	Automobile carburetors
Arakawa Auto Body, Ltd.	Buses, land cruisers, specially equipped vehicles
Daiho Industries, Ltd.	Automobile bearings
Asahi Denso, Ltd.	Lighting fixtures
Asahi National Lighting Co., Ltd.	Lighting fixtures and lighting equipment
Hosei Brake Industries, Ltd.	Automobile brakes
Kanto Auto Works, Ltd.	Passenger car assembly and parts manufacture
Kubota, Ltd.	Agricultural machinery and diesel engines
Matsushita Electric Industrial Co., Ltd./Vacuum Cleaner Div.	Household and industrial electric vacuum cleaners
Matsushita Electric Industrial Co., Ltd./Washing Machine Division/Mikuni Plant	Aisai brand twin-tub washing machines, dishwashers

Matsushita Electric Industrial Co., Ltd./Washing Machine Division/Shizuoka Plant	Aisai brand full automatic washing machines, dryers
Saga Tekkohsho Co., Ltd.	Ordinary and specialty bolts
Toyoda Gosei Co., Ltd.	Rubber automobile parts and plastic products
Toyota Auto Body Co., Ltd.	Passenger car and truck assembly, parts manufacture

POKA-YOKE DEVICES AND EXAMPLES OF POKA-YOKE SYSTEMS

The relationships among Zero Quality Control, poka-yoke devices, and poka-yoke systems may be described in the following way.

The Relationship Between Poka-yoke Devices, Poka-yoke Systems, and Inspection Systems

Poka-yoke devices. The following are characteristics of poka-yoke devices:

- They have the capacity for 100 percent inspections.
- In SQC, sampling techniques are used to reduce the trouble involved in checking, but poka-yoke devices can carry out 100 percent inspections with significantly less bother.
- In general, poka-yoke devices can be put in place at an extremely low cost.

Poka-yoke systems. Compared with SQC systems, in which fairly long periods of time elapse between the "check" stage and the execution of feedback and action, poka-yoke systems utilizing poka-yoke devices minimize defects by carrying out feedback and action immediately:

- In control systems, operations are halted and feedback and action have to be performed before processing can resume.
- When defects occur in warning systems, the need for immediate feedback and action is promptly signaled by means of buzzers or lights.

Combinations with inspection systems. The occurrence of defects will vary depending on the type of inspection system with which poka-yoke devices or poka-yoke systems are combined.

- Combination with *source inspection systems* makes it possible to achieve zero defects.
- Combination with *informative inspections — self-check methods* can reduce defects to a minimum. If defective items can be fixed, zero defects can be attained.
- Combination with *informative inspections — successive check methods* can do nothing about single occurrences of defects, but otherwise, defects can be reduced to a minimum. Again, if defective items can be fixed, zero defects can be attained.

Ultimately, however, the adoption of source inspections and poka-yoke methods is an absolutely essential condition for those who wish to achieve zero defects. Only when this is done will a Zero Quality Control system take shape.

Thus, the need today is to pursue some basic questions:

- Can we take current informative inspections with successive check methods and improve them to get a system of informative inspections with self-check methods?
- Can we take current informative inspections with self-check methods and improve them to get source inspections?
- Since informative inspections tolerate the occurrence of defects, can we take these methods and improve them to get source inspections in which the errors that cause defects are detected and prevented from turning into defects?

As I look at the examples illustrated below, I still feel that zero defects cannot be attained with SQC methods. In the case of high-diversity, low-volume production — and especially in so-called mixed production systems where a number of different products are simultaneously moving along the same line — control chart systems are totally ineffective if the goal is to reach zero defects. I feel more keenly than ever that one has to use a Zero QC system, i.e., a combination of source inspections and poka-yoke methods.

I hope that this will be the approach with which readers refer to the examples in the second section of this book and that they will make all-out efforts to attain the goal of zero defects.

POKA-YOKE EXAMPLES CLASSIFIED ACCORDING TO METHOD

As a reference aid, all of the examples that follow are classified according to method.

Source Inspection Examples

Contact Methods – Control Type	Examples 1-39
Contact Methods – Warning Type	Examples 40-44
Fixed Value Methods – Control Type	Examples 45-49
Fixed Value Methods – Warning Type	Examples 50-52
Motion-Step Methods – Control Type	Examples 53-76
Motion-Step Method – Warning Type	Example 77

Informative Inspection (Self-Check) Examples

Contact Methods – Control Type	Examples 78-85
Contact Methods – Warning Type	Examples 86-96
Fixed Value Methods – Control Type	Example 97
Fixed Value Methods – Warning Type	Examples 98-101
Motion-Step Methods – Control Type	Examples 102-103
Motion-Step Methods – Warning Type	Examples 104-106

Informative Inspection (Successive-Check) Examples

Contact Methods – Control Type	Examples 107-110
Contact Methods – Warning Type	Examples 111-112

Inspection Method		Setting Function		Regulative Function		Company Name
Source Inspection	●	Contact Method	●	Control Method	●	Aisan Industries, Ltd./ Yasushiro Plant
Informative Inspection (self)		Constant Value Method		Warning Method		**Proposed by**
Informative Inspection (successive)		Motion-Step Method				Tatsuya Tsutsumi

Theme   Ensuring Inclusion of Link No. 1 Clips

Before Improvement

1. Clips would sometimes be left off in an operation in which clips were to be mounted at four sites on a link.
2. Such errors were corrected by worker vigilance.

After Improvement

The clip press was made so that a pin would protrude at any site lacking a clip underneath.

1. Clips are set at four sites and the clip press is lowered.
2. Since a pin will protrude whenever a clip is missing, the link can be inserted only as far as the pin.
3. Consequently, proximity switch Sw is not activated, the clip bending machine will not operate, and it will not unclamp.

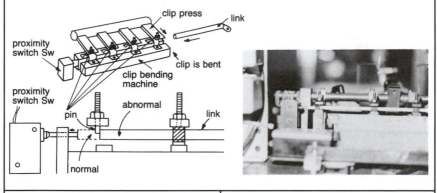

Effects	Cost
Clip omission was eliminated.	¥ 2,000 ($10)

Example 1

Inspection Method		Setting Function		Regulative Function		Company Name
Source Inspection	●	Contact Method	●	Control Method	●	Aisan Industries, Ltd./ Yasushiro Plant
Informative Inspection (self)		Constant Value Method		Warning Method		**Proposed by**
Informative Inspection (successive)		Motion-Step Method				Tatsuo Egawa

Theme   Preventing Flange Mounting Defects

Before Improvement

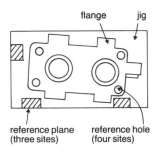

flange   jig

reference plane (three sites)   reference hole (four sites)

1. Reference holes were drilled at four locations on a multi-axis drill press, but occasionally processing would proceed despite faulty attachment to the jig. This would lead to problems at subsequent processes.

2. Faulty mounting was prevented through worker vigilance, but sometimes flanges would leave reference planes as they were mounted on jigs, causing hole-machining positions to shift.

After Improvement

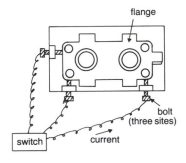

flange

bolt (three sites)

switch   current

1. Flange is set on jig.

2. The "on" switch causes a weak electric current to flow to bolts attached to the three reference planes.

3. If the flange does not make contact with the three bolts, the current will not flow and processing will not proceed even though the switch has been turned on.

Effects	Cost
Mounting errors disappeared.	¥ 5,000 ($25)

Example 2

Inspection Method		Setting Function		Regulative Function		Company Name
Source Inspection	●	Contact Method	●	Control Method	●	Aisan Industries, Ltd./ Yasushiro Plant
Informative Inspection (self)		Constant Value Method		Warning Method		**Proposed by**
Informative Inspection (successive)		Motion-Step Method				Sadamu Kamiya

Theme	
	Preventing Backward Casting of Engine Valve FL Material

Before Improvement

1. Backward strikes occasionally cropped up in a process for casting engine valves.
2. A worker would check the orientation of the workpiece visually and then place it in a hopper.

After Improvement

1. Workpieces consist of both material that is susceptible to magnetism and material that is not, and the nonsusceptible ends are cast.
2. Workpieces are placed by a hopper on an elevator and transported to the casting operation. A magnetic sensor is installed along the elevator so that whenever a workpiece pointing in the wrong direction (i.e., with the end made of material susceptible to magnetism facing forward) tries to pass by, it shuts down the elevator.

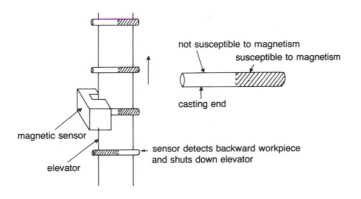

Effects	Cost
Backward strikes disappeared.	¥ 10,000 ($50)

Example 3

Inspection Method		Setting Function		Regulative Function		Company Name
Source Inspection	●	Contact Method	●	Control Method	●	IW Ceramics
Informative Inspection (self)		Constant Value Method		Warning Method		**Proposed by**
Informative Inspection (successive)		Motion-Step Method				Tetsuo Tatebayashi

Theme Preventing Tile Thickness Defects

Before Improvement

1. Considerable numbers of defective tiles (nicknamed "widows") cropped up whose thicknesses were outside the specified range.
2. The thicknesses of liquid glazes were determined by workers' intuitions.
3. A glaze was pumped directly from a large reservoir and fed to a nozzle by means of air piped throughout the plant.
4. The nozzle sprayed glaze onto dried tile substrate, but the degree to which the nozzle was opened was determined only by "feel."
5. Since the glaze was wet immediately after being sprayed on, its thickness was not known. The worker, therefore, used his intuition to judge the thickness after the glaze had partially dried, and adjusted the nozzle opening accordingly.
6. Since the true thickness was not known until after firing, thickness defects appeared quite often.

After Improvement

1. A densitometer was purchased for the glaze reservoir, so that a numerical value, e.g. "6", could be set, eliminating reliance on worker intuition.
2. Glaze was delivered from a large reservoir to a small supply tank by air pressure. A proximity switch continually kept volume in this supply tank constant.
3. A separate air stream was directed to the small tank and constant pressure was maintained through the use of a pressure monitor.
4. A large, 200 mm ϕ disk was mounted on the open/shut knob of the nozzle. A scale divided into 100 parts was attached to the disk in such a way that by connecting it to a reference indicator, a turn of the disk would move the nozzle mouth 1/100 mm. As a result, the degree of nozzle opening no longer depended on the worker's intuition and could be displayed both numerically and accurately.

Example 4

5. This substitution of numerical nozzle-setting capability for intuition and the standardization of volume and air pressure in glaze resupply tanks combined to reduce defects dramatically.

6. The improvements were obtained by substituting numerical and physical methods for intuitive qualitative and functional checks and by using source inspections to control operating conditions that influence quality.

Effects Thickness defects fell from 15% to 0.2%, for a monthly profit increase of ¥ 150,0000 ($750).	**Cost** approx. ¥ 350,000 ($1750), of which ¥ 30,000 ($150) were for a densitometer to measure reservoir liquid density

Example 4 cont.

Inspection Method		Setting Function		Regulative Function		Company Name
Source Inspection	●	Contact Method	●	Control Method	●	Aisan Industries, Ltd./ Yasushiro Plant
Informative Inspection (self)		Constant Value Method		Warning Method		**Proposed by**
Informative Inspection (successive)		Motion-Step Method				Sadame Kamiya

Theme   Preventing Outflows of Items with Uncut Cotter Grooves

Before Improvement

cotter groove

There was no way to prevent the outflow of items with uncut cotter grooves, and such items ended up moving on to the next process.

After Improvement

photoelectric tube

chute (A)

groove diameter check pin

engine valve

V-angle

chute (B)

groove diameter check pin

1. Engine valve drops from chute (A) to the top of the V-angle.

2. If the cotter groove has been machined, the valve will pass through check pins the diameter of the groove, turn 90° and drop into chute (B) in a vertical position.

3. Whenever an item arrives on which a cotter groove has not been cut, it cannot pass through the groove diameter check pins and does not move on to chute (B).

4. The groove-cutting machine shuts down whenever an engine valve fails to pass by a photoelectric tube.

Effects	**Cost**
Outflows of uncut items were eliminated.	¥ 10,000 ($50)

Example 5

Inspection Method		Setting Function		Regulative Function		Company Name
Source Inspection	●	Contact Method	●	Control Method	●	Aisan Industries, Ltd./ Yasushiro Plant
Informative Inspection (self)		Constant Value Method		Warning Method		**Proposed by**
Informative Inspection (successive)		Motion-Step Method				Hisashi Danmatsu

Theme
Ensuring that Screws are Tightened on Electromagnetic Valves

Before Improvement

1. An electromagnetic valve assembly line included an operation to tighten screws, but occasionally products would show up on which insufficient torque had been applied.

2. Products were verified visually in a successive-type inspection at the next process on the line, but this was not a failsafe check method.

After Improvement

1. When an electromagnetic valve is set on a jig, a photoelectric tube is activated and the tip of a pen cylinder advances.

2. When two screws are tightened to the specified torque by means of a torque driver, an electric signal causes a chime to sound and the tip of the cylinder retreats.

3. If either of the two screws has not been tightened to the specified torque, the tip of the pen cylinder does not retreat and the electromagnetic valve cannot be removed from the jig.

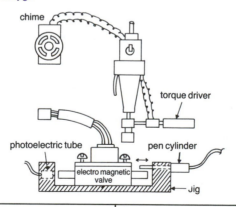

Effects	Cost
Screw-tightening defects were eliminated.	¥ 25,000 ($125)

Example 6

Inspection Method	Setting Function	Regulative Function	Company Name
Source Inspection ●	Contact Method ●	Control Method ●	Asahi Denso, Ltd.
Informative Inspection (self)	Constant Value Method	Warning Method	**Proposed by**
Informative Inspection (successive)	Motion-Step Method		Zenshi Matsubashi Katsuyasu Kitamura

Theme   Preventing Backward Attachment of Yokesets

Before Improvement

1. Attachment was performed by visual verification of indicators on the yoke cover. In addition, errors occurred in the attachment of yokes to yoke covers and in polarity indicators (processed outside the plant), as well as in polarity mounting.

2. Inspection took place after the fact, with a jig with polarity sensors being fitted to the finished product after assembly.

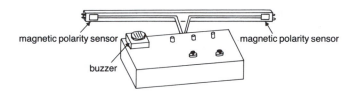

magnetic polarity sensor   magnetic polarity sensor

buzzer

After Improvement

Magnets with their poles oriented to attract both ends of the yokes were mounted on either side of the mounting jig for both L-14s and yokesets. This permitted source inspections by making it impossible, through the use of the repellent force of the magnets, to attach the yokeset backward.

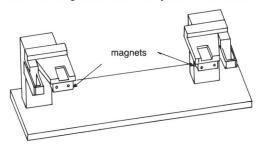

magnets

Effects	Cost
Yoke polarity errors were eliminated.	none

Example 7

Inspection Method		Setting Function		Regulative Function		Company Name
Source Inspection	●	Contact Method	●	Control Method	●	Asahi National Lighting Co., Ltd.
Informative Inspection (self)		Constant Value Method		Warning Method		**Proposed by** Katsumi Muneyasu, Interior Lighting Development Department
Informative Inspection (successive)		Motion-Step Method				

Theme	Preventing Backward Mounting of S194 Switches

Before Improvement

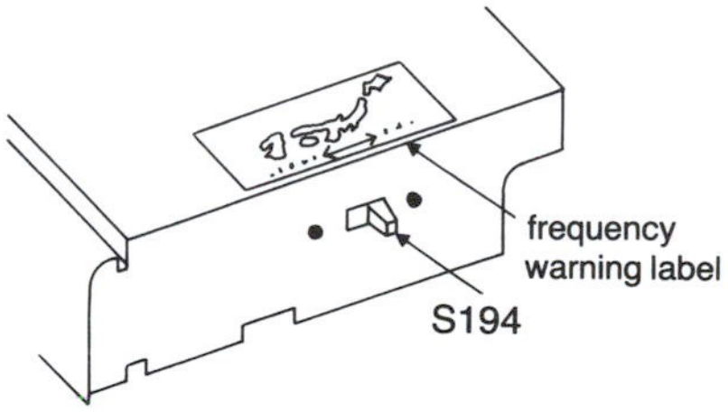

frequency warning label

S194

An S194 switch that has been mounted backward no longer matches the indicators on the frequency warning label.

After Improvement

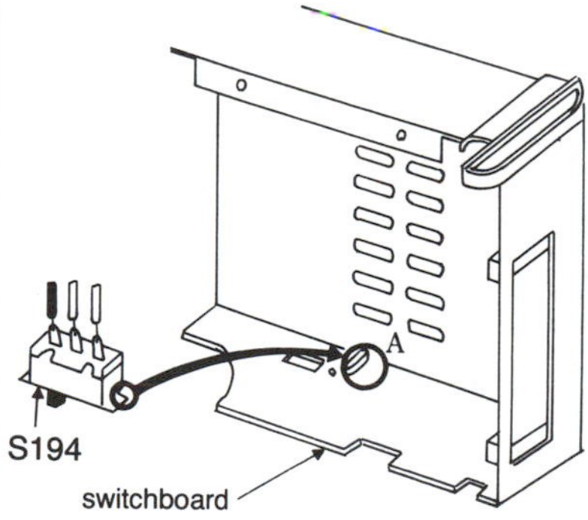

S194

switchboard

A

An S194 put in backward will ride up on lug A in the figure at left and will be impossible to attach.

Effects	Backward mountings were eliminated.	Cost	none

Example 8

Inspection Method		Setting Function		Regulative Function		Company Name
Source Inspection	●	Contact Method	●	Control Method	●	Asahi National Lighting Co., Ltd.
Informative Inspection (self)		Constant Value Method		Warning Method		**Proposed by** Kenji Uesada, Interior Lighting Manufacturing Technology Department
Informative Inspection (successive)		Motion-Step Method				

Theme
Preventing Failure to Attach Kicksprings

Before Improvement

Kickspring mountings were sometimes left out when using a shield plate caulking device (set shield plate → set kickspring → switch on → press operates) and this was linked to claims made against the company.

After Improvement

A touch sensor was attached to the shield plate caulking device. The presence or absence of the kickspring is detected by the sensor and caulking cannot proceed if the kickspring is not seated.

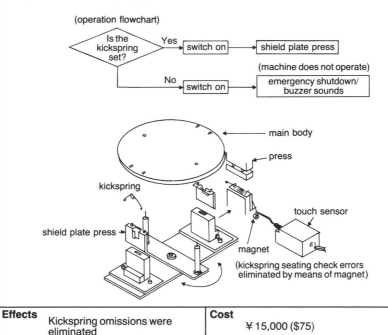

(operation flowchart)

Is the kickspring set? — Yes → switch on — shield plate press

(machine does not operate)

Is the kickspring set? — No → switch on — emergency shutdown/ buzzer sounds

main body
press
kickspring
shield plate press →
touch sensor
magnet
(kickspring seating check errors eliminated by means of magnet)

Effects	Cost
Kickspring omissions were eliminated	¥ 15,000 ($75)

Example 9

Inspection Method		Setting Function		Regulative Function		Company Name
Source Inspection	●	Contact Method	●	Control Method	●	Asahi National Lighting Co., Ltd./
Informative Inspection (self)		Constant Value Method		Warning Method		**Proposed by** Setsuo Iwamuro, Interior Lighting Manufacturing Technology Department
Informative Inspection (successive)		Motion-Step Method				

Theme	Ensuring Proper Positioning of Blanks for House Number Plates

Before Improvement

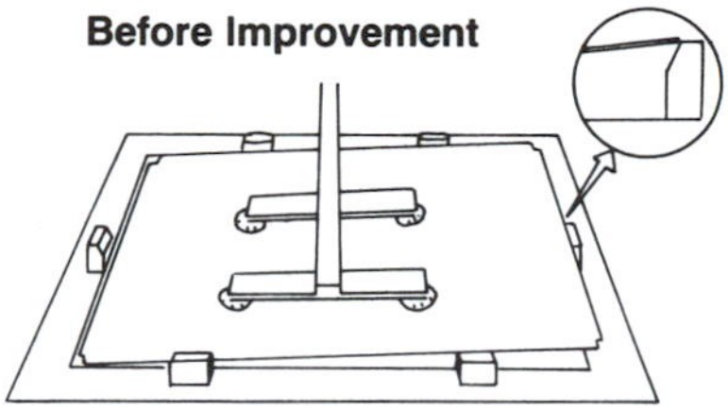

Poor alignment on an automatic line for house number plates occasionally caused defects in machining because plates would catch near the die.

After Improvement

Proximity switches were mounted on either side of the die to assure correct positioning of the blanks.

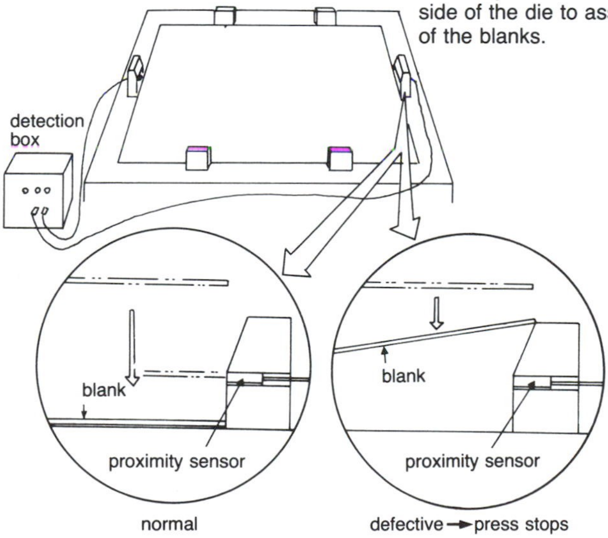

detection box

blank

proximity sensor

normal

blank

proximity sensor

defective → press stops

Effects	Errors due to feed misalignment were eliminated.	Cost	¥ 50,000 ($250)

Example 10

Inspection Method		Setting Function		Regulative Function		Company Name
Source Inspection	●	Contact Method	●	Control Method	●	Asahi National Lighting Co., Ltd. Gunma Plant
Informative Inspection (self)		Constant Value Method		Warning Method		**Proposed by**
Informative Inspection (successive)		Motion-Step Method				Mizuide

Theme	Preventing Failures to Caulk and Cut Terminals Arising from Erroneous Feeding of 62-Type Terminal Boards

Before Improvement

Since terminal boards were fed by a terminal board pitch feed method, it was possible for caulking and cutting to be omitted when the pitch feed was off alignment.

After Improvement

A photoelectric switch detects the absence of a cut and shuts down the machine. When this happens, the omission of caulking at the previous process can also be corrected.

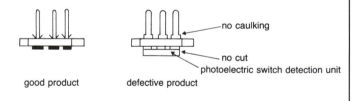

good product   defective product

Effects	Terminal caulking and cutting omissions were eliminated.	Cost	none

Example 11

Inspection Method		Setting Function		Regulative Function		Company Name
Source Inspection	●	Contact Method	●	Control Method	●	Asahi National Lighting Co., Ltd.
Informative Inspection (self)		Constant Value Method		Warning Method		**Proposed by** Keiji Nakai, Interior Lighting Manufacturing Technology Department
Informative Inspection (successive)		Motion-Step Method				

Theme	Ensuring the Attachment of HA3130-Type Glove Fastenings

Before Improvement

The operation depended on the worker's vigilance.

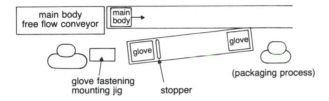

main body free flow conveyor / main body / glove / glove / (packaging process) / glove fastening mounting jig / stopper

After Improvement

A metal sensor was attached to the glove fastening mounting jig so that a stopper would prevent movement to the next process if two glove fastenings were not attached.

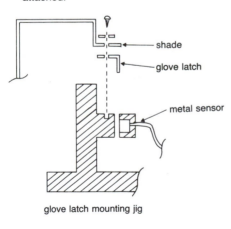

shade / glove latch / metal sensor / glove latch mounting jig

Effects	Cost
Claims were eliminated.	¥ 40,000 ($200)

Example 12

Inspection Method		Setting Function		Regulative Function		Company Name
Source Inspection	●	Contact Method	●	Control Method	●	Asahi National Lighting Co., Ltd.
Informative Inspection (self)		Constant Value Method		Warning Method		**Proposed by** Kentaro Shimada, Interior Lighting Manufacturing Technology Department
Informative Inspection (successive)		Motion-Step Method				

Theme   Preventing Backward Attachment of Stabilizers and L-428 Sockets

Before Improvement

upper-type driver

Socket mounts, stabilizers and L-428 sockets were attached by means of an upper-type driver, but it was possible to attach the L-428 sockets backward.

After Improvement

special jig to prevent backward attachment of L-428 sockets

special jig to prevent backward attachment of stabilizers

Backward attachment was prevented and worker time was cut by cradling stabilizers and L-428 sockets in special jigs and then carrying out attachment operations from above with an air driver.

Effects	Cost
Backward attachment of sockets was eliminated.	¥ 50,000 ($250)

Example 13

Inspection Method		Setting Function		Regulative Function		Company Name
Source Inspection	●	Contact Method	●	Control Method	●	Asahi National Lighting Co., Ltd.
Informative Inspection (self)		Constant Value Method		Warning Method		**Proposed by** Shizuo Tsujinaka, Commercial Lighting Plant, Technology Department
Informative Inspection (successive)		Motion-Step Method				

Theme	Preventing Orientation Errors in Silk Screen Printing

Before Improvement

decorative board

printing surface

tabs for caulking

panel

holes for caulking decorative board

silk screen printing surface becomes interior of unit

panel holder

The orientations of panel holes and printing surfaces were verified visually.

After Improvement

panel

panel holder

dowel to control orientation

Errors in panel printing orientation are prevented by providing a dowel to control orientation on the panel holder, so that the panel cannot be set on the holder unless the panel hole matches the dowel. Proper positioning is further determined by the product's silk screen printing orientation and by the orientation of tabs on the decorative board.

Effects Orientation errors were eliminated.	**Cost** none

Example 14

Inspection Method		Setting Function		Regulative Function		Company Name
Source Inspection	●	Contact Method	●	Control Method	●	Asahi National Lighting Co., Ltd./ Gunma Plant
Informative Inspection (self)		Constant Value Method		Warning Method		**Proposed by**
Informative Inspection (successive)		Motion-Step Method				Mizuide

Theme   Preventing Damage to Door Switch Molds

Before Improvement

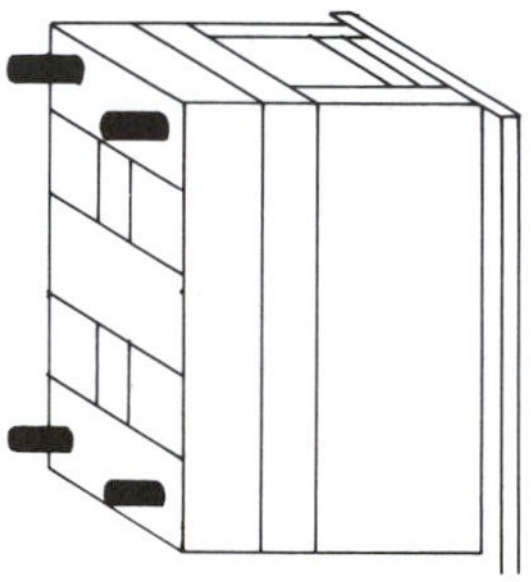

Ejection operations were verified visually.

After Improvement

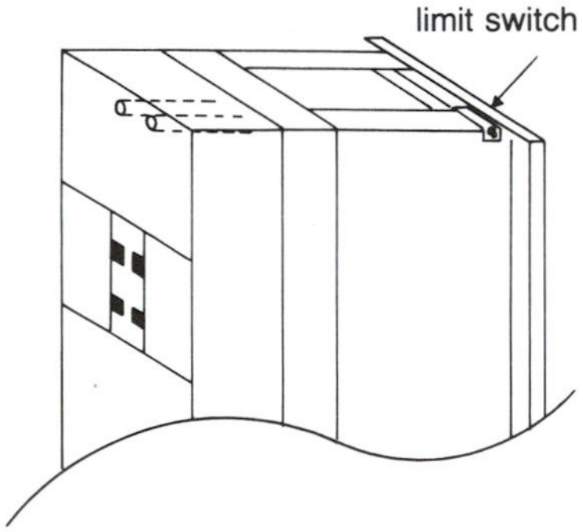

limit switch

The operation of the ejector plate is verified by means of a limit switch, so that the molding machine shuts down if the operation is unsatisfactory.

Effects	Cost
Damage to molds was eliminated.	¥ 1,500 ($7.50)

Example 15

Inspection Method		Setting Function		Regulative Function		Company Name
Source Inspection	●	Contact Method	●	Control Method	●	Asahi National Lighting Co., Ltd.
Informative Inspection (self)		Constant Value Method		Warning Method		**Proposed by** Keiji Nakai, Interior Lighting Manufacturing Technology Department
Informative Inspection (successive)		Motion-Step Method				

Theme   Controlling the Orientation of Lights

Before Improvement

could be attached even if rotated 180°

The fact that arms and lights can be attached in either direction meant that the orientation of finished bulbs was inconsistent.

After Improvement

limit switch

1. Attaching a limit switch to the jig cradling the light caused relays and electromagnetic valves to function only when a light was set in the proper direction. This also permitted the use of electric drivers and air drivers.

2. Screws cannot be tightened when a light is set in backward, because electricity and air do not flow to the electric and air drivers.

air driver snap-in socket

electric driver plug socket

A-A cross-section light

bulb

jig   limit switch

Effects		Cost	
Backward attachment of lights was eliminated.		¥ 8,000 ($40)	

Example 16

Inspection Method		Setting Function		Regulative Function		Company Name
Source Inspection	●	Contact Method	●	Control Method	●	Toyoda Gosei Co., Ltd.
Informative Inspection (self)		Constant Value Method		Warning Method		**Proposed by**
Informative Inspection (successive)		Motion-Step Method				

Theme Preventing Attachment Errors on an Automatic Tray Clip Attachment Machine

Before Improvement

clips (four)

tray clip attachment process

clips are automatically fitted onto conveyor-fed trays

1. Even though the operation was carried out by machine, clips failed to be attached in about one unit in every few hundred.

2. Molded trays were fed to part A by conveyor.

3. The part B loader transported the unit from part A to part C and set it on a jig.

4. Attachment head D took clips from part E and attached them at designated locations on the tray.

5. When four clips had been attached, the unit was ejected from the jig at part C, slid down a chute, and came to part F.

   Steps 2-5 were repeated automatically.

6. The problem was that the unit would be ejected even if no clips had been attached during the operation to attach clips at four sites.

After Improvement

1. Part C was enhanced by the addition of a device to verify the presence or absence of clip F.

2. When the clip attachment operations are completed, the presence or absence of clips is verified before the unit is ejected.

   If clips are present the unit is ejected.

   If clips are absent the attachment operation is carried out once more and the unit is ejected after the presence of the clips has been verified.

Effects Clip attachment failures were eliminated.	**Cost** approx. ¥ 40,000 ($200)

Example 17

Inspection Method		Setting Function		Regulative Function		Company Name
Source Inspection	●	Contact Method	●	Control Method	●	Arakawa Auto Body Industries, Ltd./ Sarunage Plant
Informative Inspection (self)		Constant Value Method		Warning Method		**Proposed by**
Informative Inspection (successive)		Motion-Step Method				

Theme　　Preventing Omission of Wire Stop Caulking

Before Improvement

wire stop punch, left side
during caulking
wire stop punch, right side
rivet caulking punch
caulking omitted
caulking holder

When switching processing from left to right, a punch would be removed manually and goods without caulking would show up whenever a worker to set the punch.

After Improvement

1. The position of the product's wire set determines the position of the wire stop punch.
2. With a half turn of the caulking holder, the position of the upper caulking punch is automatically changed by means of a cylinder and detector limits.
3. If setting is left out, then the product will drop and setting will be impossible.

cylinder
wire stop punch
half turn
caulking holder
setting cannot take place

Effects　Reduction in omitted wire stopper caulking. Shortening of product RL changeover setting times.	**Cost**　　¥ 35,000 ($175)

Example 18

Inspection Method		Setting Function		Regulative Function		Company Name
Source Inspection	•	Contact Method	•	Control Method	•	Kanto Auto Works, Ltd./ Yokosuka Plant
Informative Inspection (self)		Constant Value Method		Warning Method		**Proposed by**
Informative Inspection (successive)		Motion-Step Method				Kazuo Suzuki

Theme Preventing the Defective Clamping of Bolts on Rear Brake Drums and Rear Shock Absorbers

Before Improvement

1. Because of the importance of these parts, defective tightening of bolts must not occur. (defect prevention)

2. Although clamping of rear brake drums and rear shock absorbers was carried out with a jig like the one depicted below, the importance of these parts meant that workers always stayed alert so that bolt-tightening defects would not occur. Very occasionally, however, such defects did show up.

After Improvement

1. addition of microsensors   2. addition of reaction force detector

double-checks 1 item in 30

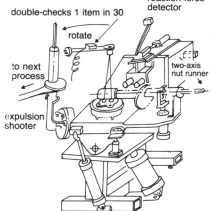

rotate

to next process

two-axis nut runner

expulsion shooter

1. For tightening the parts in question, a reaction force detector switch was added to a two-axis nut runner so that the jig would not rotate if there was any defect in the number (2) of items tightened (N) or in torque values (T).

2. A warning is automatically issued at every thirtieth item and the jig will not rotate unless a process worker personally double-checks the part in question.

Effects	Defects involving missing bolts and nuts were eliminated, along with deviations from torque specifications.	**Cost**	approx. ¥ 20,000 ($100) (three microswitches, machining of two reaction force sensor bars)

Example 19

Inspection Method		Setting Function		Regulative Function		Company Name
						Kanto Auto Works, Ltd./ Yokosuka Plant
Source Inspection	●	Contact Method	●	Control Method	●	
Informative Inspection (self)		Constant Value Method		Warning Method		**Proposed by**
Informative Inspection (successive)		Motion-Step Method				Sakae Kawana

Theme	Preventing the Defective Tightening of Bolts on Shock Absorber Shafts and Bearing Supports

Before Improvement

1. Because of the importance of these parts, defective tightening of bolts must not occur. (defect prevention)

2. After coil springs were compressed onto rear shock absorbers by means of jigs like the one depicted below, absorber shafts and bearing supports were bolted together so that the springs would not fly off. When the nuts were inadequately tightened, springs would occasionally fly off and strange noises would occasionally crop up.

After Improvement

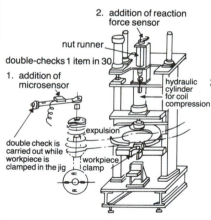

2. addition of reaction force sensor

nut runner

double-checks 1 item in 30

1. addition of microsensor

hydraulic cylinder for coil compression

expulsion

double check is carried out while workpiece is clamped in the jig

workpiece clamp

1. To deal with tightening on the parts in question, a reaction force sensor switch was added to the nut runner so that whenever tightening was inadequate, the workpiece would not unclamp and could not proceed to the next process.

2. A warning is automatically issued at every thirtieth item and the workpiece will not unclamp unless a process worker personally performs a double check by means of a QL wrench equipped with a sensor.

Effects	Both occurrences of strange noises due to clamping defects and flying out of coil springs were eliminated.	**Cost**	approx. ¥ 10,000 ($50) (two micro-switches, machining of one reaction-force sensor bar)

Example 20

Inspection Method		Setting Function		Regulative Function		Company Name
Source Inspection	●	Contact Method	●	Control Method	●	Kanto Auto Works, Ltd./ Yokosuka Plant
Informative Inspection (self)		Constant Value Method		Warning Method		**Proposed by**
Informative Inspection (successive)		Motion-Step Method				Makoto Hishikura

Theme	Ensuring Proper Attachment of Parts Inside Auto Body Engine Housings

Before Improvement

1. Different automobile models use different types of brackets in their body engine housings and backward attachment would occasionally occur with a parts jig.
2. The workpiece indicated on a light board was set into the jig.
3. A visual check was made to verify that a bracket conforming to specifications was attached.
4. Attachment errors were prevented through worker vigilance.

After Improvement

1. When the initial workpiece specified is set into the front fender S/A apron attachment jig, all bracket types are detected by means of a limit switch.
2. A match between the specification indicators from the control light board and the specifications detected by the limit switch is confirmed.
3. If the confirmation checks, then the jig automatically clamps and the operation can begin.
4. If the confirmation does not check, the jig cannot clamp and the situation is indicated by means of a buzzer and a display.

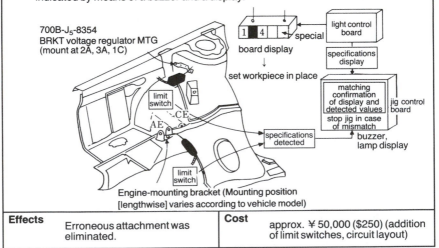

700B-J₅-8354
BRKT voltage regulator MTG
(mount at 2A, 3A, 1C)

light control board

1 4   special
board display

specifications display

set workpiece in place

limit switch

matching confirmation of display and detected values — jig control board
stop jig in case of mismatch

specifications detected

buzzer, lamp display

limit switch

Engine-mounting bracket (Mounting position [lengthwise] varies according to vehicle model)

Effects	Erroneous attachment was eliminated.	Cost	approx. ¥ 50,000 ($250) (addition of limit switches, circuit layout)

Example 21

Inspection Method		Setting Function		Regulative Function		Company Name
						Kubota, Ltd./Sakai Manufacturing Facility
Source Inspection	•	Contact Method	•	Control Method	•	
Informative Inspection (self)		Constant Value Method		Warning Method		**Proposed by**
Informative Inspection (successive)		Motion-Step Method				

Theme	Preventing Slippage of Products in a Punching Process

Before Improvement

Defects were feared if processing were to occur when the mounting of housing cases had slipped; avoidance of this problem depended on worker vigilance.

After Improvement

1. A touch switch was mounted on the former contact point so that a seating signal could be detected.
2. Defects are prevented by making the machine inoperable when a mounting is unacceptable.

Effects	Processing defects were eliminated	Cost	approx. ¥ 15,000 ($75)

Example 22

Inspection Method		Setting Function		Regulative Function		Company Name
Source Inspection	●	Contact Method	●	Control Method	●	Kubota, Ltd./Sakai Manufacturing Facility
Informative Inspection (self)		Constant Value Method		Warning Method		**Proposed by**
Informative Inspection (successive)		Motion-Step Method				

Theme	Preventing Duplicate Cutting of Spline Grooves

Before Improvement

Identical spline grooves must be cut on both ends of each axle, but occasionally the same end would be cut twice. In the past, worker vigilance guarded such errors.

After Improvement

1. A reflective photoelectric switch was installed to detect the difference between items on which grooves had and had not been cut.
2. If an item was mounted in the wrong way, the machine would not operate.

Effects	Processing defects due to mounting errors were eliminated.	Cost	approx. ￥25,000 ($125)

Example 23

Inspection Method		Setting Function		Regulative Function		Company Name
Source Inspection	●	Contact Method	●	Control Method	●	Taiho Industries, Ltd.
Informative Inspection (self)		Constant Value Method		Warning Method		**Proposed by** Forming Dept. 2, Line No. 21, Metals Production Division No. 2
Informative Inspection (successive)		Motion-Step Method				

Theme	Preventing Reversal Errors in a Forming Process

Before Improvement

1. With parts made of bonded steel and aluminum, the steel side of the material had to face upward. Sometimes, however, the aluminum side would be up and this would lead to damage to tools in later processes and cause production to fall.

2. We decided to deal with this problem by building a poka-yoke device into the process itself.

After Improvement

As illustrated in Figure A, the machine shuts down and a warning message is when the aluminum side is facing up.
Operation proceeds normally when the situation is as shown in Figure B.

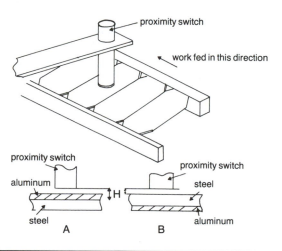

Effects Damage to tools has been eliminated because abnormal items can be detected and are no longer fed to subsequent processes.	Cost ¥ 12,000 ($60)

Example 24

Inspection Method		Setting Function		Regulative Function		Company Name
Source Inspection	●	Contact Method	●	Control Method	●	Taiho Industries, Ltd.
Informative Inspection (self)		Constant Value Method		Warning Method		**Proposed by**
Informative Inspection (successive)		Motion-Step Method				

Theme	Preventing Cutting Length Defects in a Press Process

Before Improvement

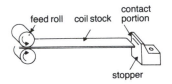

feed roll   coil stock   contact portion

stopper

The fact that the material was coiled meant that roll imperfections and the like sometimes caused the material to be cut before it reached the stopper, resulting in lengths that were too short.

After Improvement

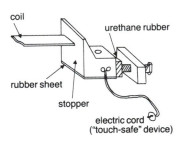

coil

urethane rubber

rubber sheet

stopper

electric cord ("touch-safe" device)

A "touch-safe" method has been adopted in which electric current is used to shut down the machine whenever the material does not come in contact with the stopper.

Effects Short lengths due to material feed mechanisms were eliminated	**Cost** ¥ 108,000 ($540)

Example 25

Inspection Method		Setting Function		Regulative Function		Company Name
Source Inspection	●	Contact Method	●	Control Method	●	Toyoda Gosei Co., Ltd.
Informative Inspection (self)		Constant Value Method		Warning Method		**Proposed by**
Informative Inspection (successive)		Motion-Step Method				

Theme	Preventing Backward Attachment of Brake Hose Mouthpieces

Before Improvement

1. This operation involved fitting a mouthpiece to a hose and then caulking it by machine. Since sections A and B resembled one another, however, mouthpieces would sometimes be attached backward.
2. Prevention of such backward attachment depended on worker vigilance.
3. In the event that backward attachment did occur, it was discovered at subsequent processes. (successive check)

After Improvement

1. The mouthpiece and hose are joined.
2. They are passed through a poka-yoke jig.
   [Since section A and B differ in shape, the assembly does not pass through the jig when a mouthpiece has been attached backward.]
3. The assembly is positioned on a caulking machine.
4. Section B is automatically caulked and ejected.
   [A proximity switch is attached to the poka-yoke jig, so that the caulking machine does not operate whenever an assembly does not pass through the jig.]

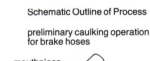

Schematic Outline of Process

preliminary caulking operation for brake hoses

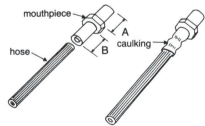

Effects	Backward attachment was eliminated.	**Cost**	approx. ¥ 20,000 ($100)

Example 26

Inspection Method		Setting Function		Regulative Function		Company Name
Source Inspection	•	Contact Method	•	Control Method	•	Toyoda Gosei Co., Ltd.
Informative Inspection (self)		Constant Value Method		Warning Method		**Proposed by**
Informative Inspection (successive)		Motion-Step Method				

Theme   Ensuring the Complete Installation of Heater Controls

Before Improvement

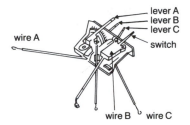

1. Workers would occasionally install parts incorrectly or neglect to install parts both because of the large number of parts and because some parts resembled others.

2. The failure to install parts was prevented through worker vigilance.

After Improvement

1. Levers A, B, and C are installed.

2. Wires A, B, and C are installed.

3. The switch is provisionally installed in its specified position, set in a bolting machine, and then clamped.

   [A proximity switch mounted in the bolting machine checks for the presence or absence of levers and wires, as well as for faulty installation.]

4. When two bolts are tightened and the switch is secured, it is unclamped and the workpiece is ejected.

Effects	Cost
Instances of neglected installation were eliminated.	approx. ¥ 120,000 ($600)

Example 27

Inspection Method		Setting Function		Regulative Function		Company Name
Source Inspection	•	Contact Method	•	Control Method	•	Toyoda Gosei Co., Ltd.
Informative Inspection (self)		Constant Value Method		Warning Method		**Proposed by**
Informative Inspection (successive)		Motion-Step Method				

Theme   Preventing Defects in Brake Hose Mouthpiece Angle

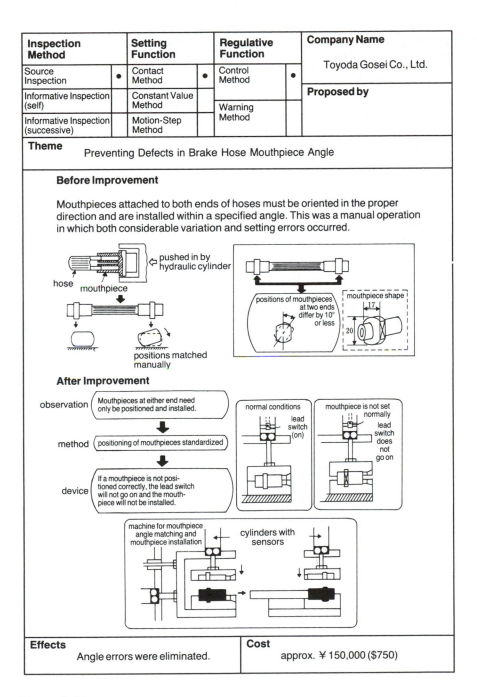

Before Improvement

Mouthpieces attached to both ends of hoses must be oriented in the proper direction and are installed within a specified angle. This was a manual operation in which both considerable variation and setting errors occurred.

pushed in by hydraulic cylinder

hose   mouthpiece

positions matched manually

positions of mouthpieces at two ends differ by 10° or less

mouthpiece shape

After Improvement

observation — Mouthpieces at either end need only be positioned and installed.

method — positioning of mouthpieces standardized

device — If a mouthpiece is not positioned correctly, the lead switch will not go on and the mouthpiece will not be installed.

normal conditions — lead switch (on)

mouthpiece is not set normally — lead switch does not go on

machine for mouthpiece angle matching and mouthpiece installation

cylinders with sensors

Effects	Cost
Angle errors were eliminated.	approx. ¥ 150,000 ($750)

Example 28

Inspection Method		Setting Function		Regulative Function		Company Name
Source Inspection	●	Contact Method	●	Control Method	●	Toyota Auto Body Co., Ltd.
Informative Inspection (self)		Constant Value Method		Warning Method		**Proposed by**
Informative Inspection (successive)		Motion-Step Method				Body Division No. 31

Theme	Ensuring Proper Installation of Retainer Drivers' Seats

Before Improvement

1. Retainers for left-hand steering wheels were sometimes installed in right-hand drive vehicles.

2. Operating Procedure: 1.) Look at work-in-process tag.
                               2.) Paint sealer on floor assembly.
                               3.) Remove retainer seat.
                               4.) Attach retainer seat to floor assembly.

3. Conditions for Installation: Right-hand drive vehicles: floor of right seat
                                               Left-hand drive vehicles: floor of left seat

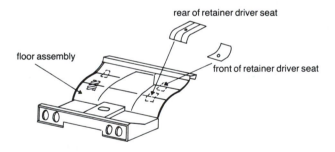

Example 29

After Improvement

1. A proximity switch senses the different shapes of floor assemblies for left-hand steering wheels and right-hand steering wheels.

2. The signal from the proximity switch activates an air cylinder mounted on a jig and a stopper designed to prevent backward attachment springs out to make positioning of the part impossible.

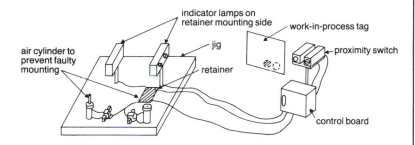

Effects	Cost
Faulty mountings were eliminated.	¥ 30,000 ($150) (for proximity switch)

Example 29 cont.

Inspection Method		Setting Function		Regulative Function		Company Name
Source Inspection	●	Contact Method	●	Control Method	●	Toyoda Gosei Co., Ltd.
Informative Inspection (self)		Constant Value Method		Warning Method		**Proposed by**
Informative Inspection (successive)		Motion-Step Method				

Theme	Preventing Drilling Defects through the Detection of Damage to Drills

Before Improvement

1. Processing took place on a six-axis automatic machine. Thin drills would sometimes break, leading to a series of processing defects.

2. All holes were automatically checked at the next process, but by that time a series of defects had already occurred.

2.3 ϕ mouthpiece hole boring process (automatic line)

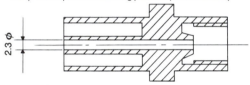

After Improvement

1. A mechanism was devised to check whether or not the drill tip is broken each time processing takes place.

2. In the event that a drill is broken, the machine shuts down and a light board (information relay device) summons a worker. Consequently, only one defective item is produced and series of two or more defects do not occur.

Effects	Serial defects were eliminated	**Cost**	approx. ¥ 10,000 ($50)

Example 30

Inspection Method		Setting Function		Regulative Function		Company Name
Source Inspection	●	Contact Method	●	Control Method	●	Toyota Auto Body Co., Ltd.
Informative Inspection (self)		Constant Value Method		Warning Method		**Proposed by**
Informative Inspection (successive)		Motion-Step Method				Body Department No. 31

Theme   Preventing Use of the Wrong Frame Back Weld Nuts

Before Improvement

1. In mounting 8φ frame back weld nuts, 6φ weld nuts were sometimes attached by mistake.
2. Although a single welding machine could mount both 6φ and 8φ weld nuts, which type was mounted depended on worker vigilance.

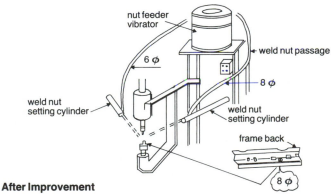

After Improvement

Using the size of the holes in the section of the frame back to which weld nuts are to be attached, 7φ pins are attached, so that the frame back cannot be positioned when 6 weld nuts are used.

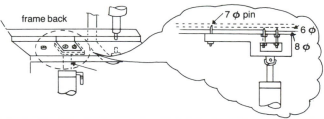

Effects	Cost
Defects involving the wrong item were eliminated.	none (scrap materials used)

Example 31

Inspection Method		Setting Function		Regulative Function		Company Name
Source Inspection	●	Contact Method	●	Control Method	●	Toyota Auto Body Co., Ltd.
Informative Inspection (self)		Constant Value Method		Warning Method		**Proposed by**
Informative Inspection (successive)		Motion-Step Method				Body Department No. 41

Theme
Ensuring Proper Installation of Apron Cowls

Before Improvement

upper apron cowl
welding machine

1. Eight weld nuts are attached to upper apron cowls, but occasionally weld nuts would be missing.
2. Because apron cowls were box-shaped, it was impossible to tell whether lost strikes were taking place.

After Improvement

arm
limit switch
welder

1. When there is no weld nut, the arm falls and comes in contact with a limit switch that detects the presence or absence of nuts. A buzzer sounds and electric current is shut off.
2. When a nut is present, the detector arm comes in contact with the nut and so does not touch and activate the limit switch.

Effects	Cost
Missing weld nuts were eliminated.	¥ 30,000 ($150)

Example 32

Inspection Method		Setting Function		Regulative Function		Company Name
Source Inspection	●	Contact Method	●	Control Method	●	Hosei Brake Industries, Ltd.
Informative Inspection (self)		Constant Value Method		Warning Method		**Proposed by**
Informative Inspection (successive)		Motion-Step Method				Naoteru Ochiai

Theme	Ensuring Activation of a Selector Switch

Before Improvement

1. This is a process in which plates and dust collars are welded both for vehicle model A, which uses a checker, and for vehicle model B, which does not. It sometimes happened that a worker would forget to use the checker.

2. Welding for both vehicle models was done by the same machine.

3. A worker switched from one model to the other by means of a selector switch.

4. Occasionally, the worker would fail to throw the selector switch for welding because A and B are similar in shape.

After Improvement

A limit switch is positioned below of a special jig used for vehicle type A at the next process. Since the limit switch is off while model A processing is under way, the welder operates when this condition is fulfilled and when the use of the checker is verified.

Effects	Defects involving skipping the checker process were eliminated.	Cost	approx. ¥ 2,500 ($12.50)

Example 33

Inspection Method		Setting Function		Regulative Function		Company Name
Source Inspection	●	Contact Method	●	Control Method	●	Hosei Brake Industries, Ltd.
Informative Inspection (self)		Constant Value Method		Warning Method		**Proposed by**
Informative Inspection (successive)		Motion-Step Method				Naoteru Ochiai

Theme Preventing Painting of the Wrong Vehicle Model Identification Color (Painting Mistakes)

Before Improvement

paint containers

1. Defects cropped up that involved identifying paint color errors and items left unpainted.
2. A worker checked a kanban (tag) and then selected a paint container for painting.

After Improvement

color identification machine

assembly kanban

photo-electric tube

cylinder

The placement of holes punched in an assembly kanban identifies vehicle body type and indicates the specified color to the worker by using air cylinders to raise the correct container. To guard against unpainted items, photoelectric tubes verify the removal of paint containers.

assembly kanban

Effects Painting errors involving the wrong color or the failure to apply paint were eliminated.	**Cost** approx. ¥ 150,000 ($750)

Example 34

Inspection Method		Setting Function		Regulative Function		Company Name
Source Inspection	●	Contact Method	●	Control Method	●	Hosei Brake Industries, Ltd.
Informative Inspection (self)		Constant Value Method		Warning Method		**Proposed by**
Informative Inspection (successive)		Motion-Step Method				Toshihiro Nabeta

Theme	Preventing Upside-Down Welding of Plates

Before Improvement

plate

1. Welding defects due to upside-down positioning of plates occasionally occurred in a hardware projection welding process.
2. Although welding was done after a check was made to ensure that the side of a plate with welding projections was on top when the plate was positioned on the welding jig, sometimes a plate would inadvertently be set upside down and then welded.

After Improvement

Normal

chute

plate

Upside-down positioning

plate

stopper

chute

welding jig

1. When a plate is positioned on the jig, a chute prevents the finished product from proceeding if the plate is upside down.
2. A plate that is upside down hits a block on the top of the chute and cannot be positioned in the jig.

normal

upside down

Effects Upside down plate weldings were eliminated.	**Cost** ¥ 500 ($2.50)

Example 35

Inspection Method		Setting Function		Regulative Function		Company Name
Source Inspection	●	Contact Method	●	Control Method	●	Matsushita Electric Industrial Co., Ltd./ Mikuni Plant
Informative Inspection (self)		Constant Value Method		Warning Method		**Proposed by**
Informative Inspection (successive)		Motion-Step Method				Yukio Yagyu, Assembly Manufacturing Department

Theme	
	Preventing Body Damage with a Sensor-Equipped Automatic Fastening Machine

Before Improvement

automatic machine (fastening machine)

body

pallet

chain conveyor

Body defects occurred when the automatic fastening machine operated while bodies were tilted or otherwise misplaced on pallets.

After Improvement

pallet

body

photoelectric tube   photoelectric tube

automatic machine (fastening machine)

photoelectric tube sensor

body

chain conveyor

A photoelectric tube senses whether the body has correctly entered the pallet and, in the normal case, the machine proceeds with its work. When the body is tilted or out of position, the photoelectric tube is not activated and the machine shuts down.

Effects	Cost
Body defects due to automatic machine operation were eliminated.	¥ 20,000 ($100)

Example 36

Inspection Method		Setting Function		Regulative Function		Company Name
Source Inspection	●	Contact Method	●	Control Method	●	Matsushita Electric Industrial Co., Ltd./ Mikuni Plant
Informative Inspection (self)		Constant Value Method		Warning Method		**Proposed by**
Informative Inspection (successive)		Motion-Step Method				Osamu Tsuchiya, Assembly Manufacturing Department

Theme   Preventing Packing Material Machine Type Errors

Before Improvement

74300

74400

74100

1. Identical shapes of body covers for packing material led to errors in machine type selection.
2. These errors occurred even though selections were made after parts numbers on the backs of the parts were checked.

After Improvement

74300

cut notch

74400

cut notch

74100

cut notch

A design-level poka-yoke device was set up, which by means of a sensor distinguishes among different notches cut into body covers and then indicates which packing material should be used.

Effects	Cost
Packing material machine type errors were eliminated.	¥ 15,000 ($75)

Example 37

Inspection Method		Setting Function		Regulative Function		Company Name
Source Inspection	●	Contact Method	●	Control Method	●	Matsushita Electric Industrial Co., Ltd./ Mikuni Plant
Informative Inspection (self)		Constant Value Method		Warning Method		**Proposed by**
Informative Inspection (successive)		Motion-Step Method				Tetsuo Nonoguchi, Assembly Manufacturing Department

Theme Ensuring the Fastening of Staples on an Automatic Packaging Machine

Before Improvement

1. When an automatic carton-sealing machine ran out of staples, it would continue operating, but without staples.

2. Although a limiter to detect staple shortages was installed in the machine's magazine unit, deterioration or bending of the limiter lever caused sensing to fail and the machine would continue operating without staples.

After Improvement

The limiter to detect staple shortages in the magazine unit of the carton-sealing machine was exchanged for a proximity switch, improving the accuracy with which staple shortages were detected. To prevent the machine from operating without staples, the machine stops and a buzzer signal sounds whenever the supply of staples is exhausted.

Effects	Cost
Operation of the machine without staples was eliminated.	¥ 15,000 ($75)

Example 38

Inspection Method		Setting Function		Regulative Function		Company Name
Source Inspection	●	Contact Method	●	Control Method	●	Matsushita Electric Industrial Co., Ltd. / Washing Machine Division
Informative Inspection (self)		Constant Value Method		Warning Method		**Proposed by**
Informative Inspection (successive)		Motion-Step Method				Yasufumi Nakahara

Theme   Preventing Inadequate Water Levels in a Package-Sealing Machine

Before Improvement

Workers carried out water-level checks visually.

After Improvement

Inadequate water volume activates a water-level sensor and a valve opens automatically to supply water.

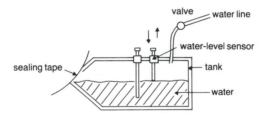

Effects	Cost
Instances of inadequate water levels were eliminated.	approx. ¥ 10,000 ($50)

Example 39

Inspection Method		Setting Function		Regulative Function		Company Name
Source Inspection	●	Contact Method	●	Control Method		Asahi National Lighting Co., Ltd.
Informative Inspection (self)		Constant Value Method		Warning Method	●	**Proposed by** Keiji Nakai, Interior Lighting Manufacturing Technology Department
Informative Inspection (successive)		Motion-Step Method				

Theme	
	Preventing Wiring Errors on Multiple Light Fixtures

Before Improvement

A lighting inspection process involved verifying that each lamp lit and then successively inserting the remaining lamps and lighting them. Wiring errors could not be found, however, in instances where workers made mistakes with the operating procedure.

After Improvement

A warning light rotates to warn the operator whenever wiring errors prevent all lamps from lighting.

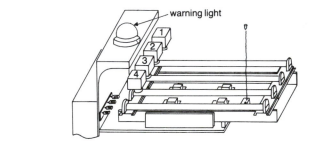

warning light

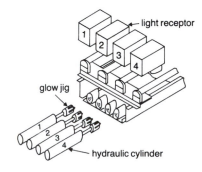

light receptor

glow jig

hydraulic cylinder

Outline of Operation

1. hydraulic cylinder 1 causes glow jig to move
2. light receptor 1 verifies that lamp has lit
3. cylinder 2 causes glow jig to move
4. light receptor 2 verifies that lamp has lit
5. cylinder 3 causes glow jig to move
6. light receptor 3 verifies that lamp has lit
7. cylinder 4 causes glow lamp to move
8. light receptor 4 verifies that lamp has lit
9. current, insulation, pressure proof inspections

Effects	Cost
Wiring errors were eliminated.	¥ 120,000 ($600)

Example 40

Inspection Method		Setting Function		Regulative Function		Company Name
Source Inspection	●	Contact Method	●	Control Method		Asahi National Lighting Co., Ltd./ Gunma Plant
Informative Inspection (self)		Constant Value Method		Warning Method	●	**Proposed by**
Informative Inspection (successive)		Motion-Step Method				Tool Plant

Theme Preventing the Omission of Tension Inspections after L420 Units Are Soldered

Before Improvement

In soldering 504 lead wires to the L420, the lead wires were held by hand while the soldering took place.

After the soldering was over, the lead wires were pulled by hand to verify the state of the solder.

After Improvement

steel ball
L420
spring

1. Steel balls and springs hold the L420 in place once it is positioned in a jig.

lead wires

L420

2. 504 lead wires are soldered to the L420's terminals.

L420

3. The lead wires are pulled out of the tension jig. When they are, the resistance of the springs guarantees the tensile force.

Effects	Cost
Post-soldering tension inspections became reliable and soldering defects decreased.	¥ 5,000 ($25)

Example 41

Inspection Method		Setting Function		Regulative Function		Company Name
Source Inspection	●	Contact Method	●	Control Method		Toyota Auto Body Co., Ltd.
Informative Inspection (self)		Constant Value Method		Warning Method	●	**Proposed by**
Informative Inspection (successive)		Motion-Step Method				Body Department No. 34

Theme   Preventing Attachment of the Wrong Front Guard Frame

Before Improvement

1. Front guard frame types DB and DBL vary in the heights of their grills, and occasionally the wrong frame was attached.
2. This problem involved errors in loading frames on pallets; workers would sometimes attach the wrong frame when different frame types were used on the same vehicle model (type DB or type DBL can be mounted on the same model).

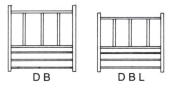

D B   D B L

After Improvement

Making use of the height difference between front guard frame types DB and DBL, Photoelectric tubes mounted along the path of the transport device determine whether the frame is of type DB or type DBL by sensing its height, which differs by type. If the frame is not of the specified type, the operator is alerted by means of a buzzer and a rotating warning light.

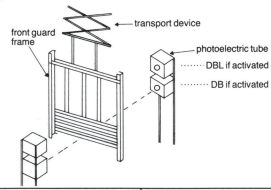

Effects Attachment errors were eliminated.	**Cost** ¥ 130,000 ($650)

Example 42

Inspection Method		Setting Function		Regulative Function		Company Name
Source Inspection	●	Contact Method	●	Control Method		Matsushita Electric Industrial Co., Ltd./ Washing Machine Division, Mikuni Plant
Informative Inspection (self)		Constant Value Method		Warning Method	●	**Proposed by**
Informative Inspection (successive)		Motion-Step Method				Hisao Akiyama, Assembly Manufacturing Department

Theme   Preventing Suction Defects in Vacuum Transfer

Before Improvement

Since vacuum transfer of finished washing machines was carried out by fixed-type pads, suction errors occurred when products were tilted, leading to either defective products or abnormal shutdowns.

After Improvement

Fixed-type pads were replaced by a tilting pad method. Along with improving suction, it was possible to provide for defect prevention and running time increases by using a photoelectric tube and a buzzer to check for suction defects.

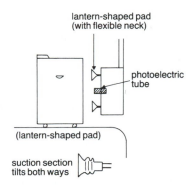

lantern-shaped pad (with flexible neck)

photoelectric tube

(lantern-shaped pad)

suction section tilts both ways

Effects	Cost
Suction errors involving finished washing machines were eliminated.	¥ 10,000 ($50)

Example 43

Inspection Method		Setting Function		Regulative Function		Company Name
Source Inspection	●	Contact Method	●	Control Method		Arakawa Auto Body Industries, Ltd./ Main Plant
Informative Inspection (self)		Constant Value Method				**Proposed by**
				Warning Method	●	
Informative Inspection (successive)		Motion-Step Method				

Theme	Preventing Installation Errors Through a Continuous Pokayoke Device

Before Improvement

1. On a front-end fittings line, errors were sometimes made in the installation of glass and electrical fittings.
2. Installation errors had been prevented through worker vigilance.

After Improvement

Outline

Using the movement of the installation line, instructions are sent one after another to parts racks along the entire process as a single information packet, and errors in the selection and installation of parts are prevented by opening the needed hose-shaped gates of the parts racks.

Mechanism

Limit switches linked to the parts racks are recessed below the conveyor and rods—called detector rods—that operate the limit switches are positioned at needed locations on the information set plates mounted at designated sites on the conveyor. This allows *on* and *off* signals to be repeated by means of the conveyor's movement and uses one packet of information continuously.

Operation

1. At the first process, workers on either side of the conveyor look at the body specifications tag and set the information signals. To prevent errors in setting information signals, doublechecking is performed so that the operation does not proceed if information from the two workers does not match.
2. Air hoses that function as gates are attached to the parts racks and those at needed locations activate the limit switches underneath the conveyor. When a switch is turned on, air escapes, the rod-shaped hose gate bends, and the part can be taken out.

Example 44

3. A reset rod is provided after the input rod which, by turning the limit switch off, allows air to enter the hose. The hose then extends and blocks the parts rack.

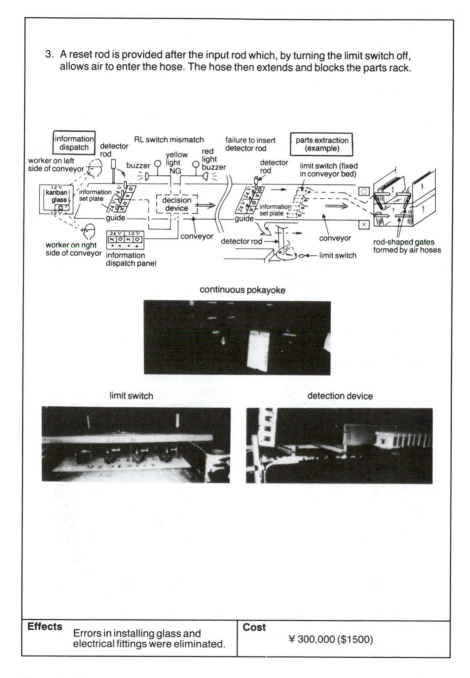

continuous pokayoke

limit switch

detection device

Effects	Cost
Errors in installing glass and electrical fittings were eliminated.	¥ 300,000 ($1500)

Example 44 cont.

Inspection Method		Setting Function		Regulative Function		Company Name
Source Inspection	●	Contact Method		Control Method		Arakawa Auto Body Industries, Ltd./Sanage Plant
Informative Inspection (self)		Constant Value Method	●	Warning Method	●	**Proposed by**
Informative Inspection (successive)		Motion-Step Method				

Theme	Preventing the Omission of Spot Welding

Before Improvement

Workers would sometimes forget the number of spot welds to be made when the order of operations changed.

welds missed

After Improvement

1. A control board counter detects the number of welds and operates clamps.

2. The control board counts whenever the portable spot welder is operated and clamps are loosened only when the count reaches 10.

operation valve

control board

clamp cylinder

10 welds

portable spot welder

Effects	Defects due to insufficient spot welds dropped from two per month to zero.	Cost	¥ 8,500 ($42.50)

Example 45

Inspection Method		Setting Function		Regulative Function		Company Name
Source Inspection	●	Contact Method		Control Method	●	Arakawa Auto Body Industries, Ltd./Sanage Plant
Informative Inspection (self)		Constant Value Method	●	Warning Method		**Proposed by**
Informative Inspection (successive)		Motion-Step Method				

Theme	Preventing Failure to Change Tips

Before Improvement

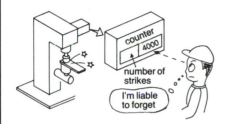

Wear and tear necessitates changing tips, and when workers forgot to change tips, tips slipped off specification. When this happened, nugget diameters were no longer within specifications.

After Improvement

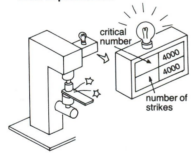

1. A control board remembers a fixed value and when that tip-changing value is reached, it stops the machine.

2. When the critical number is reached
   • a lamp lights
   • the machine ceases operation
   • the worker changes the tip

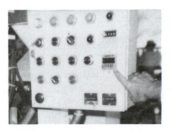

Effects	Cost
The problem of forgetting to change tips was resolved and defects were eliminated.	¥ 15,000 ($75)

Example 46

Inspection Method		Setting Function		Regulative Function		Company Name
Source Inspection	●	Contact Method	●	Control Method	●	Kanto Auto Works, Ltd./ Yokosuka Plant
Informative Inspection (self)		Constant Value Method	●	Warning Method		**Proposed by**
Informative Inspection (successive)		Motion-Step Method				Satoaki Masumoto

Theme	Ensuring the Tightening of Drive Plates

Before Improvement

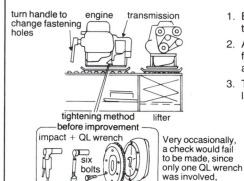

turn handle to change fastening holes   engine   transmission

tightening method before improvement — impact + QL wrench

six bolts

Very occasionally, a check would fail to be made, since only one QL wrench was involved.

lifter

1. Bolts came out because workers forgot to check drive plate torque. (prevention)
2. As shown in the figure at left, the fastening of the drive plate took place on a conveyor.
3. Tightening errors were difficult to find at later processes.

After Improvement

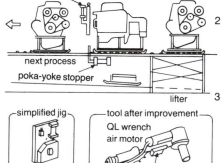

angle of lead simplification jig

next process

poka-yoke stopper

lifter

simplified jig

to crankshaft

tool after improvement — QL wrench air motor

microsensor

air motor is set lower than preset torque

1. The QL wrench was provided with an air motor and a microsensor was attached.
2. As shown in the figure at left, a simplified jig was made up to match the angles of lead at 60° from crank handles. The simplified jig's angle of lead was stepped up by means of a verification signal as each was checked with a QL wrench.
3. Unless both the number (N) of bolts and the preset torque are satisfied, the pokayoke stopper will not open and the engine cannot move on to the next process.

Effects	Cost
The number of bolts that were not tightened or that came out fell to zero.	approx. ¥ 80,000 ($400) (construction of simplified jig, stopper; rebuilding QL wrench)

Example 47

Inspection Method		Setting Function		Regulative Function		Company Name
Source Inspection	●	Contact Method		Control Method	●	Toyoda Gosei Co., Ltd.
Informative Inspection (self)		Constant Value Method	●	Warning Method		**Proposed by**
Informative Inspection (successive)		Motion-Step Method				

Theme   Ensuring the Installation of Radiator Grill Parts

Before Improvement

1. Where nine clips, two screws and one insignia were to be installed, some parts would occasionally be left out.

2. Prevention of inadvertent failure to install parts depended on worker vigilance.

3. Inspection personnel performed visual checks to prevent such installation deficiencies and to keep incomplete grills from being sent out.

After Improvement

1. The nine clips are installed and then the grill is positioned on a workbench.

   { Clips come in contact with limit switches mounted on the workbench and nine lamps light up on the box at right.
   When a clip is missing, the corresponding lamp does not light and a buzzer sounds. }

2. One insignia is mounted while the grill is on the workbench.

3. A driver is used to fasten two screws.

   { To check the insignia at this point, a clamp with a proximity switch comes forward to keep the grill from being removed from the workbench. }

4. The two screws are fastened and the driver is returned to its original position.

   { When the presence of the insignia and the fact that the driver has been used twice have been verified, the clamp retreats. Otherwise, the clamp cannot be released and a buzzer sounds. }

5. The grill is taken off the workbench and placed in a box.

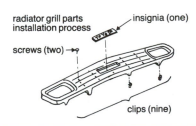

radiator grill parts installation process

insignia (one)

screws (two) →

clips (nine)

Effects	Cost
Failures to install parts were eliminated.	approx. ¥ 90,000 ($450)

Example 48

Inspection Method		Setting Function		Regulative Function		Company Name
Source Inspection	•	Contact Method		Control Method	•	Toyota Auto Body Co., Ltd.
Informative Inspection (self)		Constant Value Method	•	Warning Method		**Proposed by**
Informative Inspection (successive)		Motion-Step Method				Body Department No. 21

Theme	Preventing Missing Weld Nuts on Panel Front Floors

Before Improvement

1. Workers would sometimes forget to attach weld nuts in an operation in which such nuts were to be attached to panel front floors.
2. Worker Y counts out 10 6ϕ weld nuts for model A and 12 weld nuts for model B and attaches them.
3. Worker Z attaches one 8ϕ weld nut.

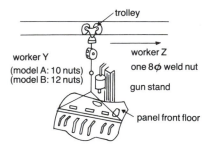

trolley

worker Y
(model A: 10 nuts)
(model B: 12 nuts)

worker Z
one 8ϕ weld nut

gun stand

panel front floor

Example 49

After Improvement

1. Worker X (at the process before Y) looks at the model indicator label affixed to the body. The number of 6ϕ weld nuts is both shown on the label and displayed on a light board (an information display device).
2. The stopper opens when worker Y correctly welds the indicated number of nuts.
3. The indicators can then move on to worker Z.

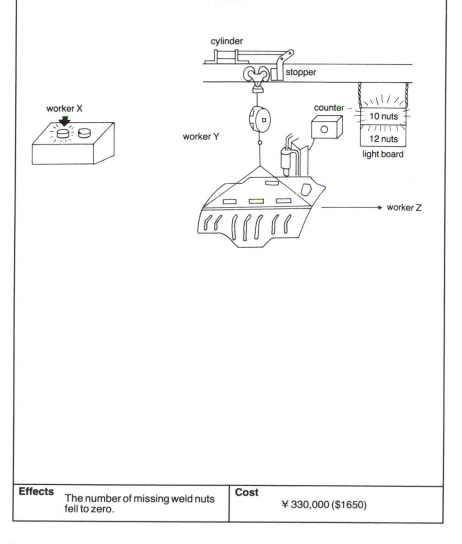

Effects		Cost	
	The number of missing weld nuts fell to zero.		¥ 330,000 ($1650)

Example 49 cont.

Inspection Method		Setting Function		Regulative Function		Company Name
Source Inspection	●	Contact Method		Control Method	●	Asahi National Lighting Co., Ltd.
Informative Inspection (self)		Constant Value Method	●	Warning Method		**Proposed by** Keiji Nakai, Interior
Informative Inspection (successive)		Motion-Step Method				Lighting Manufacturing Technology Department

Theme	Preventing Errors in Balancer Quantities

Before Improvement

In an operation involving the attachment of five balancers to balance instruments, errors in the number of balancers would cause instruments to tilt and might be the source of claims against the company.

After Improvement

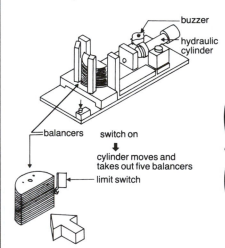

buzzer

hydraulic cylinder

balancers

switch on
↓
cylinder moves and takes out five balancers

limit switch

A jig was devised to attach only the needed number of balancers (five). A limit switch was provided to ensure that only five would be attached and a supply buzzer would provide notice if there were too few balancers remaining.

The operation was at first performed manually.

To forestall the possibility that either unplugging or forgetting to plug in the system might keep the supply buzzer from sounding, a cylinder was provided that would not operate if the system were not plugged in.

Effects	Errors in the required number of balancers were eliminated; as a consequence, instrument defects also were eliminated.	Cost	¥ 20,000 ($100)

Example 50

Inspection Method		Setting Function		Regulative Function		Company Name
Source Inspection	●	Contact Method		Control Method		Toyoda Gosei Co., Ltd.
Informative Inspection (self)		Constant Value Method	●	Warning Method	●	**Proposed by**
Informative Inspection (successive)		Motion-Step Method				

Theme	
	Ensuring the Installation of Spoiler Mounting Bolts

Before Improvement

1. In an operation to install nine mounting bolts used for attachment to automobiles, too few bolts were sometimes used.
2. The operation was performed by taking bolts directly out of a bin containing many bolts.
3. Inadvertent failures to install bolts were prevented through worker vigilance.

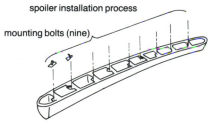

spoiler installation process

mounting bolts (nine)

After Improvement

1. Nine bolts come out when a parts feeder lever is pressed.
2. The nine mounting bolts are held in the left hand and all are installed with the right hand.

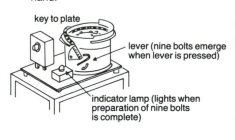

key to plate

lever (nine bolts emerge when lever is pressed)

indicator lamp (lights when preparation of nine bolts is complete)

Effects	Cost
Instances of inadvertent failure to install bolts were eliminated.	approx. ¥ 40,000 ($200)

Example 51

Inspection Method		Setting Function		Regulative Function		Company Name
Source Inspection	●	Contact Method		Control Method		Toyota Auto Body Co., Ltd.
Informative Inspection (self)		Constant Value Method	●	Warning Method	●	**Proposed by**
Informative Inspection (successive)		Motion-Step Method				Assembly Department No. 36

Theme	Preventing Shortages of Small Parts

Before Improvement

1. In operations involving the collection of small parts (such as bolts and nuts), fewer than the standard number would occasionally be collected.

2. Items were collected on the basis of weight comparisons with standard numbers of items. Yet error increased along with the number of items involved because of differences in the weights of individual items.

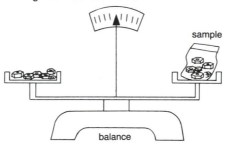

sample

balance

After Improvement

The balance was replaced by a scale that displays the number of items weighed.

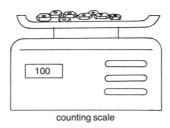

counting scale

Effects	Cost
Defects were eliminated.	¥ 450,000 ($2250)

Example 52

Inspection Method		Setting Function		Regulative Function		Company Name
Source Inspection	•	Contact Method		Control Method	•	Aisan Industries, Ltd./ Main Plant
Informative Inspection (self)		Constant Value Method		Warning Method		**Proposed by**
Informative Inspection (successive)		Motion-Step Method	•			Terukatsu Asakura

Theme Preventing Omission of Acceleration Out Balls

Before Improvement

1. Small balls are needed in the installation of carburetors and occasionally workers would omit these balls.
2. The prevention of such omissions depended on worker vigilance.

After Improvement

Order of installation:

① out ball ② small spring ③ stopper ④ large spring ⑤ rod pump

A shutter was attached to the stopper bin so that the next stopper cannot be taken out unless an out ball is removed.

1. A limit switch senses the removal of an out ball and the shutter on the bin containing stoppers opens.
2. A pneumatic micro measuring device is in contact with the workpiece as the stopper and other parts are installed. When the workpiece is withdrawn, a limit switch is activated and the shutter on the stopper bin closes.

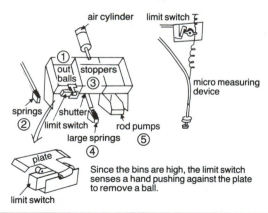

Effects	**Cost**
Omissions of balls were eliminated.	¥ 50,000 ($250)

Example 53

Inspection Method		Setting Function		Regulative Function		Company Name
Source Inspection	•	Contact Method		Control Method	•	Asahi National Lighting Co., Ltd.
Informative Inspection (self)		Constant Value Method		Warning Method		**Proposed by** Kenji Uesaka, Interior Lighting Manufacturing Technology Department
Informative Inspection (successive)		Motion-Step Method	•			

Theme	Preventing Electric Shock in a Lighting Test

Before Improvement

lighting jig

The fact that the contacts on a lighting jig protruded led to fears of electric shock and damage to testing apparatus due to shorting.

After Improvement

start switch

A method was worked out in which, when the start switch was turned on, current would flow to the lighting jig terminals only when necessary.

◯ current off
◯ current on

(summary of motions)

1. position lighting jig
2. turn start switch on
3. automatic inspection
   (lighting ⟶ current ⟶ insulation pressure-proof)
4. end

Effects	Instances of electric shock and damage to testing apparatus due to shorting were eliminated.	Cost	¥ 15,000 ($75)

Example 54

Inspection Method		Setting Function		Regulative Function		Company Name
Source Inspection	•	Contact Method		Control Method	•	Arakawa Auto Body, Ltd.
Informative Inspection (self)		Constant Value Method		Warning Method		**Proposed by**
Informative Inspection (successive)		Motion-Step Method	•			Shūya Sugiyama

Theme	Preventing Omission of Board Set Mounting Holes

Before Improvement

1. Workers occasionally neglected to drill mounting holes in board sets.
2. After the board set was spot-welded, the multispot (multiple electrode spot welding) machine started operating regardless of the presence or absence of holes.

After Improvement

After the board set is spot-welded, the multispot machine will not work—even if it is turned on—unless holes are present.

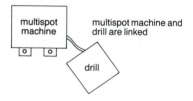

Effects	Hole omission was eliminated.	**Cost**	relay: ¥ 1,450 ($7.25) cable: ¥ 300 ($1.50) for 3 meters

Example 55

Inspection Method		Setting Function		Regulative Function		Company Name
Source Inspection	●	Contact Method		Control Method	●	Arakawa Auto Body, Ltd.
Informative Inspection (self)		Constant Value Method		Warning Method		**Proposed by**
Informative Inspection (successive)		Motion-Step Method	●			Shōgo Takagi Mitsuyoshi Narita

Theme	
	Preventing Undercoating Application Errors

Before Improvement

1. Several times a month, a body not needing undercoating would be coated and had to be discarded.

2. Procedure

   1.) Looking at the procedural chart, worker A hooked with two rings only those bodies that required undercoating.

   2.) After the body had been rinsed and dried, worker B performed a double check by removing one of the rings.

   3.) Worker C applied coating only to those bodies with a single ring remaining.

   4.) Roughly ¥ 300,000 ($1500) were lost each month because mistakenly coated bodies had to be discarded.

After Improvement

1. Noticing that there were two types of mistakes here—visual mistakes and mental mistakes—we constructed a sliding frame that allowed only the section of the procedural chart necessary for the operation to be seen. This prevented visual errors.

2. Since mental errors were more likely to occur the longer workers had to use their memories, a worker had, for example, to put an S-ring in the specified receptacle immediately after looking at the procedural chart.

3. Where in the past final checks had been relegated to a single line and column, placing the designations "coated" and "uncoated" in separate columns made rechecking at the next operation possible.

4. After the rinsing and drying, worker B hooks a short-volume checker to A's ring in accordance with the procedural chart. B's procedural chart, too, calls for a sliding frame that masks all but the required information. Thus, B carries out an independent check where in the past he might have put too much confidence in A's check and inadvertently unhooked the ring.

Example 56

5. The spray gun can be removed when C detaches the "short-volume checker" and inserts it into a detector. In addition, a timer allows only one coating's worth of undercoating material to be used.

6. The spray gun holder locks as soon as the spray gun is inserted.

Looking at his procedural chart, A immediately takes out an S-shaped checker. (sliding frame in use)

After the rinsing process is completed, B hangs a short-volume checker on the S-shaped checker.

C inserts the short-volume checker in the detector and removes the spray gun.

Effects The incidence of coating errors fell to zero after these pokayoke devices were put in place; this made it possible to avoid annual losses of approximately ¥ 4 million ($20,000)	Cost approx. ¥ 30,000 ($150)

Example 56 cont.

Inspection Method		Setting Function		Regulative Function		Company Name
Source Inspection	●	Contact Method		Control Method	●	Arakawa Auto Body, Ltd./ Toyohashi Plant
Informative Inspection (self)		Constant Value Method		Warning Method		**Proposed by**
Informative Inspection (successive)		Motion-Step Method	●			

Theme	Preventing Omission of Door Pockets

Before Improvement

1. An operation in which pockets are mounted on door trim involves three specifications, and workers occasionally neglected to mount pockets.
2. The prevention of such omissions depended on worker attentiveness to production work-in-process kanban.

After Improvement

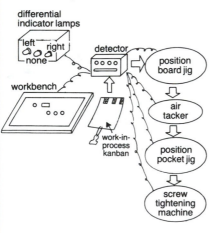

1. Production work-in-process kanban are inserted into a detector that remembers whether either left or right pockets are missing.
2. If a pocket is missing, a lamp lights.
3. If a pocket's right and left have been reversed on the door trim or if a pocket has not been mounted, a buzzer sounds, air stops flowing to the screw-tightening tool, and the operation cannot proceed.

Effects	Instances of pocket omission were eliminated.	Cost	¥ 32,000 ($160)

Example 57

Inspection Method		Setting Function		Regulative Function		Company Name
Source Inspection	●	Contact Method		Control Method	●	Arakawa Auto Body, Ltd./ Kotobuki Plant
Informative Inspection (self)		Constant Value Method		Warning Method		**Proposed by**
Informative Inspection (successive)		Motion-Step Method	●			

Theme   Preventing Errors in Mounting Front S Springs

Before Improvement

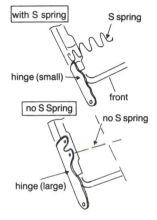

1. Specifications call for S springs to be mounted or not on the front, but S springs were occasionally mounted where specifications did not call for them.

2. A worker would look at the hinge section of the front and make a judgment either to mount an S spring or not. Mounting errors, however, sometimes occurred.

After Improvement

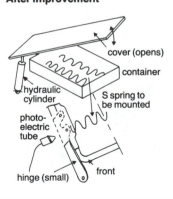

1. When the front is set on the jig, a photoelectric tube checks the shape of the hinge section.

2. If an S spring is not required, the cover of the S spring container remains closed; it opens only when an S spring is needed.

Effects S spring mounting errors were eliminated.	**Cost** approx. ¥ 100,000 ($500)

Example 58

Inspection Method		Setting Function		Regulative Function		Company Name
Source Inspection	●	Contact Method		Control Method	●	Arakawa Auto Body, Ltd./ Kotobuki Plant
Informative Inspection (self)		Constant Value Method		Warning Method		**Proposed by**
Informative Inspection (successive)		Motion-Step Method	●			

Theme   Preventing Erroneous Side Seal Attachment

Before Improvement

1. With many types of side seal in use, the wrong type was occasionally attached.
2. A worker would look at a kanban and take the corresponding side seal from a rack. Sometimes, however, a worker would take the wrong type of side seal.

After Improvement

1. A kanban with a steel plate glued to it is inserted into a slot and the kanban is read by a proximity switch.
2. On the basis of this electrical judgment, the cover of the bin for parts corresponding to the kanban indication opens.
3. The part is taken out and attached.

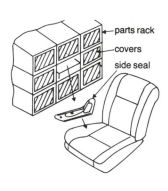

parts rack
covers
side seal

Effects	Cost
Side seal errors were eliminated.	approx. ¥ 300,000 (1500)

Example 59

Inspection Method		Setting Function		Regulative Function		Company Name
Source Inspection	●	Contact Method		Control Method	●	Arakawa Auto Body, Ltd./ Main Plant
Informative Inspection (self)		Constant Value Method		Warning Method		**Proposed by**
Informative Inspection (successive)		Motion-Step Method	●			

Theme	A Side Member Pokayoke for Preventing the Omission of Holes

Before Improvement

1. In a side member installation process, workers would occasionally forget to punch holes for trim attachment.

2. A worker would look at an indicator card and then press the required start button.

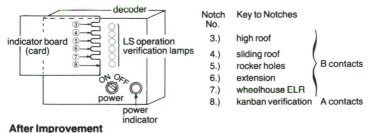

Notch No.	Key to Notches	
3.)	high roof	
4.)	sliding roof	
5.)	rocker holes	B contacts
6.)	extension	
7.)	wheelhouse ELR	
8.)	kanban verification	A contacts

After Improvement

1. The indicator card is placed in a decoder equipped with limit switches.

2. The limit switches detect the presence or absence of notches in the indicator card.

3. The workpiece verification limit switch is triggered when a worker sets a workpiece in the hole-punching machine.

4. An air cylinder starts the hole-punching machine by pressing the start switch only when there is a notch present in the indicator card.

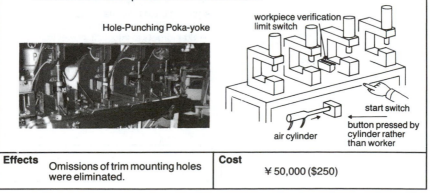

Hole-Punching Poka-yoke

Effects	Omissions of trim mounting holes were eliminated.	Cost	¥ 50,000 ($250)

Example 60

Inspection Method		Setting Function		Regulative Function		Company Name
Source Inspection	●	Contact Method		Control Method	●	Kanto Auto Body, Ltd.
Informative Inspection (self)		Constant Value Method		Warning Method		**Proposed by**
Informative Inspection (successive)		Motion-Step Method	●			Tomio Endō

Theme	Preventing Differential Oil Omission

Before Improvement

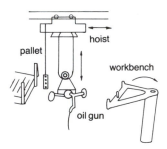

1. Although assembly included the injection of oil into differentials, this operation was occasionally neglected.

2. A worker uses a hoist to take a differential from a pallet and then pours in oil in front of a workbench. When this is done, the worker transports the differential to the workbench and adjusts the brakes. Sometimes, though, workers forgot the oil on several differentials, this error was be discovered during an inspection process.

After Improvement

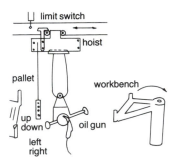

A worker takes a differential from a pallet and, in transporting it to the site of the oil gun, strikes a limit switch. This cuts power to the hoist. The power comes on when oil is inserted, enabling the differential to be transported to the workbench. If a worker forgets to inject oil, power to the hoist remains off and the differential cannot be transported to the workbench.

Effects	Instances of failure to add oil were eliminated.	**Cost**	¥ 6,800 ($34)

Example 61

Inspection Method		Setting Function		Regulative Function		Company Name
Source Inspection	●	Contact Method		Control Method	●	Kanto Auto Works, Ltd.
Informative Inspection (self)		Constant Value Method		Warning Method		**Proposed by**
Informative Inspection (successive)		Motion-Step Method	●			Tomio Endō

Theme   Preventing Errors in Body Number Stamping

Before Improvement

1. A stamping machine stamps body numbers into the surfaces of support radiators, but occasionally worker misunderstandings would cause the machine to stamp in the absence of a part, to double stamp, or to omit stamping.

2. The stamping machine was set up to operate when the start button was pressed, regardless of whether a support radiator was in place or not. Double stamping sometimes occurred as well.

After Improvement

When a support radiator is placed on the jig, it strikes a limit switch and a cylinder rod emerges to make it impossible for the part to be removed from the jig. (This ensures that the part will be stamped.) Next, the cylinder rod withdraws when the body number has been stamped. In this state, the machine will not start up even if the start button is pressed. The support radiator, therefore, has to be taken off the jig. (This prevents double stamping.) Finally, the machine will not start unless the limit switch is struck. (This prevents stamping when no part is present.)

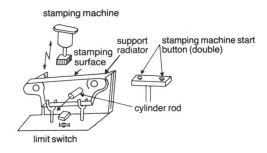

Effects	Cost
Stamping errors were eliminated.	approx. ¥ 25,000 ($125)

Example 62

Inspection Method	Setting Function	Regulative Function	Company Name
Source Inspection ●	Contact Method	Control Method ●	Kanto Auto Works, Ltd./ Yokosuka Plant
Informative Inspection (self)	Constant Value Method	Warning Method	**Proposed by**
Informative Inspection (successive)	Motion-Step Method ●		Hideo Suzuki

Theme　Preventing Omission of Silencers Inside Automobile Doors

Before Improvement

1. In an operation in which silencers are to be glued to the inside of doors according to the class of the car, workers would occasionally forget to glue in silencers.
2. Worker A verifies specifications printed by a terminal and pastes a gluing instruction kanban to bodies that require silencers.
3. Worker B visually checks the gluing instruction kanban and glues a silencer to the door.
4. Occasional failures to glue in silencers involved worker A's forgetting the instructions or worker B's overlooking the instruction kanban.

After Improvement

1. When a door requiring a silencer comes down the line, the terminal causes a signal lamp on a light board (information display device) above a silencer storage bin to light up.
2. The signal light is turned off by a photoelectric switch tripped by a hand reaching into the door silencer bin.
3. A body advancing to the next process while the signal light is still on means that an operation has been missed and so the line shuts down.
4. If a hand reaching into the bin activates the photoelectric switch even though the signal light is off, then a specification mismatch is assumed and a warning buzzer sounds.

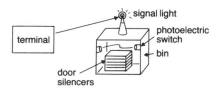

Effects	Cost
Cases of omitted door silencers were eliminated.	approx. ¥ 120,000 ($600) (control items, bin, other)

Example 63

Inspection Method		Setting Function		Regulative Function		Company Name
Source Inspection	●	Contact Method		Control Method	●	Kubota, Ltd./ Sakai Plant
Informative Inspection (self)		Constant Value Method		Warning Method		**Proposed by**
Informative Inspection (successive)		Motion-Step Method	●			

Theme	
	Preventing Skipped Processes

Before Improvement

Drilling and tapping processes were sometimes inadvertently skipped, leading to damaged workpieces or unfinished products. The prevention of this problem depended on worker vigilance.

After Improvement

1. Stoppers were installed above the conveyor to control flow.
2. When processing is over and machines withdraw, stoppers drop and the workpieces flow to the next process. When they have passed through, the stoppers return to their previous position to prevent processing gaps. As a consequence, it has become impossible for processes to be skipped.

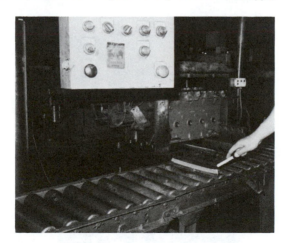

Effects	Cost
Processing gaps and damage defects were eliminated.	approx. ¥ 15,000 ($75) per machine

Example 64

Inspection Method		Setting Function		Regulative Function		Company Name
Source Inspection	●	Contact Method		Control Method	●	Kubota, Ltd./ Sakai Plant
Informative Inspection (self)		Constant Value Method		Warning Method		**Proposed by**
Informative Inspection (successive)		Motion-Step Method	●			

Theme	Ensuring the Tightening of Engine Flywheel Nuts

Before Improvement

In an operation in which engine flywheel nuts are tightened, it was feared that workers would sometimes forget to tighten the nuts. Tightening was verified through worker vigilance.

After Improvement

1. When a flywheel is in place, a limit switch causes a barrier to descend. Nuts are then installed and tightened with an air wrench.
2. The barrier in front of the flywheels ascends.
3. This barrier will not ascend and the next flywheel will not be accessible unless the nuts have been tightened.

Effects	Cases in which workers forget to tighten nuts were eliminated.	Cost	approx. ¥ 30,000 ($150)

Example 65

Inspection Method		Setting Function		Regulative Function		Company Name
Source Inspection	●	Contact Method		Control Method	●	Kubota, Ltd./ Sakai Plant
Informative Inspection (self)		Constant Value Method		Warning Method		**Proposed by**
Informative Inspection (successive)		Motion-Step Method	●			

Theme   Preventing Errors in Selecting Cultivator Tire Sizes

Before Improvement

In an operation for mounting tires on cultivators, the use of different tire sizes on different models made it easy to select the wrong tire. In the past, such errors were prevented through worker vigilance.

After Improvement

1. Cards were made up for each model type, so that when the required card is inserted in a card reader:
2. A light goes on above the needed tires and barrier rods open.
3. When a worker takes a tire, the light goes out and the barrier rods close.

Effects	Cost
Tire selection errors were eliminated.	approx. ¥ 30,000 ($150)

Example 66

Inspection Method		Setting Function		Regulative Function		Company Name
Source Inspection	●	Contact Method		Control Method	●	Kubota, Ltd./ Sakai Plant
Informative Inspection (self)		Constant Value Method		Warning Method		**Proposed by**
Informative Inspection (successive)		Motion-Step Method	●			

Theme   Preventing Errors in Parts Selection

Before Improvement

In operations for mounting parts on cultivators, gears, bearings, collars, clips, and the like each had their own place, but many parts had double uses or resembled one another, so errors were apt to occur. In the past, workers paid close attention as they selected and attached parts.

After Improvement

1. A rack of parts bins equipped with shutters was constructed and parts were kept in each bin.
2. Pressing a control box switch for a particular model opens shutters for all the needed parts.
3. At the same time, a display lights up on an installation procedures chart provided above the rack.
4. When all parts have been removed, the shutters automatically close and the light turns off.

Effects	Cost
Parts installation errors were eliminated and the operation became one that even a novice could perform without mistakes.	approx. ¥ 100,000 ($500)

Example 67

Inspection Method		Setting Function		Regulative Function		Company Name
Source Inspection	●	Contact Method		Control Method	●	Toyoda Gosei Co., Ltd.
Informative Inspection (self)		Constant Value Method		Warning Method		**Proposed by**
Informative Inspection (successive)		Motion-Step Method	●			

Theme	Ensuring that Foam Pad Screws are Tightened

Before Improvement

Schematic view of foam pad forming and installation process

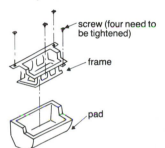

screw (four need to be tightened)

frame

pad

1. The operation involved placing a foam pad in a frame and then securing it with screws. Sometimes, however, not enough screws would be put in.
2. Four screws were tightened manually.
3. Errors were prevented through worker vigilance.

After Improvement

1. The frame is placed on the pad and then positioned in a screw tightening machine. The start button is pressed.
2. A clamp comes down and holds down the workpiece.
3. The four screws are tightened automatically. (Automotating this operation ensures that all screws will be tightened. The machine stops automatically when screws are not present.)
4. An air cylinder immobilizes the pad from below and the foam is tested.
5. If the product passes the foam test, the clamp returns to its original position.

Effects	Screw omissions were eliminated.	**Cost**	approx. ¥ 50,000 ($250)

Example 68

Inspection Method		Setting Function	Regulative Function		Company Name
Source Inspection	●	Contact Method	Control Method	●	Toyota Auto Body Co., Ltd.
Informative Inspection (self)		Constant Value Method	Warning Method		**Proposed by**
Informative Inspection (successive)		Motion-Step Method	●		Body Department No. 41

Theme   Preventing Installation of the Wrong Header Linings

Before Improvement

1. In an operation for the installation of header linings, parts for the wrong model would occasionally be attached.

2. Procedure

    1.) Read model with model indicator.

    2.) Looking at a model specifications chart, find the header lining part number. Rare errors or misunderstandings would show up at this stage.

    3.) Sometimes, then, the wrong header liners would be attached.

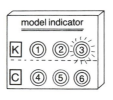

model indicator

order of operations

1.)

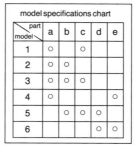

model specifications chart

part model	a	b	c	d	e
1	○		○		
2	○	○			
3	○	○	○		
4	○				○
5		○	○	○	
6				○	○

2.)

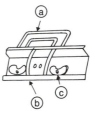

3.)

Example 69

After Improvement

1. Model is displayed on model indicator board.

2. Linked to the model indicator board, parts rack covers for required parts only open and a light comes on. The worker can then remove a header liner from the open section of the rack. The body to which the liner is to be attached, moreover, is clamped down at this point.

3. When a liner is removed the lid closes automatically and the mounting clamp will not open if a header liner is not taken out within one minute.

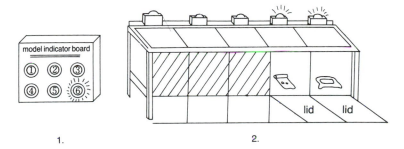

1.   2.

Effects	Cost
Cases of erroneous installation were eliminated.	none; all materials used were lying idle

Example 69 cont.

Inspection Method		Setting Function		Regulative Function		Company Name
Source Inspection	●	Contact Method		Control Method	●	Toyota Auto Body Co., Ltd.
Informative Inspection (self)		Constant Value Method		Warning Method		**Proposed by**
Informative Inspection (successive)		Motion-Step Method	●			Painting Department No. 32

Theme

Preventing Erroneous and Missing Asphalt Sheets

Before Improvement

1. Asphalt sheets are introduced into auto bodies, but as many as 36 different patterns are involved and sometimes either the pattern would be wrong or no sheet at all would be put in.

2. Procedure

   1.) Read model number from the work-in-process slip.

   2.) On a model specifications chart, find and remember the number of the asphalt sheet.

   3.) Take out an asphalt sheet whose number corresponds to the one on the model specifications chart.

These operations, then, relied mainly on the attentiveness of the worker.

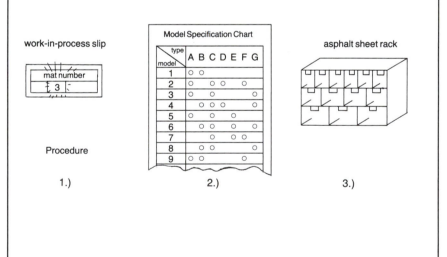

work-in-process slip

mat number

Model Specification Chart

asphalt sheet rack

Procedure

1.)   2.)   3.)

Example 70

After Improvement

1. Read model number from work-in-process slip.
2. Immediately press the model button on the model indicator board. This prevents misunderstood numbers.
3. When the asphalt sheet indicator light comes on, the worker can take out the specified sheet without having to remember anything.

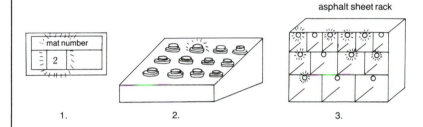

asphalt sheet rack

mat number

2

1.   2.   3.

Effects	Instances of erroneous and missing items were eliminated.	Cost	¥ 490,000 ($2450)

Example 70 cont.

Inspection Method		Setting Function		Regulative Function		Company Name
Source Inspection	●	Contact Method		Control Method	●	Hosei Brake Industries, Ltd.
Informative Inspection (self)		Constant Value Method		Warning Method		**Proposed by**
Informative Inspection (successive)		Motion-Step Method	●			Katsumi Hirata

Theme　　Preventing Assembly Errors Due to the Wrong Assembly Kanban

Before Improvement

Assembly Procedures Chart (in 5 car units)

order of delivery →	No.	Vehicle model number (in 5 car units)				
	1	35	36	37	38	71
	2	42	42	36	35	42
	3	70	71	35	36	71

→ order of installation

1. When a worker on a diversified production line looked at a brake assembly procedures chart and selected an assembly kanban, sometimes took a kanban other than the one indicated on the chart and the order of assembly went awry.

2. When, for example, assembly kanban no. 71 (the vehicle model number) was to be taken from the shelf in accordance with the indication on the procedures chart, the wrong kanban (no. 70, say) could be put into a parts reader and thus cause part no. 70 to be displayed and then installed.

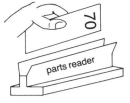

parts reader

Example 71

After Improvement

1.)

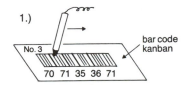

bar code kanban

1. The system of displaying parts on an assembly procedures chart was abandoned in favor of a method of bar codes and interlocks.

2. Procedure
   1.) Bar code causes reading order to be remembered.
   2.) Kanban shelf indicator light goes on.
   3.) Take assembly kanban from compartment indicated by light and place in parts reader.
   4.) The part is indicated only when matched with the assembly kanban shown on the procedures chart. A mismatch causes a buzzer to sound.

2.)

35	36	37	38	70	71	42
○	○	○	○	○	○	○

3.) 4.)

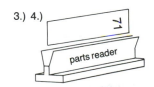

parts reader

Effects	**Cost**
Assembly errors due to procedural mistakes were eliminated.	approx. ¥ 3 million ($15,000)

Example 71 cont.

Inspection Method		Setting Function		Regulative Function		Company Name
Source Inspection	●	Contact Method		Control Method	●	Toyota Auto Body Co., Ltd.
Informative Inspection (self)		Constant Value Method		Warning Method		**Proposed by**
Informative Inspection (successive)		Motion-Step Method	●			Assembly Department No. 23

Theme   Preventing Installation of the Wrong Driven Gears

Before Improvement

1. In attaching driven gears to engines, the fact that six types of gear were involved meant that sometimes the wrong gears would be mounted.

2. Procedure:
   1.) Worker B looks at the work-in-process slip.
   2.) He then takes type B driven gear from the parts rack.
   3.) He attaches the driven gear to the engine.

After Improvement

1. Worker A looks at the work-in-process slip and presses, say, button F on a specification indicator box.

2. Worker B looks at the work-in-process slip and presses button F on his specification indicator box, thus heading off errors by double-checking A's action.

3. The cover to the F bin on the driven gear rack opens. (If workers A and B press different buttons, then a buzzer rings and the rack cover does not open.)

Effects	Cost
Cases of attachment of the wrong parts were eliminated.	¥ 490,000 ($2450)

Example 72

Inspection Method		Setting Function		Regulative Function		Company Name
Source Inspection	●	Contact Method		Control Method	●	Hosei Brake Industries, Inc.
Informative Inspection (self)		Constant Value Method		Warning Method		**Proposed by**
Informative Inspection (successive)		Motion-Step Method	●			Yorifumi Ishikawa

Theme	Preventing Parts Errors in Assembly

Before Improvement

reader

After Improvement

kanban

reader

assembly kanban

1. Since there are as many as 100 kinds of parts involved on a single line, workers take parts indicated by lights. Assembly defects would sometimes occur because workers would take the wrong parts.

2. When assembly kanban were inserted in a reader, lights above the parts would go on as signals to workers. (Workers sometimes took the wrong parts even with the signal lights.)

When an assembly kanban is inserted in the reader, air cylinders push out only the parts boxes needed. (Parts cannot be taken out of boxes that are not protruding.)

Effects	Assembly errors due to the wrong parts were eliminated.	Cost	approx. ¥ 2 million ($10,000)

Example 73

Inspection Method		Setting Function		Regulative Function		Company Name
Source Inspection	•	Contact Method		Control Method	•	Matsusita Electric Industrial Co., Ltd./ Washing Machine Division/ Shizuoka Plant
Informative Inspection (self)		Constant Value Method		Warning Method		**Proposed by**
Informative Inspection (successive)		Motion-Step Method	•			

Theme   Ensuring Attachment of Cock Springs

Before Improvement

With 11 cock-U components—including internal cock springs, the failure to attach parts 1 or 2 would invite deterioration of product performance. The difficulty of verification meant that avoidance of the problem in the past depended mainly on worker vigilance.

After Improvement

1. Photoelectric switches were provided on parts boxes to signal each step of the operation.
2. If a worker does not follow predetermined procedures, a buzzer sounds to signal an abnormal condition. In such a situation, the final operation of tightening the cock cover cannot be carried out, for the driver will not start even when the "on" switch is thrown.

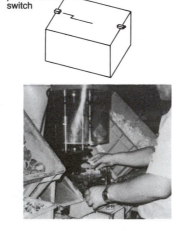

photoelectric switch

Effects	Cost
Worker failure to attach cock springs was eliminated.	¥ 10,000 ($50)

Example 74

Inspection Method		Setting Function		Regulative Function		Company Name
Source Inspection	●	Contact Method		Control Method	●	Matsusita Electric Industrial Co., Ltd./ Vacuum Cleaner Division
Informative Inspection (self)		Constant Value Method		Warning Method		**Proposed by** Improvement Group, Assembly Manufacturing Department
Informative Inspection (successive)		Motion-Step Method	●			

Theme	Ensuring the Attachment of Handle Set Screws

Before Improvement

Failure to attach screws was prevented through worker vigilance.

After Improvement

1. A stopper was installed that prevents a product from moving to the next process unless the handle screw has been tightened.

2. If a set screw is not taken out of the parts box, the stopper descends and the tightening operation cannot take place.

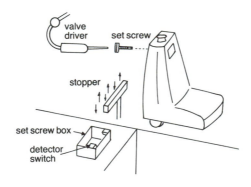

Effects	Worker failure to attach screws was eliminated.	Cost	approx. ¥ 10,000 ($50)

Example 75

Inspection Method		Setting Function		Regulative Function		Company Name
Source Inspection	●	Contact Method		Control Method	●	Matsushita Electric Industrial Co., Ltd./ Vacuum Cleaner Division
Informative Inspection (self)		Constant Value Method		Warning Method		**Proposed by** Toshio Yamamoto, Assembly Manufacturing Division
Informative Inspection (successive)		Motion-Step Method	●			

Theme   Ensuring Pad Printing

Before Improvement

Switches needed to be pressed on both the right and left sides of the body, but sometimes one side would be printed and the other side forgotten.

After Improvement

A single motion, two-stroke system was devised, in which stepping on a switch once causes two pad movements and eliminates one-sided printing.

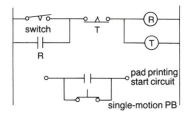

Effects	**Cost**
One-side printing was eliminated.	approx. ¥ 5,000 ($25)

Example 76

Inspection Method		Setting Function		Regulative Function		Company Name
Source Inspection	●	Contact Method		Control Method		Hosei Brake Industries, Ltd.
Informative Inspection (self)		Constant Value Method		Warning Method	●	**Proposed by**
Informative Inspection (successive)		Motion-Step Method	●			Toshihiro Nabeta

Theme   Ensuring Proper Installation of Washers

Before Improvement

1. In an operation for installing brake struts, defects occurred when washers were either omitted or installed on top of one another.

2. Workers took washers from a box and attached them with great care. Each washer was 0.6mm thick and had an outside diameter of 16mm.

After Improvement

When a strut assembly machine is turned on, a single washer is fed from a cartridge.

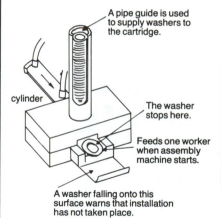

A pipe guide is used to supply washers to the cartridge.

cylinder

The washer stops here.

Feeds one worker when assembly machine starts.

A washer falling onto this surface warns that installation has not taken place.

Effects	Cost
Defects involving doubled and missing washers were eliminated.	approx. ¥5,000 ($25)

Example 77

Inspection Method		Setting Function		Regulative Function		Company Name
Source Inspection		Contact Method	●	Control Method	●	Arakawa Auto Body, Ltd./ Kotobuki Plant
Informative Inspection (self)	●	Constant Value Method		Warning Method		**Proposed by**
Informative Inspection (successive)		Motion-Step Method				

Theme Ensuring that a QL Wrench is Tightened

Before Improvement

1. After bolts are impact-tightened, torque is checked by means of a QL wrench. Occasionally, however, workers would forget to tighten the QL wrench.
2. The prevention of this sort of omission depended on worker vigilance.

After Improvement

1. When an impact wrench is used to tighten bolts, limit switch no. 1 is activated. (starts timer)
2. When the QL wrench is used to check torque, limit switch no. 2 is activated. (clears timer)

When a worker neglects to use the QL wrench, the timer is not cleared and, when a predetermined period elapses, a buzzer sounds, air is cut off, and movement to the next process becomes impossible.

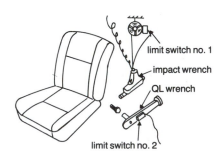

limit switch no. 1
impact wrench
QL wrench
limit switch no. 2

Effects Instances of failure to check torque with a QL wrench were eliminated.	**Cost** approx. ¥ 100,000 ($500)

Example 78

Inspection Method		Setting Function		Regulative Function		Company Name
						Saga Tekkohsho Co., Ltd/ Fujisawa Plant
Source Inspection		Contact Method	●	Control Method	●	
Informative Inspection (self)	●	Constant Value Method		Warning Method		**Proposed by**
Informative Inspection (successive)		Motion-Step Method				Shōri Koga

Theme	
	Preventing the Intrusion of Items with Defective Cross Recesses

Before Improvement

1. Numerous defective items would be produced whenever a cross-recess punch broke off.
2. Workers regularly conducted checks at the rate of about once every 15 minutes.

After Improvement

1. Cross-recess punch breakage is detected electrically and the machine shuts down.
2. In the ordinary case, the punch comes in contact with an electric terminal when it advances. No contact is made when the punch is broken, however, and this is detected electrically and causes the machine to shut down.

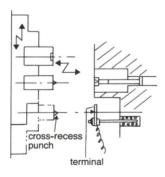

cross-recess punch

terminal

Effects The defect rate fell, as the only defective goods produced are those made while the machine is operating by inertia. Defective items are no longer sent to the next process. There is no longer any need, moreover, for workers to check the machine every 15 minutes.	Cost ¥ 30,000 ($150)

Example 79

Inspection Method		Setting Function		Regulative Function		Company Name
Source Inspection		Contact Method	●	Control Method	●	Taiho Industries, Ltd.
Informative Inspection (self)	●	Constant Value Method		Warning Method		**Proposed by**
Informative Inspection (successive)		Motion-Step Method				Metal Production Division No. 1

Theme   Eliminating Unfininshed Tabs

Before Improvement

When something went wrong with tab protrusion forming, products with unfinished tabs flowed to the next process and, even with intermediate inspection processes, to customers. Such problems gave rise to claims against the company and lowered confidence in the product.

After Improvement

When a workpiece passes through, it trips a side-mounted limit switch. This switch checks for the presence of tabs and the machine shuts down if tabs are not found.

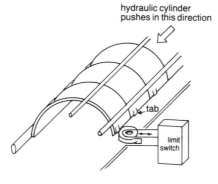

hydraulic cylinder
pushes in this direction

tab

limit switch

Effects	Cost
Unfinished tabs were eliminated.	1 limit switch used electric circuit rebuilt

Example 80

Inspection Method		Setting Function		Regulative Function		Company Name
Source Inspection		Contact Method	●	Control Method	●	Hosei Brake Industries, Ltd.
Informative Inspection (self)	●	Constant Value Method		Warning Method		**Proposed by**
Informative Inspection (successive)		Motion-Step Method				Naoteru Ochiai

Theme	Preventing Double Welding and Omissions of Disk Cover Retainers

Before Improvement

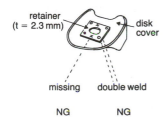

retainer (t = 2.3 mm)   disk cover

missing   double weld

NG   NG

1. In welding disk covers and retainers, defects would occasionally arise involving missing retainers or double welds.

2. Electrodeposition painting follows welding in a multiprocess operation, but movement in slinging and boxing operations would occasionally deviate from standards and workers would make careless errors.

After Improvement

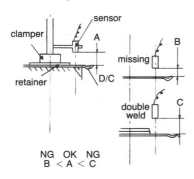

sensor
clamper   A   B
                missing
retainer   D/C

double weld   C

NG OK NG
 B < A < C

1. A positioning sensor was mounted on the clamper of a multiple electrode spot welding machine.

2. The clamper operates outside of A, but the welding gun does not pressurize.

3. The welder starts up only if the sensor is off; this prevents erroneous spotter movement.

Effects Defects involving missing and double welded retainers were eliminated.	**Cost** approx. ¥116,000 ($580)

Example 81

Inspection Method		Setting Function		Regulative Function		Company Name
Source Inspection		Contact Method	●	Control Method	●	Hosei Brake Industries, Ltd.
Informative Inspection (self)	●	Constant Value Method		Warning Method		**Proposed by**
Informative Inspection (successive)		Motion-Step Method				Norio Katō

Theme	Preventing Omission of Engine Mounting Washers

Before Improvement

1. Workers would occasionally forget washers in attaching hardware to vulcanized rubber mountings.
2. At the next process—a tapping process—a wax pencil was used to check the workpiece, but sometimes items without washers were inadvertently boxed.

After Improvement

When the workpiece has been positioned in the tapping process, a proximity switch checks for the presence or absence of washers. If a washer is missing, the start switch for the tapping operation will not turn on.

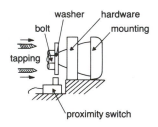

Effects	Defects involving missing washers were eliminated.	Cost	approx. ¥ 2,500 ($12.50)

Example 82

Inspection Method		Setting Function		Regulative Function		Company Name
Source Inspection		Contact Method	●	Control Method	●	Matsushita Electric Industrial Co., Ltd./Washing Machine Division/Shizuoka Plant
Informative Inspection (self)	●	Constant Value Method		Warning Method		**Proposed by**
Informative Inspection (successive)		Motion-Step Method				

Theme   Preventing Pulley-Tightening Defects

Before Improvement

1. Torque is set with a nut runner and, if satisfactory, a clutch goes to work and a switch turns on.

2. The problem was that only the force of the torque was measured, so that as long as torque was sufficient, the result would be judged satisfactory even if, for example, pulleys were attached at an angle.

After Improvement

In addition to the previous torque check, a contact and photoelectric switch were provided to verify the height of nuts that had been tightened.

Procedure

The nut runner descends and when tightening is completed

1. a contact touches the flange of the tightening bit,
2. a photoelectric switch is activated, and
3. the clutch starts.

If these three conditions are fulfilled, then everything is all right and the stopper withdraws to permit movement to the next process. (If not, then a buzzer sounds and the product comes to a halt.)

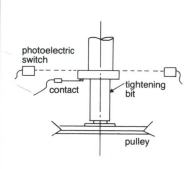

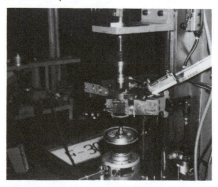

Effects	Cost
Tightening errors due to skewed tightening and the like were eliminated.	¥ 20,000 ($100)

Example 83

Inspection Method		Setting Function		Regulative Function		Company Name
Source Inspection		Contact Method	●	Control Method	●	Hosei Brake Industries, Ltd.
Informative Inspection (self)	●	Constant Value Method		Warning Method		**Proposed by**
Informative Inspection (successive)		Motion-Step Method				Mimio Nakamura

Theme	Preventing Installation of the Wrong Engine Bracket

Before Improvement

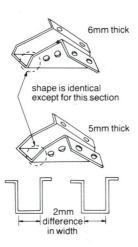

6mm thick

shape is identical
except for this section

5mm thick

2mm
difference
in width

1. When attaching a bracket to a vulcanized rubber mounting, similar mountings were occasionally attached instead of the correct one.

2. Visual checks were carried out when brackets were packed in boxes.

Example 84

After Improvement

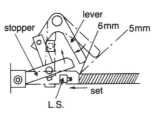

1. A poka-yoke jig is fitted on the nut runner used for bolt installation and when the wrong mounting is present, the jig detects differences in bracket shape and dimension and blocks operation of the nut runner.

   (e.g., a 6mm bracket cannot be used when a 5mm bracket is called for)

2. For 6mm brackets, a lever operates, the stopper opens, and the workpiece is set in position. Operation can begin when the limit switch is set.

   For 5mm brackets, the lever does not operate and the stopper does not open. The difference in inside dimensions makes positioning impossible and thus prevents installation of a 6mm bracket when a 5mm bracket is called for.

Effects	Cost
Defects involving the wrong bracket were eliminated.	approx. ¥ 2,000 ($10)

Example 84 cont.

Inspection Method		Setting Function		Regulative Function		Company Name
Source Inspection		Contact Method	●	Control Method	●	Hosei Brake Industries, Ltd.
Informative Inspection (self)	●	Constant Value Method		Warning Method		**Proposed by**
Informative Inspection (successive)		Motion-Step Method				Naoteru Ochiai

Theme	Ensuring Drum-in-Disk Bracket Welding

Before Improvement

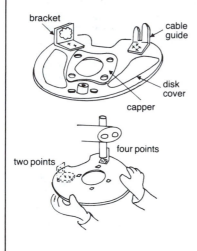

1. Workers occasionally forgot to carry out welding in a plate processing operation.
2. Brackets were welded to dust covers.
3. Two types of jig were used on a spot welding machine to weld on cable guides and then brackets. The welding of brackets was sometimes neglected.

Example 85

After Improvement

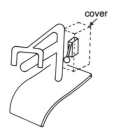

cover

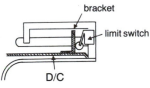

bracket

limit switch

D/C

1. After welding, the bracket hole is moved over a poka-yoke bar.
2. When a bracket is absent, the limit switch is not activated and the next welding machine cannot start. (interlock)

Effects	Cost
Missing brackets and defects were eliminated.	approx. ¥ 2,000 ($10)

Example 85 cont.

Inspection Method		Setting Function		Regulative Function		Company Name
Source Inspection		Contact Method	●	Control Method		Asahi Electric Fixtures
Informative Inspection (self)	●	Constant Value Method		Warning Method	●	**Proposed by**
Informative Inspection (successive)		Motion-Step Method				

Theme   Preventing the Backward Attachment of Faceplates

Before Improvement

formed knob

aluminum faceplate

After assembly, an operation was conducted in which a worker turned a knob, felt its surface with his fingers, and estimated where to apply the faceplate before actually attacking on.

After Improvement

Faceplates are notched and joggled onto knobs. A photoelectric tube senses when positions match and a signal light goes on.

formed knob
joggle added

aluminum faceplate
notch added

Effects Accurate positioning was made possible merely by joining knob joggles and faceplate notches. Faceplate and knob defects involving the replacement of parts put on backward or those that had slipped out of place were eliminated.

Cost
¥ 20,000 ($100)

Example 86

Inspection Method		Setting Function		Regulative Function		Company Name
Source Inspection		Contact Method	●	Control Method		Asahi National Lighting Co., Ltd
Informative Inspection (self)	●	Constant Value Method		Warning Method	●	**Proposed by**
Informative Inspection (successive)		Motion-Step Method				Metalwork Department

Theme	Prevention of Hole Slippage in a Press-Punching Operation

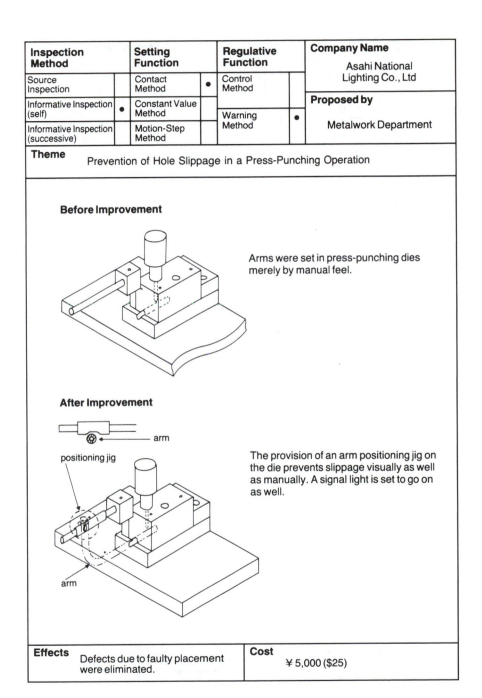

Before Improvement

Arms were set in press-punching dies merely by manual feel.

After Improvement

arm

positioning jig

arm

The provision of an arm positioning jig on the die prevents slippage visually as well as manually. A signal light is set to go on as well.

Effects	Defects due to faulty placement were eliminated.	Cost	¥ 5,000 ($25)

Example 87

Inspection Method		Setting Function		Regulative Function		Company Name
Source Inspection		Contact Method	●	Control Method		Asahi National Lighting Co., Ltd.
Informative Inspection (self)	●	Constant Value Method		Warning Method	●	**Proposed by** Kentaro Shimada, Interior Lighting Manufacturing Technology Department
Informative Inspection (successive)		Motion-Step Method				

Theme   Ensuring 100 Percent Inspections of Arm Shapes, Overall Lengths and Hole Positions

Before Improvement

100 percent inspections of arm shapes, overall lengths, and hole positions are required in the assembly process.

After Improvement

In addition to securing and immobilizing the arm during the arm cord passage operation, arm shapes, overall lengths, and hole positions are controlled.

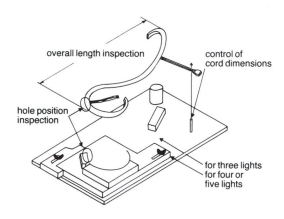

overall length inspection

control of cord dimensions

hole position inspection

for three lights
for four or five lights

Effects Instances in which workers forgot to inspect arm shapes, overall lengths, and hole positions were eliminated and, as a consequence, cord dimension defects also were eliminated.	**Cost** ¥ 25,000 ($125)

Example 88

Inspection Method		Setting Function		Regulative Function		Company Name
Source Inspection		Contact Method	●	Control Method		Saga Tekkohsho Co., Ltd./ Fujisawa Plant
Informative Inspection (self)	●	Constant Value Method		Warning Method	●	**Proposed by**
Informative Inspection (successive)		Motion-Step Method				

Theme	Eliminating Abnormal Screw Threads

Before Improvement

1. Chamfer defects during rolling would cause doubled threads and bead-shaped threads to crop up and be mixed in with good items.
2. It was extremely difficult both to find the cause of this problem and to come up with countermeasures.

After Improvement

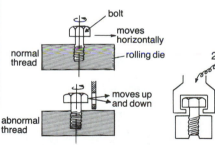

1. An automatic detection device like the one in the figure to the left was provided and set up so that, in the unlikely event of a defect, a shutter will drop and keep defective screws from mixing in with good ones.

2. When an abnormal situation occurs, the bolt does not rise to the reworking process. Making use of its downward motion, a gate-type electrode and sensor are provided along the way. When the bolt comes in contact with these, a shutter attached to the chute automatically drops and a buzzer sounds.

Effects	Along with preventing items from moving to the next process if an abnormal situation occurs, the improvement reduced defects because it became easier to root out the sources of problems.	Cost	¥ 50,000 ($250)

Example 89

Inspection Method		Setting Function		Regulative Function		Company Name
Source Inspection		Contact Method	●	Control Method		Asahi National Lighting Co., Ltd.
Informative Inspection (self)	●	Constant Value Method		Warning Method	●	**Proposed by** Kenji Uesaka, Interior Lighting Manufacturing Technology Department
Informative Inspection (successive)		Motion-Step Method				

Theme	Device for Verifying Lighting Sequences

Before Improvement

Claims arose because of reversed lighting sequences due to erroneous stabilizer wiring (no. 1 ◄───► no. 2).

body of round 60W type

 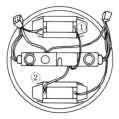

Example 90

After Improvement

The lighting sequences of lamps are detected electrically and a buzzer notifies workers when faulty wiring causes a sequence to be reversed.

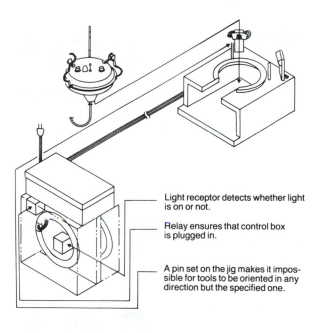

Light receptor detects whether light is on or not.

Relay ensures that control box is plugged in.

A pin set on the jig makes it impossible for tools to be oriented in any direction but the specified one.

Effects	**Cost**
Wiring errors were eliminated.	¥ 35,000 ($175)

Example 90 cont.

Inspection Method		Setting Function		Regulative Function		Company Name
Source Inspection		Contact Method		Control Method		Saga Tekkohsho Co., Ltd./ Fujisawa Plant
Informative Inspection (self)		Constant Value Method		Warning Method		**Proposed by**
Informative Inspection (successive)		Motion-Step Method				Katsuhiko Miura

Theme   Eliminating Bolts with Uncut Grooves

Before Improvement

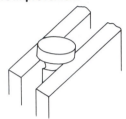

1. In the automated cutting of grooves under bolt heads, uncut items would very infrequently creep in because of chucking defects on the machine.
2. Such defects were uncovered during visual inspections after processing. (judgment inspection)

After Improvement

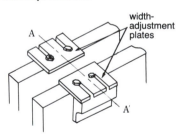

width-adjustment plates

A

A'

A-A' cross-section

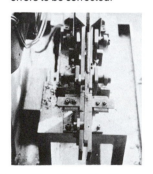

1. A poka-yoke device was installed on the top of the chute leading to the product holder.
2. Plates adjusted to match the width of bolts with grooves under their heads were set so as to halt the outflow of uncut items. A bolt caught on this device sets off a buzzer, which allows chucking errors to be corrected.

Effects After installation, the inclusion of bolts with uncut grooves was eliminated.	**Cost** ¥ 15,000 ($75)

Example 91

Inspection Method		Setting Function		Regulative Function		Company Name
Source Inspection		Contact Method	●	Control Method		Saga Tekkohsho Co., Ltd./ Fujisawa Plant
Informative Inspection (self)	●	Constant Value Method		Warning Method	●	**Proposed by**
Informative Inspection (successive)		Motion-Step Method				Kunihiro Hisadomi, Heat Treatment Chief

Theme　A Device to Warn of Heat Treatment Mesh Conveyor Belt Slippage

Before Improvement

1. Defects resulted when the mesh belt in a heat treatment process occasionally got caught and stopped.

2. Defective goods would show up because the problem was be discovered too late.

After Improvement

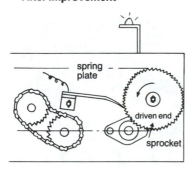

spring plate

driven end

sprocket

1. As shown at left, sprockets are provided on the drum shaft on the driven end, so electrical detection can set off a warning signal.

2. When the conveyor is turning normally, the spring plate and sprockets regularly come into contact with one another. This contact comes to a halt when the conveyor stops and, if this abnormal condition occurs, it is picked up electrically, a warning signal is issued, and the conveyor drive is shut down. Thus, no damage to the mesh belt takes place and product defects are reduced.

Effects　This did away with the tardy discovery of problems; measures could be taken early enough to prevent defects.

Cost　¥ 40,000 ($200)

Example 92

Inspection Method		Setting Function		Regulative Function		Company Name
Source Inspection		Contact Method	●	Control Method		Hosei Brake Industries, Ltd.
Informative Inspection (self)	●	Constant Value Method		Warning Method	●	**Proposed by**
Informative Inspection (successive)		Motion-Step Method				Mimio Nakamura

Theme   Preventing Cutting and Welding Defects in Suspension Parts

Before Improvement

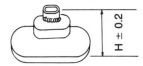

$H \pm 0.2$

1. Visual checks could not uncover cutting flaws and missing welds, and products with such defects flowed off the production line.
2. After welding, products were checked visually and finished items were placed on pallets.

After Improvement

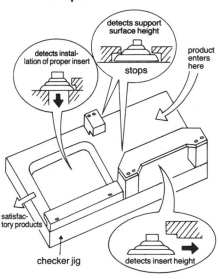

detects support surface height

detects instal-lation of proper insert

stops

product enters here

satisfac-tory products

checker jig

detects insert height

After welding, finished products are sent down a chute from which defective goods are expelled. When defective items show up, a light comes on and the information is relayed to the previous process.

Effects Defects sent on to subsequent processes were eliminated and the occurrence of defects was reduced.	**Cost** approx. ¥ 1,000 ($5)

Example 93

Inspection Method		Setting Function		Regulative Function		Company Name
Source Inspection		Contact Method	●	Control Method		Matsushita Electric Industrial Co., Ltd./ Washing Machine Division/ Mikuni Plant
Informative Inspection (self)	●	Constant Value Method		Warning Method	●	**Proposed by** Tetsuo Nonoguchi, Assembly Manufacturing Department
Informative Inspection (successive)		Motion-Step Method				

Theme	Preventing Slippage Defects in Support Block Positioning

Before Improvement

Slippage would occasionally occur in gluing support blocks into a pedestal unit used in packing finished washing machines. This made it difficult for the washing machine to fit into the unit.

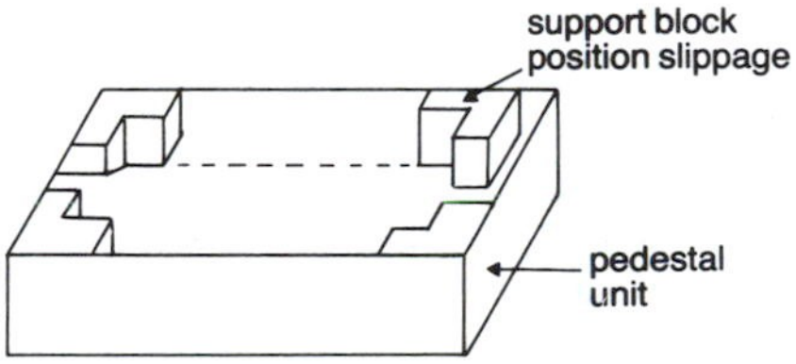

support block position slippage

pedestal unit

After Improvement

The installation of a support block detector like the one shown below makes it possible to discover defects after gluing.

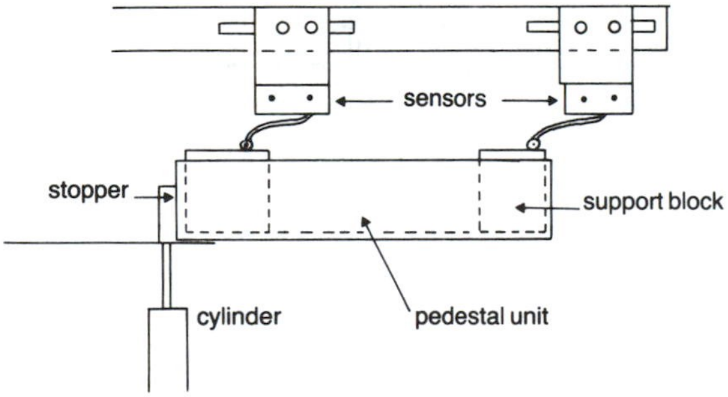

sensors

stopper

support block

cylinder

pedestal unit

Effects	Packing defects associated with block slippage were eliminated.	Cost	¥ 10,000 ($50)

Example 94

Inspection Method		Setting Function		Regulative Function		Company Name
Source Inspection		Contact Method	●	Control Method		Matsushita Electric Industrial Co., Ltd./ Vacuum Cleaner Division
Informative Inspection (self)	●	Constant Value Method		Warning Method	●	**Proposed by**
Informative Inspection (successive)		Motion-Step Method				Noriko Nishi Tatsuo Mōri

Theme   Ensuring Verification of Switch Lever Action

Before Improvement

Inspection checks of finished products were carried out by hand only.

After Improvement

1. The completed handle guarantees switch lever action
2. Assembly of the finished handle provides a 1.5mm clearance for switch lever action and makes verification with a detector switch possible.

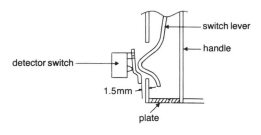

Effects	**Cost**
Action defects were eliminated.	approx. ¥ 2,000 ($10)

Example 95

Inspection Method		Setting Function		Regulative Function		Company Name
Source Inspection		Contact Method	•	Control Method		Matsushita Electric Industrial Co., Ltd./ Vacuum Cleaner Division
Informative Inspection (self)	•	Constant Value Method		Warning Method	•	**Proposed by**
Informative Inspection (successive)		Motion-Step Method				Yūyō Ogawa

Theme	
	Preventing Air Pressure Abnormalities

Before Improvement

Visual control was maintained with an air pressure gauge.

After Improvement

When air pressure falls below 5 kg/cm², a rotating light comes on and workers are warned by a buzzer. This brings drops in pressure to the workers' attention immediately.

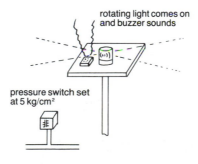

rotating light comes on and buzzer sounds

pressure switch set at 5 kg/cm²

Effects		Cost	
	Defects due to drops in pressure were eliminated.		approx. ¥ 10,000 ($50)

Example 96

Inspection Method		Setting Function		Regulative Function		Company Name
Source Inspection		Contact Method		Control Method	●	Asahi National Lighting Co., Ltd.
Informative Inspection (self)	●	Constant Value Method	●	Warning Method		**Proposed by** Kenji Uesaka, Interior Lighting Manufacturing Technology Department
Informative Inspection (successive)		Motion-Step Method				

Theme	Detecting the Absence of Sealing Pins on Cases

Before Improvement

Since cases continued to move along the line even when sealing pins had not been inserted, it was especially difficult to verify the presence of pins on the bottoms of cases.

After Improvement

A sensor for detecting sealing pins was mounted at the rear of the packing machine. This sensor, linked to a counter, verifies the number of sealing pins and stops the cases if a shortage occurs.

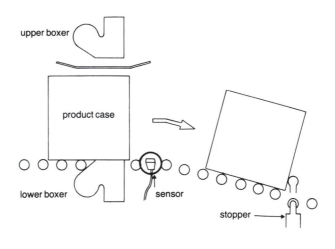

Effects	Cost
Instances of missing packing pins fell to zero.	¥ 80,000 ($400)

Example 97

Inspection Method		Setting Function		Regulative Function		Company Name
Source Inspection		Contact Method		Control Method		Taiho Industries, Ltd.
Informative Inspection (self)	●	Constant Value Method	●	Warning Method	●	**Proposed by**
Informative Inspection (successive)		Motion-Step Method				Assembly Parts Department, Production Division

Theme	Ensuring the Presence of Needed Parts on an EGR Assembly Line

Before Improvement

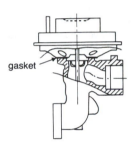

gasket

1. On an EGR assembly line, errors would occur involving either missing parts or double installation of parts, and the resulting defective goods would be sent on to customers.

2. Missing or doubled gasket assembly errors would show up once or twice a month in the assembly process.

After Improvement

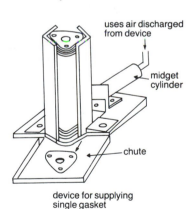

uses air discharged from device

midget cylinder

chute

device for supplying single gasket

After assembly, one gasket is supplied to each unit by using air discharged from the cylinder that carries out welding on the same jig. The presence of one gasket at the top of the chute during assembly is normal. If two or more are present, the worker knows that the previous unit is missing a gasket.

Effects	The regular supply of parts eliminated assemblies with missing parts.	**Cost**	In-house construction; no electrical conversion; effective use of air discharged under pressure

Example 98

Inspection Method		Setting Function		Regulative Function		Company Name
Source Inspection		Contact Method		Control Method		Aisan Industries, Ltd./ Main Plant
Informative Inspection (self)	●	Constant Value Method	●	Warning Method	●	**Proposed by**
Informative Inspection (successive)		Motion-Step Method				Kikuo Hattori

Theme   Ensuring Attachment of PTC Plates

Before Improvement

eight PTC plates attached

PTC plate

1. In an operation involving the attachment of eight PTC plates to the main CMH body, one plate was sometimes left out in the trial manufacture stage.

2. Measures for preventing such shortages needed to be worked out prior to production.

After Improvement

PTC plate

advances and retreats by means of an air cylinder driven by the previous process

expulsion plate

4 rows × 2 plates/ 1 row = 8 plates

1. A device like the one shown at left was built to expel eight plates at a time.

2. After the main body is removed at the previous process, the start switch is turned on and the air cylinder pushes out eight PTC plates by means of expulsion plate A.

3. All eight PTC plates are attached to the main body.

4. If no PTC plates remain, none will be missing from the assembly.

Effects	Cost
Missing PTC plates were eliminated.	¥ 40,000 ($200)

Example 99

Inspection Method		Setting Function		Regulative Function		Company Name
Source Inspection		Contact Method		Control Method		Toyota Auto Body Co., Ltd.
Informative Inspection (self)	●	Constant Value Method	●	Warning Method	●	**Proposed by**
Informative Inspection (successive)		Motion-Step Method				Body Department No. 41

Theme	
	Ensuring the Presence of Weld Nuts on Support Front Springs

Before Improvement

1. Occasionally, workers would inadvertently leave out some of the 11 weld nuts to be attached to each support front spring.

2. A worker would count nuts one by one and then attach them.

support front spring

After Improvement

A strike counter was installed and a buzzer warns the worker if the specified number of nuts has not been attached.

counter

Effects		Cost	
	Instances of missing nuts were eliminated.		¥ 120,000 ($600)

Example 100

Inspection Method		Setting Function		Regulative Function		Company Name
Source Inspection		Contact Method		Control Method		Hosei Brake Industries, Ltd.
Informative Inspection (self)	●	Constant Value Method	●	Warning Method	●	**Proposed by**
Informative Inspection (successive)		Motion-Step Method				Kaoru Hasebe

Theme   Ensuring the Correct Number of Fittings in Boxes

Before Improvement

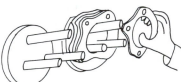

capacity: 150

1. The wrong number of fittings would occasionally be put into a box for 150 fittings.
2. Fittings go into the box after electrodeposition.
3. Fittings are counted by hand.

After Improvement

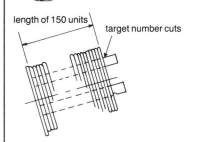

length of 150 units

target number cuts

With the attachment of a number-verification jig bar, "target number cuts" tell workers that 150 units are present.

Effects	Cost
Counting errors were eliminated.	approx. ¥ 1,500 ($7.50)

Example 101

Inspection Method		Setting Function		Regulative Function		Company Name
Source Inspection		Contact Method		Control Method	●	Matsushita Electric Industrial Co., Ltd./ Washing Machine Division/ Shizuoka Plant
Informative Inspection (self)	●	Constant Value Method		Warning Method		**Proposed by**
Informative Inspection (successive)		Motion-Step Method	●			

Theme   Preventing Tank Welder Changeover Errors

Before Improvement

Welding errors and missing welds occasionally showed up if equipment switches were not set properly for model changeovers.

After Improvement

When the model selector switch on the equipment control box is not operated (i.e., set to the correct position), a rotating light comes on to warn of an abnormal situation and product flow is halted.

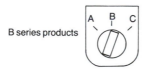

B series products

Comparison with a signal from the moving product line verifies that the above (three-position) selector switch is correctly set.

Effects	Cost
Welding errors and missing Welds were eliminated.	¥ 15,000 ($75)

Example 102

Inspection Method		Setting Function		Regulative Function		Company Name
Source Inspection		Contact Method		Control Method	•	Matsushita Electric Industrial Co., Ltd./ Washing Machine Division/ Shizuoka Plant
Informative Inspection (self)	•	Constant Value Method		Warning Method		**Proposed by**
Informative Inspection (successive)		Motion-Step Method	•			

Theme
  Ensuring that Cotter Pins are Bent

Before Improvement

Valve magnets (electromagnetic valves) are used in operating drain taps. The electromagnetic valves are linked by cotter pins; a claim was once made because a pin had not been bent after it was inserted. (The pin is located where its orientation cannot be checked visually on the inspection line.)

After Improvement

1. Stoppers (product jig pallets) for workers are provided in such a way that they will not operate unless pins are bent. This ensures that pins are bent.

2. The removal of a tool to bend a cotter pin displaces a switch and causes the stopper switch to move.

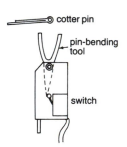

Effects	Cost
Cotter pin errors were eliminated.	¥ 5,000 ($25)

Example 103

Inspection Method		Setting Function		Regulative Function		Company Name
Source Inspection		Contact Method		Control Method		Toyota Auto Body Co., Ltd.
Informative Inspection (self)	●	Constant Value Method		Warning Method	●	**Proposed by**
Informative Inspection (successive)		Motion-Step Method	●			Katsuya Koide, Production Control Department

Theme	Preventing Removal of the Wrong Interior Fittings Order Card

Before Improvement

1. Errors sometimes occurred involving order cards for interior fittings.

2. A worker would look at the painted body and remember the body number. These numbers, however, were printed in an ill-lit place, and the need to use a flashlight to see them made verification difficult.

3. With the number remembered, the worker would remove an order card indicating the proper fittings. Occasionally, however, a worker would inadvertently take the wrong card and paste it on the body.

4. A worker would recheck the body number and order card number at the next process.

After Improvement

1. A lighting fixture was installed on the workplace floor at the ideal angle for increasing visibility. When a body comes along, it trips a limit switch that automatically turns on this light and makes the body number easy to see.

2. Immediately after verifying the body number, a worker stores it by keying it into a desktop calculator.

3. The worker then compares the number shown by the calculator and the order card numbers and removes the proper order card.

4. This has completely eliminated instances in which the workers inadvertently takes the wrong card.

5. The desktop calculator is extremely convenient because the number it displays can be erased at one stroke.

Effects	Cases in which the wrong card is taken were eliminated.	Cost	¥ 10,000 ($50)

Example 104

Inspection Method		Setting Function		Regulative Function		Company Name
Source Inspection		Contact Method		Control Method		Matsushita Electric Industrial Co., Ltd./ Washing Machine Division/ Shizuoka Plant
Informative Inspection (self)	●	Constant Value Method				**Proposed by**
Informative Inspection (successive)		·Motion-Step Method	●	Warning Method	●	

Theme   Preventing Inspection Gaps

Before Improvement

1. Inspection personnel performed visual inspection of a large number of sites.
2. The fact that there were almost no defects made inspections routine and workers were seen as apt to skip some items.
3. The point of poka-yoke devices is to eliminate defects, not to perform inspections.

After Improvement

By following predetermined steps in conducting inspections, inspection personnel cause "inspection OK" lights to go on in order. When all specified sites have been inspected, a large OK lamp lights and a chime sounds.

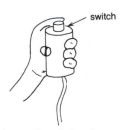

Inspection of nine sites proceeds in steps:
- A switch is pressed at each step.
- Completion of the inspection of all nine sites causes the OK signal to appear

Effects	Cost
Inspection gaps were eliminated.	¥ 5,000 ($25)

Example 105

Inspection Method		Setting Function		Regulative Function		Company Name
						Matsushita Electric Industrial Co., Ltd./Washing Machine Division/Shizuoka Plant
Source Inspection		Contact Method		Control Method		
Informative Inspection (self)	●	Constant Value Method		Warning Method	●	**Proposed by**
Informative Inspection (successive)		Motion-Step Method	●			Ken'ichi Sadamoto

Theme   Ensuring Tightening of Suction Valves

Before Improvement

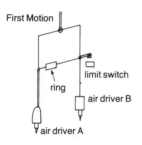

1. In this operation, which involves the tightening of two kinds of screws, workers would sometimes neglect to tighten one.

2. Air drivers A and B were to be used, but sometimes workers would, through inadvertence, use only driver A.

After Improvement

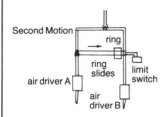

When a worker pulls down the air driver A and uses it, a ring slides forward on a steelyard-like rod. When air driver B is then pulled down for tightening, the ring slides to the opposite side and presses a limit switch to signal the end of the operation. If a worker forgets one side, then a buzzer sounds a warning after a specified period of time has elapsed.

Effects Instances of neglected tightening were eliminated.	**Cost** ¥ 3,000 ($15)

Example 106

Inspection Method		Setting Function		Regulative Function		Company Name
Source Inspection		Contact Method	●	Control Method	●	Taiho Industries, Ltd.
Informative Inspection (self)		Constant Value Method		Warning Method		**Proposed by**
Informative Inspection (successive)	●	Motion-Step Method				Assembly Parts Department, Production Division

Theme	Eliminating Uncut Housing and Lead Valve Threads

Before Improvement

In a process for cutting M28 housing threads, visual verification was inadequate for preventing uncut items from moving on to the next process and, possibly, to customers.

After Improvement

Uncut M28 threads can be discovered by a sensor at the next process. If an abnormal condition arises, automatic operation of the machine stops and a worker is warned by a buzzer and a red light.

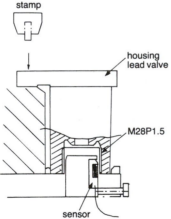

stamp

housing
lead valve

M28P1.5

sensor

Effects	Items with uncut threads no longer move to subsequent processes.	Cost	purchase of tap miss detector: ¥ 49,000 ($245)

Example 107

Inspection Method	Setting Function		Regulative Function		Company Name
Source Inspection	Contact Method	●	Control Method	●	Taiho Industries, Ltd.
Informative Inspection (self)	Constant Value Method		Warning Method		**Proposed by**
Informative Inspection (successive)	●	Motion-Step Method			

Theme   Preventing Groove Omission

Before Improvement

Groove omission defects would come back to us from customers in the form of returned goods. Each time this happened, either quality groups or line workers would go to the customer and sort the parts out. Since this damaged our relationship of trust with customers, we manufactured the poka-yoke device described below and integrated it into production.

After Improvement

1. In an oil groove cutting process, tool changes and damaged bits would lead to the occasional appearance of products missing grooves.

2. Although a principled approach to this problem would involve mounting a checking device within the process in question, space restrictions made this difficult. For this reason, a device was mounted in the next (punch) process that would catch products without grooves. The device shuts down the press and the previous process and sounds a buzzer to alert workers.

3. This approach made it possible to discover products with misplaced grooves as well as items without grooves.

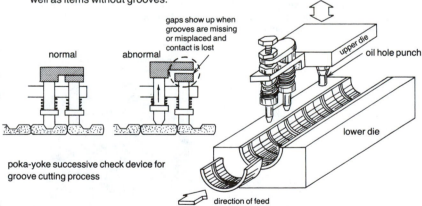

gaps show up when grooves are missing or misplaced and contact is lost

normal   abnormal

upper die

oil hole punch

lower die

poka-yoke successive check device for groove cutting process

direction of feed

Effects 1. Instances in which grooveless items moved to subsequent processes have been eliminated because missing grooves are discovered and the press is shut down. 2. grooves cut in the wrong places can be similarly discovered.	**Cost** ¥ 5,000 ($25)

Example 108

Inspection Method		Setting Function		Regulative Function		Company Name
Source Inspection		Contact Method	●	Control Method	●	Hosei Brake Industries, Ltd.
Informative Inspection (self)		Constant Value Method				**Proposed by**
Informative Inspection (successive)	●	Motion-Step Method		Warning Method		Toshihiro Nabeta

Theme   Preventing Assembly with Improper Serration Bolts

Before Improvement

1. Defects showed up when serration bolts of four different lengths were not installed as specified during assembly.
2. A check is performed at the final process on the assembly line, but this check would sometimes be overlooked.

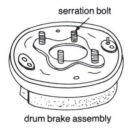

serration bolt

drum brake assembly

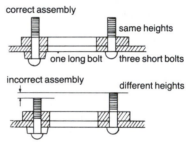

correct assembly

same heights

one long bolt — three short bolts

incorrect assembly

different heights

After Improvement

A device in a subsequent process detects serration bolt heights. The machine cannot operate when incorrect assembly takes place, and the problem is immediately corrected manually.

slide pins and contact pins touch in four places to allow operation to begin

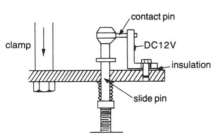

clamp

contact pin

DC12V

insulation

slide pin

slide pin and contact pin touch only when heights are normal

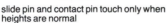

Effects	Cost
Defects involving serration bolt assembly errors were eliminated.	approx. ¥ 12,000 ($60)

Example 109

Inspection Method		Setting Function		Regulative Function		Company Name
Source Inspection		Contact Method	●	Control Method	●	Matsushita Electric Industrial Co., Ltd. / Washing Machine Division / Shizuoka Plant
Informative Inspection (self)		Constant Value Method		Warning Method		**Proposed by**
Informative Inspection (successive)	●	Motion-Step Method				

Theme	
	Ensuring Attachment of Clutch Spring Strike Plates

Before Improvement

Clutch springs and strike plates were attached manually and preventing their omission depended mainly on worker attentiveness.

After Improvement

1. Since clutch spring insertion and strike plate attachment were performed by machine, a verification device like the one in the photograph was provided in the next process. The appearance of a defect halts the pallet with a stopper and warns workers by means of a buzzer.

2. The fact that clutch springs are metal and strike plates are plastic means that the device confirms the passage of electric current between a contact and the clutch spring, while the contact is insulated from the strike plate. Thus, of course, no current passes through if the clutch spring is missing and the absence of a strike plate causes the contact to touch the brake wheel. When this happens, a buzzer sounds and the pallet is halted by means of a stopper.

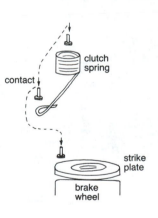

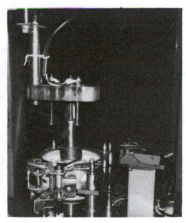

Effects	Cost
Strike plate omission was eliminated.	¥ 15,000 ($75)

Example 110

Inspection Method		Setting Function		Regulative Function		Company Name
Source Inspection		Contact Method	●	Control Method		Saga Tekkohsho Co, Ltd./ Fujisawa Plant
Informative Inspection (self)		Constant Value Method		Warning Method	●	**Proposed by**
Informative Inspection (successive)	●	Motion-Step Method				

Theme Eliminating Excessively Long Bolts

Before Improvement

1. Previously produced items involved bolts of different lengths and very rarely such bolts would find their way into the process.
2. Such problems were difficult to uncover and defective items moved on to subsequent processes.

After Improvement

An adjustable stopper was provided on a chute leading to subsequent processes to prevent defective items from moving forward. As shown below, the stopper is set so that a bolt of normal length can just barely pass through. Longer bolts are stopped and a buzzer sounds.

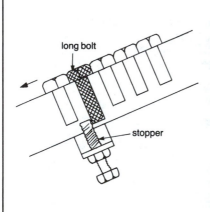
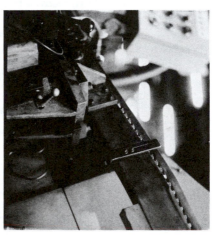

long bolt

stopper

Effects	No more excessively long bolts move to subsequent processes and this has reduced defects.	Cost	¥ 1,000 ($5)

Example 111

Inspection Method		Setting Function		Regulative Function		Company Name
Source Inspection		Contact Method	●	Control Method		Hosei Brake Industries, Ltd.
Informative Inspection (self)		Constant Value Method		Warning Method	●	**Proposed by**
Informative Inspection (successive)	●	Motion-Step Method				Akiji Kobayashi

Theme	
	Ensuring Installation of Blank Bolts in Fixtures

Before Improvement

bolt missing

chute

pallet

After Improvement

B

satisfactory product

C

A

defective product

1. Products would sometimes move to the next process without the installation of blank bolts to protect the male threads.

2. Workers occasionally forgot to install blank bolts after welding and products with this defect would be sent down a chute onto a pallet.

1. Guided by sensor rod B on the chute for finished products, satisfactory items slide onto a chute for satisfactory fixtures.

2. As they move down the chute, fixtures missing blank bolts pass underneath sensor rod B and fall into a defects box. When this happens, the worker at the next process is notified by means of a buzzer and the problem is corrected manually.

Effects	Cost
Defects involving missing blank bolts were eliminated.	approx. ¥ 200 ($1)

Example 112

8

Quality Control and QC Circles

THE DISTINCTIVE CHARACTER OF JAPANESE MANAGEMENT

During a visit I made to Cincinnati in 1983, a Mr. Tanaka from the Japan Research Center told me there had recently been a conference on "the distinctive character of Japanese management" and that talks had been given by executives of Japanese companies in America, as well as by American scholars who were doing research on Japanese management. One of the speakers had been the author of *Japan As Number One*, and his talk had been very well attended.

"What did he have to say?" I asked.

Mr. Tanaka replied that the American's principal theme was that Japanese labor-management relations were harmonious because of the country's lifetime employment system and because Japanese labor unions are company unions and so forth.

That set me to thinking.

The characterization of Japanese labor relations was certainly accurate. Yet I felt that it was emphasizing only one side of the nature of Japanese management. Another side to the contrast between Japan and the West was being overlooked.

Human deeds can be described in terms of work motivations and work methods. The lecture Mr. Tanaka described had stressed only the characteristic motivations aspect of Japanese management. I felt the need, however, to discuss the distinctive character of Japanese management in terms of methods as well.

The peculiar nature of Japanese management with respect to work motivations is something that has taken a long time to develop against a backdrop of national customs and conditions. It may well not be the sort of thing that can suddenly be adapted to the cultures of Europe and America. It occurred to me that the work methods characteristic of Japanese management, on the other hand, can be introduced in the West as along as they can be understood.

263

My view of the differences between so-called "Japanese" management and "Western" (or Euro-American) management can be illustrated as shown in *Figure 8-1*.

Comparison in Terms of Work Motivations

What follows are comparisons of general tendencies and will in many instances not necessarily be applicable to individual companies. Nor are these comparisons meant to suggest that one system is better or worse than the other.

Employment

Japan. Lifetime employment. When work is slack, personnel cuts are difficult to make. As a result, the employee's sense of belonging to the company is strong and a family atmosphere means a high level of company loyalty and harmonious labor-management relations. This may be seen as the major reason for the strong centripetal force exerted by QC circles as company-wide movements.

U.S.A./Europe. Personnel cuts are easily made when work decreases. This makes for little sense of labor-management solidarity and accounts for the feeling that workers and managers are adversaries.

Salary Systems

Japan. A monthly wage system means that daily work performance is not immediately reflected in workers' salaries. Employees can work at their own rhythms with a sense of security and their incomes are guaranteed.

U.S.A./Europe. Contract wage systems mean that daily work performance is immediately reflected in workers' salaries, and this raises the possibility of insecurity about pay.

Labor Unions

Japan. Company-internal labor unions are little influenced from the outside, so that despite a certain amount of antagonism involved in wage negotiations and the like, harmony prevails in the end and extreme confrontations do not develop.

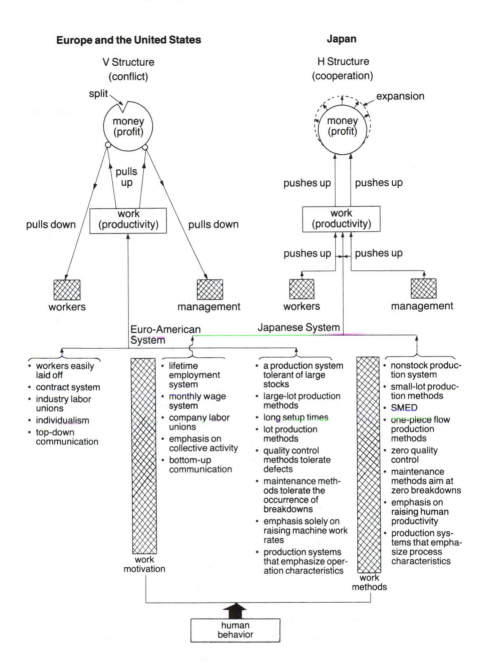

FIGURE 8-1. Characteristics of Euro-American and Japanese Production Systems

U.S.A./Europe. Conditions within companies are not reflected in industry-wide unions. This means that strikes and so forth can take place without regard to the situation inside a particular company. The intervention of external forces in wage negotiations also means that the actual state of the company may not be reflected and compromise cannot be reached.

Group Activities and Individualism

Japan. Group activities are stressed. The organization and running of circle activities is particularly easy in Japan, where there has historically been a national orientation toward group activities.

U.S.A./Europe. A historical tradition of individualism may make it comparatively difficult to organize and run group activities such as circle activities.

Communication

Japan. Communication flows from the bottom up, and this results in lengthy decision-making processes. Since the ground has been prepared in advance, however, once a decision is made, it is executed rapidly and the path to its success is smooth.

U.S.A./Europe. Communication flows from the top down, and this results in rapid policy formulation. Afterwards, it takes time for decisions to be disseminated and spread among employees, and the ultimate success of a decision will depend on whether they comply fully.

Comparison in Terms of Work Methods

Attitudes Concerning Inventory

Japan. Inventory is seen as an evil and every attempt is made to achieve production systems that don't require it. This is why SMED methods are used and efforts are made to reform conditions that lead to the generation of inventory.

U.S.A./Europe. Inventory is seen as a necessary evil, with the emphasis on "necessary." The necessary nature of inventory is legitimized by citing reasons such as long setup times, long lead times, or the occurrence of defects and breakdowns. Reforms of underlying conditions are not always carried out thoroughly.

Production Lot Sizes

Japan. Small-lot production is used. Inventory therefore decreases.

U.S.A./Europe. Large-lot production is used. Inventory therefore increases. The principal reason for the use of large-lot production is long setup times.

Length of Tooling Setups

Japan. The use of SMED methods makes setup times extremely short. On the whole, they take about one-fiftieth of the time they do in U.S. and European firms.

U.S.A./Europe. Long setup times are seen as necessary. For this reason, large-lot production is adopted and inventories grow.

The One-Piece Flow Method and the Lot Production Method

Japan. Use of the so-called one-piece flow method dramatically shortens lead times. This is also a major factor in eliminating the need for inventory.

U.S.A./Europe. Use of the lot production method lengthens lead times and results in production periods that are longer than periods between orders and deliveries. This necessitates anticipatory production, which in turn is a major cause of inventory increases.

Quality Control Approaches

Japan. Use of methods such as Zero QC systems either eliminates defects or cuts them to a minimum. As a result, production is efficient and there is little need for inventory to serve as a cushion.

U.S.A./Europe. Quality control methods that tolerate the occurrence of defects inevitably lead to defects. In addition to blocking efficient production, such methods are one of the reasons inventories are needed.

Let me illustrate the difference in attitude with this anecdote:

Around 1982, Mr. Iwasaki, an executive in charge of production at the C Company, made a visit to the American G automobile company. There, he saw a worker blithely installing a part that he clearly knew to be defective. When he asked why this was going on, the technician leading him on the plant tour gave him an answer that left him speechless.

"You see, whether a part is defective or not isn't his responsibility. It's the quality control officer's problem and it has nothing to do with the worker. His job is to install the parts. That's what he gets paid for."

In Japan, the assembly worker would exchange the defective part for a good part right away. He would then notify his foreman that a defective part had arrived, and that feedback would reach the worker in charge, who would then take corrective action.

Mr. Iwasaki told me he felt that the quality of American automobiles would never improve as long as that attitude remained.

Listening to him tell this story, I began to wonder whether the problem was one of quality control or one of the wage system. I finally concluded that it was most likely a little of each.

Equipment and Machine Maintenance

Japan. Abnormalities are distinguished from breakdowns, and measures are carried out where the abnormalities occur. This minimizes machine breakdowns and increases productivity. In addition, it eliminates the need to maintain stock in anticipation of machine breakdowns.

U.S.A./Europe. The notion of preventive maintenance originally came to Japan from the United States. Even so, people are still fairly easygoing about the idea of thoroughly eliminating breakdowns. This seems to be the number one reason for advocating the need for stock.

Machine Productivity and Human Productivity

Japan. Human productivity is given priority, even at the expense of machine work rates. This is the idea behind multiple machine operations, in which a single worker is in charge of several machines.

U.S.A./Europe. An exclusive emphasis on machine work rates means that human work rates have been slighted. Wasteful operations in which workers merely supervise machine operations are overlooked.

Operations Characteristics and Process Characteristics

Japan. Although improvements in operations characteristics are, of course, not denied, more stress is placed on improving process characteristics by harmonizing processes. The emphasis is on improvements in overall productivity. Thus, machine layouts often conform to flow operations. This results in the elimination of considerable waste and makes it possible to minimize inventories.

U.S.A./Europe. An exclusive emphasis on operations characteristics means production in which machine capacities are used to the fullest, interprocess equilibrium deteriorates, and vast inventories are generated. In many cases, moreover, machines are laid out by machine type. This gives rise to wasteful transportation and delays and incurs unnecessary manpower costs.

As in the case of comparisons regarding work motivations, the comparisons above in no way imply the superiority or inferiority of either Japanese or Western approaches. These are merely an attempt to pinpoint characteristic differences. Judgments of superiority or inferiority are rightly left to the opinions of individuals.

If one wanted to adopt the Japanese system in terms of work motivations, there would surely be many difficulties stemming from differences of historical background and national character. Yet the adoption of work methods would be relatively easy.

In short, simple comparisons are meaningless. In particular, it is surely more trouble than it is worth to emphasize only those work motivation characteristics whose adoption by other nations would be difficult. Of course, motivation is a fundamental question in labor issues, but if the idea is to adopt the advantages of Japanese management, then surely a wiser strategy is to match what is imported to conditions in one's own country.

By comparison, work methods can be introduced fairly easily. Such imports will rapidly result in increased management success, and this is why I stress that improvements in this realm are issues deserving priority consideration and exploration.

THE BIRTH OF QC CIRCLES

So-called SQC (statistical quality control) methods were introduced into Japan around 1951. Since that time, American authorities such as Dr. J.M. Juran and Dr. W. Edwards Deming have come to Japan to offer their guidance, and Japanese quality control campaigns have made great strides forward.

In the initial period, SQC ideas and techniques were taught mainly to top management people and division heads. QC leaders in Japan insisted, however, that the people who actually generate product quality are shop foremen, group leaders, and workers; by 1961, the focus of education and training began to shift to these people. In 1962, the QC circle idea was born when Professors Tetsuichi Asaka and Kaoru Ishikawa, among others, pointed out that if people on the shop floor are really the ones who generate quality, then those people should participate through circle activities.

Until that time, the sole emphasis had been on statistical aspects of quality control, and the QC movement had been dominated by technicians with theoretical leanings. The movement began to penetrate down to the workers and awareness of quality issues was heightened as everyone joined in. Circle activities permitted everyone to participate by raising quality-related issues and debating proposed improvements. The spread of this grassroots movement has improved quality in Japanese companies and has been remarkably successful in reducing defects.

In this way, international acclaim for the quality of Japanese products was an achievement no doubt due more to the impact of QC circle activities than to that of SQC methods themselves. The group-oriented character of the Japanese people presumably also contributed significantly to the success of circle activities, but we should really thank the foresight of leaders who knew how to harness these peculiarly Japanese characteristics.

Thus, the QC circle is a uniquely Japanese concept that is significant, I think, in its contention that merely fiddling around with SQC theories is meaningless, because it is people on the shop floor who really build in quality.

MOVEMENT TOWARD TOTAL QUALITY CONTROL (TQC)

The phrase "total quality control" had already been proposed by quality control specialists at General Electric in America. These experts had advocated the need to station QC workers not only in production departments, but throughout a company to carry out comprehensive quality control functions. The idea was to start from an independent QC basis and spread QC functions throughout the business.

When the expression TQC came to Japan, however, it was taken to refer to QC carried out by the business as a whole. That is to say, the company as a whole was seen as the basis and QC provided the means to improve business. Thus, QC stopped being the exclusive property of specialists and became a tool used by the whole company. It was understood as company-wide quality control and, as such, achieved considerable success. Indeed, Japanese-style TQC has recently been reimported into the United States.

The "total" element in TQC can be conceived of as having three aspects (*Figures 8-2* and *8-3*).

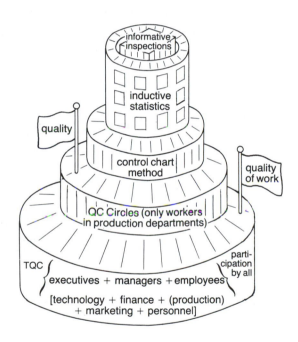

FIGURE 8-2. **Movement Toward TQC**

The spread of quality control concepts and the actual execution of quality control activities extends to all five categories of executive management — i.e., to technology, finance, production, marketing, and personnel — and is not limited to production. To accomplish this, all areas organize QC circles so that QC expands laterally.

In the past, QC activities have expanded perpendicularly when they have focused on people in the shop. This means that workers

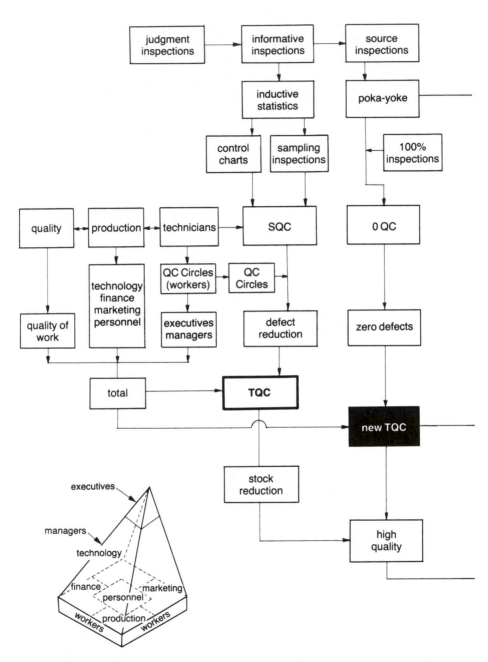

FIGURE 8-3. Just-In-Time and New Movement Toward TQC

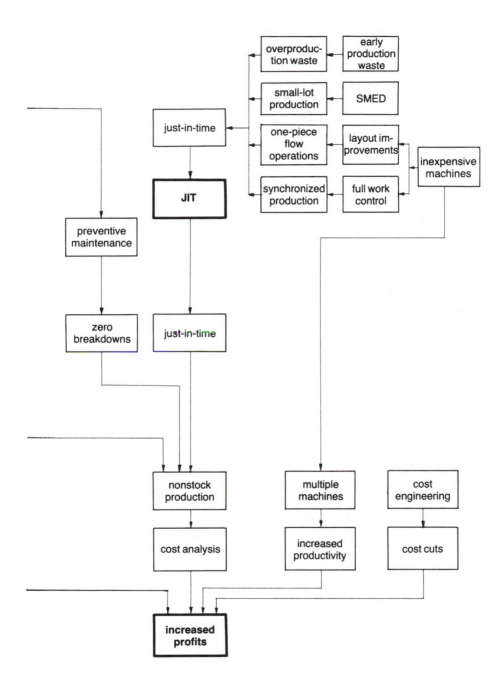

in the shop, managers, and executives united in three-dimensional activities to pursue quality control. In particular, since the success of a movement is significantly affected by leadership from the top, it has been up to executives to organize company-wide campaigns to promote quality control.

In the past, the idea of quality focused principally on improving product quality. But quality does not solely refer to product quality. QC activities also involve the use of management, business, or other methods to raise the quality of work. Company-wide efforts should be made to this end. Thus, the objectives of quality were expanded and this significantly extended the scope of the movement.

In this way, the "total" element of TQC expands QC laterally to areas of the business other than production. It expands QC vertically to include workers, managers, and executives. It organizes three-dimensional activities (e.g., company-wide campaigns) and it expands objectives beyond product quality to include the quality of work, thereby seeking to improve the efficiency of all business tasks.

This makes it possible to better understand what it means to say that the use of TQC will raise business efficiency. A TQC activity is illustrated in the oft-cited example of the office worker who judged that each flush of the office toilet used too much water and so improved the mechanism in a way that conserved water. We can easily see the effect of TQC once we think of this example as an improvement in the quality of work.

If we fail to understand that "quality" has extended beyond product quality to include the quality of work, we will be unable to appreciate why business efficiency would improve so dramatically merely by means of product quality improvements.

The content of the term "quality control" has already changed considerably since the early days. Perhaps the expression is now inappropriate and we should refer instead to "movements aimed at improving business efficiency."

The techniques of quality control in the narrow sense of the term are, of course, effective in pinpointing problems. Much more effective, however, is the application of industrial engineering (IE)-based improvement techniques. It is particularly rewarding to consider the more liberal use of IE techniques at the improvement planning stage in matters relating to goal identification, project conception, and decision making. I strongly advocate that education in IE techniques — especially improvement techniques — be incorporated into TQC campaigns.

I would also like to stress the extraordinary effectiveness of using scientific thinking mechanisms (STM).

Once, as I listened in on a QC circle improvement report session at T Motor Corporation, I began to wonder what QC activities really were. True, members of the group were making histograms to locate problem areas and drawing up element analysis charts to track down the causes of problems, but everything after that (e.g., the development of improvement approaches and the submission of proposal improvements) simply applied IE techniques.

But then I realized that the problem was lowering the defect rate. That, I persuaded myself, was ultimately what QC circles were all about. I consoled myself with the thought that the foreman who presented the problem had been able to come up with improvement proposals relatively easily because I had taught him about IE.

I felt strongly on that occasion that although there are techniques for finding and analyzing problems in the course of quality control campaigns, there are not necessarily any special techniques for solving those problems and for making improvements. It is desirable, therefore, to combine IE techniques in harmonious ways.

I, of course, do not deny that statistics provide high-level techniques, such as the experimental planning method and the determination of significant differences, and that these techniques are effective even for developing improvement proposals. I only want to stress that before and beyond these techniques there are other methods that will lead simply and easily to improvement proposals.

THE CORE OF THE TQC MOVEMENT

The basic notion lying hidden at the core of current TQC activities is that of SQC. Yet I believe that 80 percent of the success of Japanese TQC activities is due to QC circle activities and that no more than 20 percent of the credit belongs to SQC methods themselves. I think it is time for the SQC methods at the core of TQC to yield their place to Zero QC methods.

The circle activities that support the rest of the TQC structure are as significant as ever. It seems to me also natural to think that, even if the core concept shifts from SQC to TQC, the improvement of business systems will be most decisively influenced by:

- Horizontal expansion to include the five branches of business.
- Perpendicular expansion to include strata of executives, managers, and workers within companies.
- Expansion of the goal of efficiently improving the quality of work.

In short, I maintain that we have to exchange the core concept of SQC methods for a core of Zero QC methods. I am by no means suggesting that we alter the nature of the TQC movement.

In plants I have recently visited as a consultant, there are quite a number of examples in which, when defects showed up in the workplace, we would have people in QC circles think of source inspection and poka-yoke applications. Putting these techniques into effect has eliminated the defects in these plants. This has shown me that success can be dramatically improved by the synergistic combination of Zero QC and QC circle activities.

Perhaps we can say that shifting the core of TQC activities from SQC methods to Zero QC methods will greatly expand TQC effectiveness, and naturally that will have an absolute effect on business efficiency.

Expressed in another way, we can say that this is a revolutionary shift from quality control concepts that tolerate defects to an aggressive quality control philosophy that demands that defects be eliminated.

It is important not to forget that activities, such as those involving QC circles, that have quantitatively expanded the size of the movement, have also necessarily had the effect of spurring quality improvements. In that sense, the organization of group activities like QC circles remains important. In fact, it cannot be stressed enough that it is an absolutely necessary condition for the success of TQC activities with Zero QC methods at their core.

Afterword

It took 26 years from my first encounter with SQC systems before I finally arrived at the notion of a Zero QC system. In retrospect, I cannot help but marvel at how thoroughly I had been under the spell of statistics.

I can only feel that I had been so taken by the magic of statistical methods that I had forgotten to pursue the nature of quality control itself.

Only when I happened on the poka-yoke idea and the notion of trouble-free 100 percent inspections did I realize that one did not have to use statistics. Not until then did a chink appear in the wall of statistics.

That hole gradually widened as the implementation of 100 percent inspections and rapid feedback and action cut defects dramatically. At that point, I looked into the nature of quality control and arrived at the idea of a Zero QC system. This is what first made possible the attainment of zero defects.

When I think about it now, I am struck by how long 26 years seems.

Just because I had been freed from the spell of statistics, that does not mean that I discarded statistical science entirely. Scientific statistics still provide superior techniques. It is merely that now, rather than adopting the passive stance of one entranced by statistics, I think I have come back to a more objective viewpoint in which I ask how statistics may best be used.

Indeed, statistics are tremendously effective in the planning phase of the management cycle — in the establishment of standard work processes and operating procedures. Here, I think, statistical methods should by all means be applied.

The essential goal of SQC methods is to reduce defects — a passive goal that accepts some level of defects as inevitable. In contrast, a Zero QC system pursues the active objective of eliminating defects. This is what led me to arrive at the idea of Zero QC methods.

Both in Japan and abroad, whenever I claim that defects can be eliminated, there is always someone who protests that that is impossible. "Defects will always crop up," the argument goes, "in any task performed by humans."

At that point I describe suitable examples of source inspections and poka-yoke methods.

"It is possible," I say. Because what all of you are looking at as defects are really results. You aren't looking at their causes.

"Every defect that shows up is preceded by an earlier phenomenon — the error that was the cause of the defect.

"Rather than detecting resulting defects and then carrying out feedback and action, zero defects will only be achieved if you detect the causal error behind the defect at the error stage and then perform feedback and action so that the error doesn't turn into a defect. What we absolutely cannot prevent are errors, but we can keep those errors from generating defects."

Only then do people understand what I am saying.

This notion of clearly distinguishing between errors and defects and of running through control cycles at the stage of defect discovery is the most basic and important idea behind Zero QC systems. It is imperative that this point be understood clearly.

In the quality control field, one often hears reference to the *plan, do* and *check* functions of the Deming Circle.

Do, however, is an execution function and never a management function.

Planning functions are *plan, control, and check* — brainwork, in other words — while the execution function (*do*) refers to hand- and legwork. Among these management functions, moreover, the control function has a real and overall effect on execution.

It may be that in the course of operations, supervisors exercise control functions over work performed by workers when they show those workers how to do certain jobs. Workers themselves probably control their own hand- and legwork by mentally comparing what they do to their memory of standard operations. In any case, they try as hard as they can to prevent defects.

Thus, the fact that the Deming Circle views management functions and execution functions as the same leads to neglect of control functions; and, in a real sense, I think it has retarded the advance of quality control functions.

It is vital that we properly appreciate the tremendous impact that control functions have on the fruits of management activities.

Human actions are composed of work motivations and work methods. No matter how you look at it, the decisive, impulsive element in this pair is the work motivation. Nothing will get done unless people are moved to get it done. In that sense, QC circles and TQC activities operate on this work motivation. Their impact is essential, and without them QC activities would not succeed.

Still, this is a problem of a different dimension than that of work methods. The question of whether to use SQC methods or Zero QC methods lies in another realm. It follows that, even if one's basic way of thinking shifts from SQC methods to Zero QC methods, QC circles and TQC activities have a decisive impact. Thus QC circles and TQC activities should be pursued with vigor even when a switch to a Zero QC method has been made. This point is vital and should not be slighted.

In fact, a number of quality control issues are raised by QC circles in the course of my plant consultations, and there are numerous cases in which defects were then eliminated through adoption of the idea of Zero QC methods.

Quality control can never be an independent entity. It represents one functional realm within production activities and careful thought must be given to its relationship to the whole and to processes and operations. Furthermore, it is necessary to understand correctly the relationships between quality control and the management control functions: programming (or planning), control, and monitoring.

Since various detection measures are needed to set up a poka-yoke system, I thought it would be helpful to present a range of actual examples. Many companies have been kind enough to furnish me with numerous examples, and I would like to take this opportunity to express my gratitude for their generosity.

This book was published very quickly, thanks to the unstinting efforts of Kazuya Uchiyama and Eiko Shinoda of the Japan Management Association's Publishing Division. Once again, I would like to express my compliments and my thanks for their labors.

About the Author

CAREER: 50 YEARS IN FACTORY IMPROVEMENT

First Period: Private Enterprise

1924 While studying at Saga Technical High School, reads and is deeply impressed by Toshiro Ikeda's *The Secret of Eliminating Unprofitable Efforts,* said to be a translation of Taylor's thesis.

1930 Graduates from Yamanashi Technical College; goes to work for the Taipei Railway Factory.

1931 While a technician in the casting shop at the Taipei Railway Factory, observes worker operations and feels the need for improvement. Reads accounts of the streamlining of operations at Japan National Railways plants and awakens to the need for rational plant management.

Reads Taylor's *The Principles of Scientific Management* and, greatly impressed, decides to make the study and practice of scientific management his life's work.

Reads and studies many books, including the works of Yoichi Ueno and texts published by the Japan Industrial Association.

1937 For two months beginning September 1, attends the First Long-Term Industrial Engineering Training Course, sponsored by the Japan Industrial Association. Is thoroughly instructed in the "motion mind" concept by Ken'ichi Horikome.

1943 Transfers to the Amano Manufacturing Plant (Yokohama) on orders from the Ministry of Munitions. As Manufacturing Section Chief, applies flow operations to the processing of depth mechanisms for air-launched torpedoes and raises productivity by 100%.

Second Period: The Japan Management Association

1945 On orders from the Ministry of Munitions, transfers to Ishii Precision Mfg. (Niigata), a maker of similar air-launched torpedo depth mechanisms, for the purpose of improving factory operations.

With the end of the war in August, accepts a post at Yasui Kogyo (Kita Kyushu) starting in April 1946 and moves to Takanabe-cho in Miyazaki Prefecture. Stops by Tokyo at this time and visits Isamu Fukuda at the Japan Management Association, where he is introduced to Chairman of the Board Morikawa. Is asked to participate temporarily in a plant survey to improve operations at Hitachi, Ltd.'s vehicle manufacturing facility at Kasado. Afterwards enters the service of the Japan Management Association.

1946 When asked by a survey team member during process analysis at the Hitachi plant how to treat times when goods are delayed while waiting for cranes, realizes that "processes" and "operations," which had previously been thought to be separate and parallel entities, form a "network of processes and operations" — a systematic, synthetic whole. Reports this finding at a Japan Management Association technical conference.

Invents a method of classifying like operations by counting non-interventions while studying the layout of a Hitachi, Ltd. woodworking plant.

1948 Elucidates the "true nature of skill" in *A Study of 'Peko' Can Operations* at Toyo Steel's Shitamatsu plant.

Between 1948 and 1954, takes charge of Production Technology Courses. Also runs production technology classes at companies.

At a production technology course held at Hitachi, Ltd.'s Fujita plant, begins to question the nature of plant layout. Studies and reflects on the problem.

1950 Perfects and implements a method for determining equipment layout based on a coefficient of ease of transport at Furukawa Electric's Copper Refinery in Nikko.

Analyzes work at a press at Toyo Kogyo and realizes that a setup operation is composed of "internal setup" (IED) and "external setup" (OED). This concept will become the first stage of SMED.

1954 Morita Masanobu from Toyota Motor Co., Ltd. participates in a production technology course at Toyoda Automatic Loom and achieves striking results when he returns to his company. This occasions a series of productivity technology courses inaugurated in 1955. By 1982, eighty-seven sessions of the course had been held, with approximately 2,000 participants.

1955 Observes multiple machine operations at the first production technology training course at Toyota Motor Corp. and is impressed by the separation of workers and machines.

1956 From 1956 to 1958 takes charge of a three-year study of Mitsubishi Shipbuilding's Nagasaki shipyards. Invents a new system for cutting supertanker assembly from four months to three and then to two. This system spreads to Japanese shipbuilding circles and contributes to the development of the shipbuilding industry.

1957 To raise the machining efficiency of an engine bed planer at

Mitsubishi Shipbuilding's Hiroshima shipyards, constructs a spare table, conducts advance setup operations on it and changes workpiece and table together. This doubles the work rate and foreshadows a crucially decisive conceptual element of SMED, that of shifting IED to OED.

Third Period: The Institute for Management Improvement (Domestic)

1959 Leaves the Japan Management Association to found the Institute of Management Improvement.

1960 Originates the "successive inspection system" for reducing defects and implements the system at Matsushita Electric's Moriguchi plant.

1964 From Matsushita Electric's insistence that no level of defects is tolerable, realizes that although selective inspection may be a rational procedure, it is not a rational means of assuring quality.

1965 Stimulated by Toyota Motor's "foolproof" production measures, eagerly seeks to eliminate defects entirely by systematically combining the concepts of successive inspection, independent inspection, and source inspection with "foolproof" techniques.

1966 Works as a business consultant to various Taiwanese firms, including Formosa Plastic Co., Matsushita Electric (Taiwan), and China Grinding Wheel Co. Consulted annually until 1981.

1969 Improves setup change for a 1,000-ton press at Toyota Motor's main plant from four hours to one and a half. Is soon afterward asked by management to cut setup time to three minutes and in a flash of insight thinks to shift IED to OED. With this, a systematic technique for achieving SMED is born.

Notices the difference between mechanization and automation when asked by Saga Ironworks' plant manager Yaya why automatic machines needed to be manned. This observation evolves into the concept of "preautomation" which, Shingo later realizes, is identical to Toyota Motor's "human automation."

1970 Is awarded the Yellow Ribbon Medal for contributions to streamlining operations in the shipbuilding industry, etc.

Fourth Period: The Institute for Management Improvement (International Expansion)

1971 Participates in observation tour of the European machine industry.

1973 Participates in observation tours of the machine industries in Europe and the United States.

1974 Lectures on SMED at die-cast industry associations in West Germany and Switzerland.

On this visit, observes vacuum die-casting methods at Daimler Benz in West Germany and Buehler in Switzerland and grows eager to implement vacuum molding in die-casting and plastic molding.

1975 Grows more enthusiastic about the "zero defects" concept on the basis of the achievement of zero defects in one month at the Shizuoka plant of Matsushita Electric's Washing Machine Operations Division.

Works for improvement based on fundamental approaches including high-speed plating, instantaneous drying, and the elimination of layout marking.

1976 Consults and lectures widely to promote SMED in Europe and the United States.

1977   Treats Toyota Motor's *kanban* system as essentially a scheme of "nonstock" production and develops systematic techniques for the system.

1978   Visits America's Federal-Mogul Corporation to provide on-site advice on SMED.

The sale by the Japan Management Association of an audio-visual set of slides on SMED and preautomation meets with considerable success.

1979   Further success is attained by the Japan Management Association's sale of "zero defects" slides.

Visits Federal-Mogul to give follow-up guidance on SMED.

The collected results of Shingo's experiences and ideas concerning improvement are published.

1981   Makes two trips, in the spring and fall, to provide plant guidance to the French automobile manufacturers Peugeot and Citrœn.

Travels to Australia to observe Toyota (Australia) and Borg-Warner.

1982   Makes follow-up consulting visits to Peugeot and Citrœn in France and is impressed by the considerable results achieved through the application of SMED and nonstock production.

Consults and lectures at the Siemens company in Germany.

Lectures on "The Toyota Production System — An Industrial Engineering Study" in Munich.

Gives lectures at Chalmers University in Sweden.

Lectures at the University of Chicago.

Since 1982, the author has continued traveling and consulting around the world. Since 1985, he has offered seminars in the United States under the auspices of Productivity, Inc.

CONSULTING

Below is a list of companies where Shigeo Shingo has given a training course or lecture, or has consulted for productivity improvement.

Industry	Name of Company	
JAPAN		
Automobiles and Suppliers	Toyota Motor Car Co., Ltd. Toyota Auto Body Co., Ltd. Toyo Motor Car Co., Ltd. Honda Motor Co., Ltd. Mitsubishi Heavy Industries Co., Ltd. Daihatsu Motor Car Co., Ltd. Bridgestone Cycle Kogyo Co., Ltd.	Yamaha Motor Co., Ltd. Kanto Auto Works, Co., Ltd. Central Motor Car Co., Ltd. Arakawa Auto Body Co., Ltd. Koito Manufacturing Co., Ltd. (Car parts) Aishin Seiki Co., Ltd. (Parts of Motor Car, Diecast) Hosei Brake Co., Ltd.
Electric apparatus	Matsushita Electric Industrial Co., Ltd. Tokyo Shibaura Electric Co., Ltd. Sharp Electric Co., Ltd. Fuji Electric Co., Ltd. Nippon Columbia Co., Ltd. (Stereo Disk) Stanley Electric Co., Ltd. Matsushita Electric Works Co., Ltd. Matsushita Jutaku Setsubi Kiki Co., Ltd. (House equipment) Matsushita Denchi Kogyo Co., Ltd. (Lighting parts)	Hitachi Co., Ltd. Sony Electric Co., Ltd. Mitsubishi Electric Co., Ltd. Yasukawa Electric Mfg. Co., Ltd. Kyushu Matsushita Electric Co., Ltd. Asahi National Lighting Co., Ltd. Matsushita Denshi Buhin Co., Co., Ltd. (Electric parts) Sabsga Denki Co., Ltd. (Rectifier)
Precision machine	Nippon Optical Co., Ltd. Sankyo Seiki Mfg. Co., Ltd. (Music Box)	Olympus Optical Co., Ltd.
Steel, Non-ferrous Metals and Metal Products	Nippon Steel Co., Ltd. Toyo Steel Plate Co., Ltd. Mitsui Mining and Smelting Co., Ltd. Sumitomo Electric Industries, Ltd. Toyo Can Industry Co., Ltd. Nippon Spring Co., Ltd. Togo Seisakusho Co., Ltd. (Spring)	Nisshin Steel Co., Ltd. The Furukawa Electric Co., Ltd. The Fujikura Cable Works, Ltd. Hokkai Can Industry Co., Ltd. Chuo Spring Co., Ltd.
Machine	Amada Co., Ltd. (Metallic Press Machine) Iseki Agricultural Machinery Mfg. Co., Ltd.	Aida Engineering, Co., Ltd. (Metallic Press Machine) Toyota Automatic Loom Works, Ltd.

Industry	Name of Company	
	Kanzaki Kokyu Koki Co., Ltd. (Machine Tools) Nippon Seiko Co., Ltd. (Bearings) Taiho Industry Co., Ltd. (Bearings) Asian Industry Co., Ltd. (Carburetor)	Kubota Ltd. (Engine and (Farming Machinery) Daikin Kogyo Co., Ltd. (Coolers) Nach-Fujikoshi, Co., Ltd. (Bearings, Cutters, etc.)
Rubber	Bridgestone Tire Co., Ltd. Nippon Rubber Co., Ltd.	Toyota Gosei Co., Ltd. Tsuki-Boshi Shoemaking Co., Ltd.
Glass	Asahi Glass Co., Ltd. Yamamura Glass Bottle Co., Ltd. Noritake China Co., Ltd.	Nippon Sheet Glass Co., Ltd. Onoda Cement Co., Ltd.
Marine products	Taiyo Fishery Co., Ltd.	
Mining	Mitsui Mining Co., Ltd. Dowa Mining Co., Ltd.	Nippon Mining Co., Ltd.
Food	Morinage & Co., Ltd. (Confectionery) Hayashikane Sangyo Co., Ltd.	Snow Brand Milk Products Co., Ltd.
Textile	Katakura Industries Co., Ltd. Kanebo Co., Ltd. Daiwa Spinning Co., Ltd. Teikoku Jinken Co., Ltd.	Gunze Co., Ltd. Fuji Spinning Co., Ltd. Daido Worsted Mills Co., Ltd. Asahi Chemical Industry Co., Ltd.
Pulp and Paper	Jujyo Paper Co., Ltd. Rengo Co., Ltd.	Oji Paper Co., Ltd.
Chemicals	Showa Denko Co., Ltd. Tokuyama Soda Co., Ltd. Hitachi Chemical Co., Ltd. Shionogi Pharmaceutical Co., Ltd. Shiseido Cosmetics Co., Ltd.	Nippon Soda Co., Ltd. Ube Industries Co., Ltd. Nippon Kayaku Co., Ltd. Fujisawa Pharmaceutical Co., Ltd.
Others	Nippon Gakki Co., Ltd. (Yamaha Piano) Saga Tekkosho Co.,Ltd. Zojirushi Mahobin Co., Ltd. Iwao Jiki Kogyo Co., Ltd. Koga Kinzoku Kogyo Co., Ltd. (Metallic Press) Sanei Metallic Col., Ltd. (Metallic Press)	The Sailor Pen Co., Ltd. Nippon Baruka Kogyo Co., Ltd. Gihu Dai & Mold Engineering Co., Ltd. Dia Plastics Co., Ltd. Yasutaki Industrial Co., Ltd. (Metallic Press)

Industry	Name of Company	
U.S.A.	Federal-Mogul Corp.	Livernois Automation Co., Ltd.
	Omark Industries	Hewlett-Packard
	Storage Technology Corporation (Industrial products)	
FRANCE	Automobiles Peugeot	Automobiles Citrœn
WEST GERMANY	Daimler Benz Co., Ltd.	Verband Deutscher
	Bayrisches Druckguss-verk	Druckgiesseien Co., Ltd.
	Thurner KG Co., Ltd.	Beguform-Werke
SWITZERLAND	Gebr Buhler Co., Ltd.	Bucher-guyer AC Co., Ltd.
	H-Weidmann Co., Ltd.	
TAIWAN	Formosa Plastic Co., Ltd. Co., Ltd.	Nanya Plastic Fabrication
	Formosa Chemicals and Fiber Co.,Ltd.	Plywood and Lumber Co., Ltd.
	China Grinding Wheel Co., Ltd.	Sunrise Plywood Co., Ltd. Taiwan Fusungta
	Matsushita Electric (Taiwan) Co.,Ltd.	Electric Co., Ltd. (Speakers)
	Chin Fong Machine Industrial Co., Ltd. (Metallic Press)	Super Metal Industry Co., Ltd.
NETHERLANDS	Philips	

PUBLICATIONS

Mr. Shingo's books have sold more than 40,000 copies worldwide. For convenience, all titles are given in English, although most were published in Japanese.

"Ten Strategies for Smashing Counterarguments," *Sakken to Kyoryoku* [*Practice and Cooperation*], 1938.

A General Introduction to Industrial Engineering. Japan Management Association, 1949.

Improving Production Control. Nihon Keizaisha, 1950.

Production Control Handbook (Process Control). Kawade Shobo, 1953.

Technology for Plant Improvement. Japan Management Association, 1955.

"Views and Thoughts on Plant Improvement," published serially in *Japan Management*, 1957. (Through the efforts of Mr. Gonta Tsunemasa, these essays were published together in a single volume by Nikkan Kogyo Shinbun.)

Plant Improvement Embodiments and Examples. Nikkan Kogyo Shinbunsha, 1957.

Don't Discard New Ideas. Hakuto Shobo, 1959.

Key Issues in Process Control Improvement. Nikkan Kogyo Shinbunsha, 1962.

Issues in Plant Improvement. Nikkan Kogyo Shinbun, 1964.

Techniques of Machine Layout Improvement. Nikkan Kogyo Shinbunsha, 1965.

Fundamental Approaches to Plant Improvement. Nikkan Kogyo Shinbunsha, 1976.

"The Toyota Production System — An Industrial Engineering Study," published serially in *Factory Management* (Nikkan Kogyo Shinbunsha), 1979.

A Systematic Philosophy of Plant Improvement. Nikkan Kogyo Shinbunsha, 1980.

The Toyota Production System — An Industrial Engineering Study. Nikkan Kogyo Shinbunsha, 1980. (Editions in English, French and Swedish have also been produced.)

A Revolution in Manufacturing: The SMED System. Japan Management Association, 1983 (English edition Productivity, Inc., 1985).

"180 Proposals for Plant Improvement (Sayings of Shigeo Shingo)," published serially in *Factory Management* (Nikkan Kogyo Shinbunsha), 1980-83.

Turning the Key to Plant Improvement: The Sayings of Shigeo Shingo. Nikkan Kogyo Shinbunsha, 1985.

Understanding Basic Production Resources: The Essence of the Toyota Production Formula and the Challenge of Non-stock Production. Japan Management Association, 1986.

Shigeo Shingo

Index